THE DECLARATION OF ARBROATH

History, Significance, Setting

THE DECLARATION OF ARBROATH

History, Significance, Setting

Edited by
GEOFFREY BARROW

Society of Antiquaries of Scotland

Published in 2003 by Society of Antiquaries of Scotland.
Editor: Geoffrey Barrow

Society of Antiquaries of Scotland, Royal Museum of Scotland,
Chambers Street, Edinburgh EH1 1JF.
Tel 0131 247 4115
Fax 0131 247 4163
Email administration@socantscot.org
Website www.socantscot.org

British Library Cataloguing-in-Publication Data
A catalogue record for this book is available from the British Library

ISBN 0 903903 27 X

Copyright © Society of Antiquaries of Scotland 2003

All rights reserved. No part of this publication may be reproduced, stored in or introduced into a retrieval system, or transmitted, in any form, or by any means (electronic, mechanical, photocopying, recording or otherwise) without the prior written permission of the publisher. Any person who does any unauthorised act in relation to this publication may be liable to criminal prosecution and civil claims for damages.

Cover images:
THE POPES' PALACE, AVIGNON
(by courtesy of www.FranceMonthly.com)

ARBROATH ABBEY
(© Crown copyright, reproduced courtesy of Historic Scotland)

THE DECLARATION OF ARBROATH
(The National Archives of Scotland: SP13/7.
By kind permission of the Keeper of the Records of Scotland)

The Society of Antiquaries of Scotland acknowledges grant aid from Historic Scotland and Angus Council towards the publication of this volume.

Typeset by Waverley Typesetters, Galashiels
Designed by Lawrie Law and Alison Rae
Index by Anne McCarthy
Manufactured in Great Britain by CPI, Bath

CONTENTS

Contributors   vii

Foreword   ix

PREFACE   xi
    Geoffrey Barrow

THE DECLARATION OF ARBROATH: ENGLISH TRANSLATION   xiii

THE DECLARATION OF ARBROATH: PEDIGREE OF A NATION   1
    Dauvit Broun

DECLARING ARBROATH   13
    Edward J. Cowan

THE DECLARATIONS OF THE CLERGY, 1309–10   32
    Archie Duncan

ARBROATH ABBEY: A NOTE ON ITS ARCHITECTURE
AND EARLY CONSERVATION HISTORY   50
    Richard Fawcett

IMAGES OF THE DECLARATION: THE ARBROATH PAGEANT   86
    J. N. Graham Ritchie

THE DECLARATION OF ARBROATH: WHAT SIGNIFICANCE
WHEN?   108
    Grant G. Simpson

ARBROATH ABBEY IN CONTEXT, 1178–1320   116
    Keith Stringer

Index   143

CONTRIBUTORS

Geoffrey Barrow graduated at St Andrews University in 1948 and took a B.Litt. at Oxford in 1950. He taught history at University College London and the universities of Newcastle upon Tyne and St Andrews before being appointed to the Sir William Fraser Chair of Scottish History at the University of Edinburgh, which he held from 1979 to 1992. He has published ten books and over a hundred articles on many aspects of Scottish history, including one on the connection between Robert Bruce and the Declaration of Arbroath.

Dauvit Broun has a PhD from the University of Edinburgh, and has taught Scottish History at the University of Glasgow since 1990, where he is now a Senior Lecturer. His book, *The Irish Identity of the Kingdom of the Scots in the Twelfth and Thirteenth Centuries* (1999) won the Hume Brown Senior Prize. He has been editor of *The Innes Review* (1991–9), and is currently the pre-1603 editor of *The Scottish Historical Review*.

Edward J. Cowan taught at the University of Edinburgh from 1967 to 1979, and at the University of Guelph, Ontario, from 1979 to 1993 (where he was Professor of History and Chair of Scottish Studies) before his appointment as Professor of Scottish History at Glasgow. Recent publications include: *The Ballad in Scottish History*, '*For Freedom Alone': The Declaration of Arbroath 1320*, *Alba: Celtic Scotland in the Medieval Era* (with R. A. McDonald), *Scottish History: The Power of the Past* (with Richard Finlay) and *Scottish Fairy Belief: A History* (with Lizanne Henderson).

Archie Duncan was Professor of Scottish History at the University of Glasgow from 1962 to 1993, during which time he edited the charters of Robert I as volume V of *Regesta Regum Scottorum* (1988). In 1997 he published a new edition with translation and notes of John Barbour's poem, *The Bruce*.

Richard Fawcett is a Principal Inspector of Ancient Monuments with Historic Scotland. His chief research interest is in medieval ecclesiastical architecture. His publications include: *Scottish Architecture from the Accession of the Stewarts to the Reformation*, *Scottish Abbeys and Priories*, *Scottish Cathedrals* and *Scottish Medieval Churches: Architecture and Furnishings*. He is a co-author of the forthcoming volume on the Scottish Borders in the *Buildings of Scotland Series*.

Graham Ritchie was a pupil at Arbroath High School before studying Prehistoric Archaeology at the University of Edinburgh. He worked for the Royal Commission on the Ancient and Historical Monuments of Scotland from 1965 to 1998, latterly as Head of Archaeology. He was President of the Society of Antiquaries of Scotland from 1999 to 2001.

Grant G. Simpson took his first degree, in History, at the University of Glasgow; and his PhD at Edinburgh. He was an Assistant Keeper at the Scottish Record Office (now the National Archives of Scotland), then in 1969 became a Lecturer in History at the University of Aberdeen. He retired in 1995 as a Reader in Scottish History and now runs a heritage consultancy in partnership with his wife, Anne. He has published on medieval Scottish politics, Anglo-Scottish relations, baronial families, castles and early handwriting.

Keith Stringer is Reader in Medieval British History and Research Dean (Arts and Humanities) at Lancaster University. He has written extensively on state-making, noble power structures, religious change, and the construction of identities in medieval Britain and Ireland. His most recent publications include *The Reformed Church in Galloway and Cumbria from c. 1100* (Whithorn 2003). He is the editor of *Regesta Regum Scottorum*, volume III (forthcoming), and co-directs the Leverhulme-funded project 'Border Liberties and Loyalties in North-East England, 1200–1400'.

FOREWORD

I was delighted to be able to say a few words at the Conference on The Declaration of Arbroath held in Arbroath on 20 October 2000, organised by the Society of Antiquaries of Scotland and Historic Scotland with Angus Council, and to welcome delegates to a reception provided by Angus Council.

The idea of such a conference was first discussed in Angus, actually at a reception in the Glenesk Hotel, Angus, during the Ancient Monuments Board annual tour in 2000. The table at which I was sitting also had Professor Michael Lynch, the then chairman of the Board, Dr David Breeze, Director of Historic Scotland, and Norman Atkinson, then Acting Director of Cultural Services for Angus Council, and from these discussions the outline of the conference emerged.

The resurrection of the Arbroath Abbey Pageant in 1999 after some years in abeyance, and Angus Council's role in partnership with Historic Scotland in creating the new Arbroath Abbey Visitor Centre were part of the resurgence of interest in the Abbey and the famous Declaration. I was proud to be Honorary President of the Arbroath Abbey Pageant Society and doubly proud that Angus Council was able to assist both ventures, not just financially, but also in terms of advice and support from members and officers.

The Declaration of Arbroath has been a great inspiration the world over, not just to the Scots, and I was fascinated to learn of its likely use in framing the American Declaration of Independence, written some 450 years later. It is wonderful to think that the Declaration still has relevance today, which was borne out by the well-attended conference, and indeed by this publication, which contains many useful contributions to the study of the Declaration itself.

While I would not normally single out any contribution, in the circumstances I would like to mention that by Dr Graham Ritchie, the then President of the Society of Antiquaries of Scotland. Graham, a product of Arbroath High School, has, in his paper, addressed the subject dear to my heart, that is the Arbroath Pageant and its role in keeping the Declaration alive within the community today. While this clearly has tourism benefits, it is of much greater significance in bringing the town's heritage to the attention of the local population. Only by keeping our community aware of its historical past can we ensure its survival in the future.

I commend the Society of Antiquaries of Scotland in bringing the proceedings of this important conference to publication, and I trust that it will make a significant contribution to our understanding of the Declaration of Arbroath for many years to come.

Councillor Frances E. Duncan, OBE, OStJ, JP
Provost of Angus Council
April 2003

PREFACE

As long as there exists an entity which may be called Scotland, whether political, social or cultural, the letter of 6 April 1320 from the nobles of Scotland to Pope John XXII, which we call The Declaration of Arbroath, will always exert a special fascination. Well over a century before it was composed, Scotland could be given a personality – a contemporary admirer of William the Lion's chancellor, Hugh of Roxburgh, declared that Scotland rightly rejoiced to revere his name and pour out its praise for him. Forty years before the Declaration a court poet could write, with special reference to the betrothal of the king of Scots' daughter Margaret to King Eric of Norway, that from 'sweet Scotia' had shone forth light in which Norway would be happily reflected. The author of the Arbroath letter may not have personified his country in quite the same way, but even he wrote, towards the end of his magnificent flight of rhetoric, of 'this poor little Scotland, beyond which there is no dwelling place at all'.

Immeasurably as Scotland has altered since the days of Wallace and Bruce, its basic geography, its parameters and long-term features, its notion of itself as a historical entity – all these have been slow to change; while the work of generations of historians has gradually built up a picture of a country distinct and different from its neighbours although indebted to all of them in various and complex ways. Modern historians have been curiously reluctant to admit that the Declaration of Arbroath is a proclamation of Scottish nationalism. For example, in this volume Dr Grant Simpson writes, 'I personally hesitate, unlike some writers, to use the term "nationalism" in the context of the central Middle Ages. "Patriotism" could be a more acceptable word'.[1] Yet in 1309 William Lamberton, bishop of St Andrews, told the king of France in a letter that he had suffered greatly because of his love for his native land, while eight years later William Sinclair, bishop of Dunkeld, rallied the men he was leading to fight off an English incursion on the Fife coast with the cry 'Who loves his lord and his country, follow me!' Both bishops were involved in the crisis of 1319–20 when the pope threatened the king and the clergy of Scotland with severe penalties for frustrating his efforts to secure an Anglo-Scottish peace. Both bishops, along with a majority among the lay nobles whose seals were attached to the Arbroath letter, believed that Scotland was, and had the right to be internationally recognised as, an independent kingdom. That may not be the nationalism of seventeenth-century France, eighteenth-century Britain or twentieth-century Germany or Japan but it is nationalism for all that.

In this volume, seven scholars present the papers they gave at the Arbroath conference of 20 October 2000. They cover more ground than simply the Declaration itself, setting the document in its historical, ideological, architectural and environmental context. One contributor shows us, in a wealth of fascinating detail, the transatlantic ramifications and inter-connections, especially on the theme 'declaration of independence', and another essay, splendidly illustrated, takes us through the birth and growth of the Arbroath Pageant, in which since 1920 the people of Arbroath have commemorated the stirring events of seven – now nearly eight – centuries ago. No doubt in 2020 a completely new generation of historians will present completely new judgements and interpretations, but what seems absolutely certain is that the Scots barons' letter to the pope will be commemorated – possibly by means of media as yet uninvented.

Geoffrey Barrow
August 2003

NOTE

1 Below, p. 110.

THE DECLARATION OF ARBROATH
(ENGLISH TRANSLATION)

TO the most Holy Father and Lord in Christ, the Lord John, by divine providence Supreme Pontiff of the Holy Roman and Universal Church, his humble and devout sons Duncan, Earl of Fife, Thomas Randolph, Earl of Moray, Lord of Man and of Annandale, Patrick Dunbar, Earl of March, Malise, Earl of Strathearn, Malcolm, Earl of Lennox, William, Earl of Ross, Magnus, Earl of Caithness and Orkney, and William, Earl of Sutherland; Walter, Steward of Scotland, William Soules, Butler of Scotland, James, Lord of Douglas, Roger Mowbray, David, Lord of Brechin, David Graham, Ingram Umfraville, John Menteith, guardian of the earldom of Menteith, Alexander Fraser, Gilbert Hay, Constable of Scotland, Robert Keith, Marischal of Scotland, Henry St Clair, John Graham, David Lindsay, William Oliphant, Patrick Graham, John Fenton, William Abernethy, David Wemyss, William Mushet, Fergus of Ardrossan, Eustace Maxwell, William Ramsay, William Mowat, Alan Murray, Donald Campbell, John Cameron, Reginald Cheyne, Alexander Seton, Andrew Leslie, and Alexander Straiton, and the other barons and freeholders and the whole community of the realm of Scotland send all manner of filial reverence, with devout kisses of his blessed feet.

Most Holy Father and Lord, we know and from the chronicles and books of the ancients we find that among other famous nations our own, the Scots, has been graced with widespread renown. They journeyed from Greater Scythia by way of the Tyrrhenian Sea and the Pillars of Hercules, and dwelt for a long course of time in Spain among the most savage tribes, but nowhere could they be subdued by any race, however barbarous. Thence they came, twelve hundred years after the people of Israel crossed the Red Sea, to their home in the west where they still live today. The Britons they first drove out, the Picts they utterly destroyed, and, even though very often assailed by the Norwegians, the Danes and the English, they took possession of that home with many victories and untold efforts; and, as the historians of old time bear witness, they have held it free of all bondage ever since. In their kingdom there have reigned one hundred and thirteen kings of their own royal stock, the line unbroken a single foreigner.

The high qualities and deserts of these people, were they not otherwise manifest, gain glory enough from this: that the King of kings and Lord of lords, our Lord Jesus Christ, after His Passion and Resurrection, called them, even though settled in the uttermost parts of the earth, almost the first to His most holy faith. Nor would He have them confirmed in that faith by merely anyone but by the first of His Apostles – by calling, though second or third in rank – the most gentle Saint Andrew, the Blessed Peter's brother, and desired him to keep them under his protection as their patron forever.

The Most Holy Fathers your predecessors gave careful heed to these things and bestowed many favours and numerous privileges on this same kingdom and people, as being the special charge of the Blessed Peter's brother. Thus our nation under their protection did indeed live in freedom and peace up to the time when that mighty prince the King of the English, Edward, the father of the one who reigns today, when our kingdom had no head and our people harboured no malice or treachery and were then unused to wars or invasions, came in the guise of a friend and ally to harass them as an enemy. The deeds of cruelty, massacre, violence, pillage, arson, imprisoning prelates, burning down monasteries, robbing and killing monks and nuns, and yet other outrages without number which he committed against our people, sparing neither age nor sex, religion nor rank, no one could describe nor fully imagine unless he had seen them with his own eyes.

But from these countless evils we have been set free, by the help of Him Who though He afflicts yet heals and restores, by our most tireless Prince, King and Lord, the Lord Robert. He, that his people and his heritage might be delivered out of the hands of our enemies, met toil and fatigue, hunger and peril, like another Macabaeus or Joshua and bore them cheerfully. Him, too, divine providence, his right of succession according to our laws and customs which we shall maintain to the death, and the due consent and assent of us all have made our Prince and King. To him, as to the man by whom salvation has been wrought unto our people, we are bound both by law and by his merits that our freedom may be still maintained, and by him, come what may, we mean to stand.

Yet if he should give up what he has begun, and agree to make us or our kingdom subject to the King of England or the English, we should exert ourselves at once to drive him out as our enemy and a subverter of his own rights and ours, and make some other man who was well able to defend us our King; for, as long as but a hundred of us remain alive, never will we on any conditions be brought under English rule. It is in truth not for glory, nor riches, nor honours that we are fighting, but for freedom – for that alone, which no honest man gives up but with life itself.

Therefore it is, Reverend Father and Lord, that we beseech your Holiness with our most earnest prayers and suppliant hearts, inasmuch as you will in your sincerity and goodness consider all this, that, since with Him Whose Vice-Regent on earth you are there is neither weighing nor distinction of Jew and Greek, Scotsman or Englishman, you will look with the eyes of a father on the troubles and privation brought by the English upon us and upon the Church of God. May it please you to admonish and exhort the King of the English, who ought to be satisfied with what belongs to him since England used once to be enough for seven kings or more, to leave us Scots in peace, who live in this poor little Scotland, beyond which there is no dwelling-place at all, and covet nothing but our own. We are sincerely willing to do anything for him, having regard to our condition, that we can, to win peace for ourselves.

This truly concerns you, Holy Father, since you see the savagery of the heathen raging against the Christians, as the sins of Christians have indeed deserved, and the frontiers of Christendom being pressed inward every day; and how much it will tarnish your Holiness's memory if (which God forbid) the Church suffers eclipse or scandal in any branch of it during your time, you must perceive. Then rouse the Christian princes who for false reasons pretend that they cannot go to help of the Holy Land because of wars they have on hand with their neighbours. The real reason that prevents them is that in making war on their smaller neighbours they find quicker profit and weaker resistance. But how cheerfully our Lord the King and we too would go there if the King of the English would leave us in peace, He from Whom nothing is hidden well knows; and we profess and declare it to you as the Vicar of Christ and to all Christendom.

But if your Holiness puts too much faith in the tales the English tell and will not give sincere belief to all this, nor refrain from favouring them to our prejudice, then the slaughter of bodies, the perdition of souls, and all the other misfortunes that will follow, inflicted by them on us and by us on them, will, we believe, be surely laid by the Most High to your charge.

To conclude, we are and shall ever be, as far as duty calls us, ready to do your will in all things, as obedient sons to you as His Vicar; and to Him as the Supreme King and Judge we commit the maintenance of our cause, casting our cares upon Him and firmly trusting that He will inspire us with courage and bring our enemies to nought.

May the Most High preserve you to his Holy Church in holiness and health and grant you length of days.

Given at the monastery of Arbroath in Scotland on the sixth day of the month of April in the year of grace thirteen hundred and twenty and the fifteenth year of the reign of our King aforesaid.

> Endorsed: Letter directed to our Lord the Supreme Pontiff by the community of Scotland.
>
> Additional names written on some of the seal tags:
> Alexander Lamberton, Edward Keith, John Inchmartin, Thomas Menzies, John Durrant, Thomas Morham
> (and one illegible)

(Source: *The Declaration of Arbroath, 1320*, Sir James Fergusson, Edinburgh University Press, 1970.)

THE DECLARATION OF ARBROATH

PEDIGREE OF A NATION?

Dauvit Broun

It is almost impossible for us to read the most famous words of the Declaration of Arbroath without hearing in them the echo of our own modern notions of national self-determination.[1] The willingness to fight to the death for a country's survival chimes easily with the rhetoric of so many struggles for independence in the modern age of nationalism. And the remarkable statement that King Robert would be expelled if he sold out to the English, and a new king chosen who could defend Scottish independence, can readily be read as an assertion of popular sovereignty.[2] It is a matter for debate how far the prism of our own perceptions distorts or illuminates our understanding of this text. Certainly, the distance of so many centuries has inevitably obscured what would have been instantly visible between the lines to those Scottish clerics and nobles who wrote and read and listened to these words as fresh prose in 1320. They all knew about Edward Balliol, the son and heir of King John, who they or their fathers had fought for before the final surrender of the Comyn-led government to Edward I in February 1304; they would also surely have known that Edward Balliol was at large in England since being received as a guest of King Edward II in November 1318.[3] They also knew that the future of the Bruce kingship, since the death of Edward Bruce in October 1318, hung precariously on the lives of King Robert himself and the only surviving male heir of his line, his grandson Robert Stewart, who would have only just reached his fourth birthday.[4] When they heard of resisting a king who might yield to the power of the English, therefore, their minds would immediately have turned not to King Robert, but to Edward Balliol, whose potent claim to the throne was bound to mean concessions to his English hosts if he were ever to establish himself in Scotland.[5] And when they heard of making some other man king should Robert fail, they might have recognised in this a reassurance that, even if Robert I and his grandson should perish, the Bruce party meant to retain power, and might choose one of their number as king if necessary.[6]

This raises an awkward question. Would the stirring words we know so well ever have been penned had Robert I and his government not felt jeopardised by Edward Balliol and by the possibility of a dynastic crisis? The threat of a challenge to the throne was certainly very real: a few months later a conspiracy to oust King Robert was revealed. This has gone down in history as the 'Soules conspiracy', as if the object of the exercise was to put William de Soules, the king's butler, on the throne. It has recently been argued convincingly that the real objective was to restore the Balliol kingship, and that after the coup had been savagely suppressed, Robert I was eager to minimise its significance by claiming that a far less credible candidate had been its intended beneficiary.[7]

It is necessary to look elsewhere in the Declaration for reassurance that the ideal of 'national' freedom was, indeed, a central part of its argument. This can be found in one of the least well known sections of the document, in a passage which is most at odds with our modern sensibilities. To any medieval reader, however, it would almost certainly have seemed the most impressive statement of Scotland's claim to sovereignty that had ever been written. It reads as follows (in Professor Duncan's translation):[8]

> Most holy father and lord, we know, and we gather from the deeds and books of the ancients, that among other distinguished nations our own nation, namely of Scots, has been marked by many distinctions. It journeyed from Greater Scythia by the Tyrrhenian Sea and the Pillars of Hercules, and dwelt for a long span of time in Spain among the most savage peoples, but nowhere could it be subjugated by any people, however barbarous. From there it came twelve hundred years after the people of Israel crossed the Red Sea and, having first driven out the Britons and altogether destroyed the Picts, it acquired, with many victories and untold efforts, the places which it now holds, although often assailed by Norwegians, Danes and English. As the histories of old times bear witness, it has held them free of all servitude ever since. In their kingdom one hundred and thirteen kings of their own royal stock have reigned, the line unbroken by a single foreigner.

Of course, this is more or less pure fiction. It does nothing for us today, except perhaps repel us as an embarrassingly brazen piece of propaganda. There can be no denying its importance for those who drafted the Declaration, however. They chose it as their opening statement, following on immediately from the list of those in whose name the Declaration was sent (and the customary offer of devout kisses to the pontiff's feet). It defined the freedom which, in the succeeding sections of the document, we are told that Edward I had defiled, Robert Bruce had restored, and which Scots would fight for, to the death. It was the freedom to be a sovereign people: a kingdom ruled by a king of their own kind.

The notion that a kingdom had been independent since remotest times was not particularly unusual in this period. It was assumed, in the Middle Ages as much as in more modern times, that political status was justified by history. If you claimed to be an independent kingdom, then this automatically meant that you believed that you had been an independent kingdom in the deep past. This was explained with compelling candour by Scottish procurators at the papal Curia in 1301:[9]

> It is certain that, just as the kingdom of Scotland has recently been shown to have been free when its last king died [Alexander III in 1286], so it is presumed to have been free from antiquity if we make an assumption from the recent past and apply it to the more remote past before then, just as the laws dictate.

There are other examples of kingdoms at this time which boasted a long history. The Irish Remonstrance of 1317, which has been regarded as a kind of dishevelled sister of the Declaration of Arbroath, proclaimed that Ireland had an even more impressive track record of freedom, stretching back for 197 kings until, it was stated, the English Pope Adrian 'improperly conferred *de facto* lordship' on Henry II of England in 1170.[10] The English themselves regarded Geoffrey of Monmouth's vivid account of over 100 British kings spanning about 1,800 years up to the seventh century AD as the ancient history of their monarchy.[11] Further afield, we may note the amazing coincidence that King Eirik of Denmark, who was Robert Bruce's contemporary (both were born in 1274), was, like Robert in the Declaration of Arbroath, advertised as the 113th king of his country.[12] There are also instances, like the Declaration of Arbroath, in which a claim to ancient independence was elaborated precisely because the kingdom's sovereignty was at issue. Ancient Danish history, for example, was first given shape by Saxo Grammaticus sometime in or between 1208 and 1218, writing (so he tells us) at the behest of Absalon, archbishop of Lund (1178–1201), in a deliberate attempt to give substance to Denmark's independent status which Absalon was keen to advance.[13]

The significance of the Declaration of Arbroath is that it represents the high water mark of a Scottish vision of ancient independence. Nothing so uncompromising and compelling, at least to a medieval audience, had been attempted before, or would be tried again. This was not, however, achieved by making the most extreme claims for Scottish history ever. Little or nothing of any substance, in fact, had not already been anticipated in earlier attempts to set Scotland's origins in writing. The genius of the account of Scottish origins in the Declaration was in bringing a range of key elements together to produce a more potent portrayal of a primordial past. Scotland's pedigree as a sovereign kingdom had never been articulated so comprehensively and crisply before.

Let us look at each element in turn. The idea that the Scots originated in Scythia (or Greece) had been repeated for centuries. It owes its origin to the observation in the well known *Etymologies* of Isidore, bishop of Seville in the early seventh century, that the Latin word for Scythians, *Sciti*, was very close to *Scoti*. When Isidore wrote, of course, *Scoti* meant 'Irish' or 'Gaels'. The stop-off in Spain had also been a stock feature of learned Christian attempts to explain Irish/Gaelic origins from the outset.[14] So far, the account in the Declaration of Arbroath is giving a standard explanation of how *Scoti* fit into the greater scheme of peoples as this was understood in medieval Christian learning. One feature stands out, however: the idea that the Scots retained their independence in Spain despite the best efforts of savage Spaniards to subjugate them. The need to fight for their freedom at this very early stage is found in other accounts of Scottish origins. One particularly dramatic example has the Scots clinging on to dear life in the Pyrenees, depending on wild plants and robbing their neighbours for their survival, but never, no matter how desperate they became, surrendering their freedom by submitting to the rule of a king other than their own.[15] This probably belonged to a rewriting of Geoffrey of Monmouth's *History* from a Scottish point of view which has been identified by John and Winifred MacQueen, and may be dated tentatively to sometime before 1285.[16]

Much less common is the claim that the Scots reached Scotland 1,200 years after the Children of Israel crossed the Red Sea. It was not entirely unprecedented, however. In

Historia Brittonum, a seminal collection of pseudo-history written in 829 or 830, it was stated that the *Scoti* reached Ireland 1,002 years after Moses led the Israelites through the Red Sea: the crossing of the Red Sea coincided with the departure from Egypt of the eponymous Scota daughter of Pharaoh with her Scythian or Greek husband, progenitors of the *Scoti*.[17] One fundamental difference with the Declaration's account is immediately apparent. There is no mention of Ireland. In the Declaration the *Scoti* go straight from Spain to Scotland. Obviously *Scoti* in the Declaration means Scots in the same basic sense as we understand the term today. There is no suggestion that *Scoti* meant Irish or Gaels. This was something of a novelty. Up to the 1290s the Scots had been represented, in accounts of their origins, as an offshoot of the Irish, and Ireland (not Scotland) had been presented as their homeland.[18] The Declaration was not the first occasion in which Scottish origins had been focused on Scotland rather than Ireland: the Scottish procurators at the Curia in 1301, led by Baldred Bisset, had rewritten the legend of Scota, eponym of the *Scoti*, so that, for the first time, Scotland became her ultimate destination.[19] Ireland was not completely forgotten by Baldred Bisset and his team, though. It was, however, relegated to a mere staging post where Scota acquired reinforcements. The innovation in the Declaration was to omit Ireland altogether.

The figure of 1,200 years for the period between the crossing of the Red Sea and the arrival of the Scots at their homeland, rather than 1,002 years, is highly unusual. It appears to be a copying error. The fault, however, does not lie with those who drafted the Declaration. They had, it seems, inherited this mistake from their source. If we try to chase up this source, we are led to an unexpected conclusion: the author of the Declaration used a *History of the English* for most of his account of Scottish origins! The trail begins with Andrew of Wyntoun's immense poetic history written in Scots in three editions sometime between 1408 and 1424.[20] As part of his project he related a number of different accounts of Scottish origins. The third and last is derived ultimately from *Historia Brittonum*,[21] but instead of giving the figure of 1,002 years from the Red Sea crossing to final settlement, Wyntoun has 1,200 years, just as in the Declaration of Arbroath. Wyntoun's source was not, however, *Historia Brittonum* itself, but Henry of Huntingdon's *History of the English*, written in the second quarter of the twelfth century, in which the origins of the *Scoti* as given in *Historia Brittonum* is repeated with the additional information that the *Scoti* were, in fact, *Navarri* (which presumably refers to Basques)![22] The curious reference to *Navarri* by Wyntoun in very similar terms and in the same context as in Henry of Huntingdon leaves little doubt that Wyntoun was using a copy of Henry of Huntingdon. Henry of Huntingdon himself, however, correctly repeated the figure of 1,002 years given in *Historia Brittonum*. The mistake of 1,200 years instead of 1,002 years seems therefore to have occurred in a copy of Henry of Huntingdon's *History of the English* which was used not only by Wyntoun but also, about a century earlier, in the composition of the Declaration of Arbroath.

Perhaps the most brazen fiction in the Declaration's account of Scottish origins, however, is the statement that the Scots, on arrival in Scotland, not only drove out the Britons, but also destroyed the Picts.[23] It had been a commonplace to regard the Scots and Picts as originally living side-by-side for hundreds of years until the mid-ninth century; only then, and not in the primeval mists of time, were the Picts said to have been annihilated by the Scots led by Cinaed mac Ailpín. Again, however, what was said here in the Declaration was not wholly new. Such a radical rewriting of Scoto-Pictish relations had already been achieved by Baldred Bisset and his team of procurators. It is possible, indeed, to see Bisset and his colleagues making this up as they prepared their pleadings. In their first draft they routinely proposed that the Scots, on arriving in Scotland, had lived alongside the Picts. In their final text, however, they decided to make the primeval association of Scots with Scotland absolutely clear by removing the Picts immediately from the scene, insisting that the Scots destroyed them as soon as they reached Scotland.

This complete takeover of Scotland by the Scots from the very beginning went hand-in-hand with the next striking statement: namely, that there were 113 kings without the intervention of a single foreigner. This proclaimed the enduring freedom of the Scots as the rightful possessors of Scotland from the deepest past right up to Robert I himself. The figure of 113 may seem outrageous, but it was not picked at random. It was the result of a slight but hugely significant change in the way the most complete Scottish king-list was read.[24] The antecedents of Cinaed mac Ailpín's kingdom were regarded as a 'Scottish' kingdom west of Drumalban and a Pictish kingdom in the east. Ideally, the kings of these earlier kingdoms should have been listed in parallel columns, to make it clear that, in the period prior to Cinaed mac Ailpín, Scottish and Pictish kings reigned at the same time. Instead, these kings were presented in a single column: the Scottish kings before Cinaed mac Ailpín were given first, followed by Pictish kings, and then by Cinaed mac Ailpín and his successors. Nevertheless, it was made perfectly clear that the Scottish kings who preceded Cinaed were the contemporaries of Pictish kings, *not* their predecessors. At some stage in the late thirteenth century, however, this crucial detail was overlooked. Someone decided that all the kings belonged to a single series, as if they were kings of one and the same kingdom. The pre-Cinaed Scottish kings were thus presented as the predecessors of the Picts; as a result, the Scottish king Ailpín, who was obviously meant to be Cinaed's father, became separated from his son by about a millennium, with sixty Pictish kings intervening between them.[25] If all the kings, both Scots and Picts, who were thus reinterpreted as constituting a single series, were to be added up, the total (including John Balliol and Robert Bruce) would be 113. The idea of reckoning these kings in this way, with such scant regard for any sense of chronological propriety was not, however, an innovation of the Declaration of Arbroath. The earliest occasion in which it is found is in a king-list produced sometime in the reign of King John, in which it is proclaimed, in a supreme final flourish, that on the day John Balliol was inaugurated as king (30 November, 1292) the kingdom of Scotland, through its succession of Pictish and Scottish kings, was 1,976 years, 9 months and 8 days old.[26]

Any distinction between Pictish and Scottish kings was lost in the Declaration. Indeed, given that the Picts were, as we have seen, treated as foreigners who had to be rubbed out as soon as the Scots arrived in Scotland, it may seem a bit rich that the figure of 113 kings 'unbroken by a single foreigner' actually included sixty Pictish kings. But we should not rush to condemn. Such cynicism could only be imputed if the authors of the Declaration had a king-list before them. The global total of 113, however, could have been taken from an existing global figure without realising that less than half were Scots.

The idea of insisting that all kings of Scotland were Scots was not new to the Declaration. An earlier poetic account of Scottish history, written sometime between 1296 and 1306, but subsequently continued by Walter Bower, seems originally to have ended with this striking statement at the end of its comparatively modest enumeration of fifty-two kings:[27]

> Thus far these kings had all been Scots like their people, and, if God grants it, may it be henceforth just as it was before. When a body has an alien head, it is all filth: so a people is defiled when a foreigner becomes king.

There was little or nothing in terms of content or ideas, therefore, that was new in the account of Scottish origins in the Declaration of Arbroath. The only novel detail was the omission of Ireland from the itinerary before the Scots reached Scotland; the refocusing of the primordial odyssey on Scotland rather than Ireland had, however, been anticipated by Baldred Bisset and his fellow procurators in 1301. What makes the Declaration so outstanding compared to other accounts is in the range of elements that have been brought together. Only in the Declaration would you learn that Scotland and the Scots had not only been ruled by a succession of 113 kings, but also that they had never submitted to a foreign power, and that Scotland had been possessed in its entirety by the Scots, free of Picts or Britons, from 1,200 years after Moses led the Israelites across the Red Sea. Scotland's primordial integrity as an independent kingdom and people had never been stated so clearly.

Neither would it be expressed again in such an uncompromising way.[28] Later accounts allowed the Picts to populate Scottish history up to Cinaed mac Ailp'n, and fell shy of following the Declaration, or Baldred Bisset and his colleagues, in promoting Scotland's unity under the Scots as something achieved from the very beginning a millennium earlier. The Declaration's vivid outline of the kingdom's past was never made the basis of a more substantial narrative. The full-scale histories of John of Fordun and his followers made less extreme claims, particularly when it came to dealing with the Picts or adding up Scottish kings. John of Fordun, his revisers and to some extent his readers can be recognised as scholars; the vision of Scotland's ancient roots in the Declaration, however, was created by lawyers and politicians for lawyers and politicians. It was a different subspecies of regnal history to the deluxe multi-tome version elaborated by Fordun and Bower. This distinction should not be carried too far, however. The Declaration of Arbroath was bound in with some manuscripts of Fordun's chronicle, and was quoted in full by Bower and in histories derived from Bower's *Scotichronicon*. What, we may wonder, did readers of Fordun and Bower make of the Declaration's bold assertions about the kingdom's past? An innovative piece of research by Murray Tod, a teacher of History at Epsom College, is yielding some interesting answers.

One obstacle remains before the account of Scottish origins can readily be accepted as the part of the Declaration that made the greatest impact to contemporaries in 1320 as a statement of Scotland's 'nationhood'. It is a nagging question. How could Robert Bruce and the majority of those who sealed the Declaration of Arbroath *not* have noticed that, in relation to the immense span of Scottish history proclaimed in that document, their lineages were recent arrivals, and that in this sense they should have regarded themselves as foreigners? Some kind of answer might be assembled on the basis of intermarriage. Robert Bruce's ancestry from Gaelic earls of Carrick was certainly crucial for him: it gave him a political base from which he could begin to restore his fortunes after the collapse of his forces in 1306. But this, I think, would be to miss the point. Again, I suspect that our modern assumptions about nations create inappropriate expectations in the context of the Middle Ages. In the modern era it became commonplace to regard statehood as 'natural' only if it coincided with an ethnic community, typically thought of as speakers of the same language. It was assumed, moreover, that these ethnic communities constituted natural and exclusive divisions of humanity which had their origins deep in the past, whose destiny could only be fulfilled if they achieved political independence.[29] When, therefore, we read in the Declaration the claim that the Scots were an ancient sovereign people, it is tempting to understand this as expressing a sense of ethnic community. This is where the trouble begins: on these terms the statement of Scottish origins in the Declaration of Arbroath seems to fly in the face of reality so obviously that it is hard to accept that Robert Bruce and company could have meant it except as a brazen propaganda ploy. How could such a 'national' pedigree have convinced anyone?

There is a fairly straightforward response to this conundrum. It needs to be remembered that the definition of a nation as an ethnic community – the idea that sovereignty should be legitimated by language and culture – is a modern concept which was first articulated as a doctrine by Johann Gottfried Herder (1744–1803). It went hand-in-hand with a theory of government which had as its touchstone the equal participation of all inhabitants, and unenforced consent as its ideal, in deliberate opposition to the prevailing notion of an inherited ruling class who maintained their authority by coercion.[30] None of this would have made any sense to those named as the Declaration's sponsors. If we want to know what Scottish nationality meant to them, then we should look more closely at the Declaration itself, and also look at the texts which have been mentioned already as precursors of the Declaration. The core idea was of the Scots as a people obedient to the inherited authority of their king, free from the control of another king. The doctrine here was that sovereign kingdoms constituted peoples, not that ethnic communities should be politically independent; nations were communities of submission, not people bound together equally by a common culture; they were justified by lengthy king-lists, not fat dictionaries or vernacular epics.[31]

In theory, then, the family origins, mother tongue, and social *mores* of those Scots named in the Declaration were irrelevant to their sense of being Scottish. What made them Scottish was their obedience to the king of Scots.[32] This idea of Scottishness was not peculiar to the generation of 1320. It is found, for example, in Barbour's *Bruce*, written in 1375 or 1376. There we are told, for example, that Laurence of Abernethy, when he rode with his men to help Edward II at Bannockburn, 'was at that time still an Englishman'.[33] When Sir Ingram de Umfraville appeared in Robert I's court in the aftermath of the Soules conspiracy, we are told that he 'was then with the king as a Scotsman'.[34] Barbour described the changes of allegiance by these men without adverse comment: in Barbour's narrative their switch from one king to the other was made openly and for reasonable cause. The most significant text for the emergence of this definition of Scottishness is the Chronicle of Melrose, which included a century of contemporary recording from the late twelfth to the late thirteenth century. For most of this period 'Scots' is used in the chronicle as a term for the Gaelic population north of the Forth.[35] The monks of Melrose evidently regarded themselves as English, living in 'the land of England, and in the kingdom of the Scots', as the prior of neighbouring Dryburgh put it.[36] By the time the final section of the chronicle was being written up (sometime between 1285 and 1291), however, the monks of Melrose had begun to regard themselves as Scots.[37] For them, the term 'Scot' had lost its exclusive cultural associations. They were now Scots only because this term was now understood to embrace the totality of the king's subjects.

The account of Scottish origins in the Declaration of Arbroath, as the pedigree of Scottish self-determination, was not a statement of biological descent or ethnic affiliation. It was the pedigree of an allegiance, a pattern of obedience intended to demonstrate the kingdom's credentials as a thoroughbred institution with generations of history behind it. Is this the pedigree of a nation, though? Not if by 'nation' we mean an idealised ethnic community. The Declaration of Arbroath shows, however, that the idea of a sovereign community could be articulated without reference to ethnicity. This formulation was not, of course, peculiar to Scotland. Susan Reynolds has shown that the idea of sovereign peoples was deeply embedded in European political consciousness by the fourteenth century.[38] It is possible, therefore, to see the nineteenth-century ideal of nations as ethnic communities as merely a reformulation of an older idea of nationhood. At the very least, if we wish to understand the ideas which underpin the modern phenomenon of nations, consideration should be given to the medieval ancestry of some of its core concepts, not least the notion that political sovereignty and primordial communities were two sides of the same coin.

NOTES

1 See further Terry Brotherstone and David Ditchburn, '1320 and a' that: the Declaration of Arbroath and the remaking of Scottish History', in *Freedom and Authority. Scotland c. 1050 – c. 1650. Historical and Historiographical Essays presented to Grant G. Simpson*, Terry Brotherstone and David Ditchburn (eds) (East Linton 2000), 10–31, esp. 20–4.

2 Grant G. Simpson, 'The Declaration of Arbroath revitalised', *Scottish Historical Review*, 56 (1977), 11–33, at 22–4, has shown that the Declaration should be seen as belonging to a genre of government-inspired addresses to the papacy by the leading subjects of a kingdom which

was designed to add political weight to a king's resistance to papal pressure. It could be argued, however, that the framework of political assumptions which underpins the purposefully dramatised prose in such documents was significantly different in the case of the Declaration. The threat to depose the king announced in the Declaration is decidedly more radical than the parallel statements in documents cited by Simpson ('The Declaration of Arbroath', 22–3) in which the king's subjects swore to back their monarch to the death (as in the baronial letter written in support of King John of England in 1212: H. G. Richardson and G. O. Sayles, *The Irish Parliament in the Middle Ages* (2nd edn; Philadelphia 1964, 286–7), or in which they resolved to prevent their king from implementing the pope's ruling (as in the baronial response to Pope Boniface's denial of Edward I's claim to be lord superior of Scotland: *Foedera*, i, part ii, 926–7). See also G. W. S. Barrow, *Scotland and its Neighbours in the Middle Ages* (London 1992), 12–14, for the contrast between the Declaration and documents of similar type. The significance of this 'momentous clause' as evidence for the precocious development in Scotland of the 'contractual theory of monarchy' is argued by E. J. Cowan, 'Identity, freedom, and the Declaration of Arbroath', in *Image and Identity: the Making and Re-making of Scotland Through the Ages*, D. Broun, R. J. Finlay and M. Lynch (eds) (Edinburgh 1998), 38–68, esp. 51–4. For an interpretation which sees both political ideas and expediency at play, see Alexander Grant, 'Aspects of national consciousness in medieval Scotland', in *Nations, Nationalism and Patriotism in the European Past*, C. Bjørn, A. Grant and K. J. Stringer (eds) (Copenhagen 1994), 68–95, at 69–73. I would argue, however, that the radical aspect of the Declaration can be explained in the light of immediate political concerns (see below).

3   Michael Penman, '*A fell coniuracioun agayn Robert the douchty king*: the Soules conspiracy of 1318–1320', *Innes Review*, 50 (1999), 25–57, at 38–9.

4   Robert's mother, Marjorie, daughter of Robert I, was probably married not long after 27 April 1315; Robert Stewart himself was probably born before 25 March 1316. See discussion in *Scotichronicon by Walter Bower*, D. E. R. Watt (ed.), vi (1991), 465, at note on chap. 25 lines 61–2; also *Regesta Regum Scottorum*, v, *The Acts of Robert I, King of Scots, 1306–1329*, A. A. M. Duncan (ed.) (Edinburgh, 1988), 652, which shows that the date of Robert Stewart's birth is more uncertain than is apparent in *The Handbook of British Chronology*, E. B. Fryde, D. E. Greenway, S. Porter and I. Roy (eds) (3rd edn; London, 1986), 59, where it is given without comment as 2 March 1316. Detailed provision for the royal succession was made in the tailzie of 1318, adopting the principles on which the Bruce claim was based in 1291–2: see A. A. M. Duncan, *The Kingship of the Scots, 842–1292: Succession and Independence* (Edinburgh 2002), 327–8. If the direct line had died out, this would apparently have given the strongest claim to Domhnall Bán, earl of Mar, who was the son of Robert I's sister. Domhnall, however, had refused to return to Scotland after Bannockburn, and remained in England until Edward II's death in 1327.

5   It has previously been recognised that the threat to remove the king may have been directed against a Balliol, but discussion of this has hitherto focused on King John himself, and in particular the need to explain how Robert I could have become king in 1306 while John was still alive and had not been formally deposed by the 'community of the realm': see Grant, 'Aspects of national consciousness', 71–2, and R. James Goldstein, *The Matter of Scotland. Historical Narrative in Medieval Scotland* (Lincoln: Nebraska 1993), 95–7. For doubts about the retrospective intention of this key passage, see Brotherstone and Ditchburn, '1320 and a' that', 25 n. 67.

6   The most likely contender would probably have been Thomas Randolph, earl of Moray, who in the tailzies of succession of 27 April 1315 and 3 December 1318 was designated as guardian of the realm should Robert I die leaving a minor as his heir: *APS*, i, 464–5; Gordon Donaldson,

Scottish Historical Documents (reprinted with corrections; Edinburgh 1974), 52–4. Thomas Randolph's grandmother was Robert I's mother, so he would not have had the right of blood defined in the tailzie of 1318 (see Duncan, *The Kingship of the Scots*, 327, n. 47). Robert I's daughters by his second wife were not yet born: Margaret (who married William, earl of Sutherland, c. 1345) and Matilda (who married sometime in or after 1342, and died 20 July 1353): Bower, *Scotichronicon* (Watt) vi, 461, at notes on lines 231–3 and 235–8; *Scotichronicon* (Watt) vii, 471, at note on lines 54–61.

7 Penman, '*A fell coniuracioun*'. The suggestion that Edward Balliol was the intended beneficiary of the conspiracy was first made in A. A. M. Duncan, 'The war of the Scots, 1306–23', *Transactions of the Royal Historical Society*, 6th series, 2 (1992), 125–51, at 129–31.

8 John Barbour, *The Bruce*, A. A. M. Duncan (ed.) (Edinburgh 1997), 779–82.

9 *Scotichronicon* (Watt) vi, 151 (bk XI, ch. 51, lines 71–5).

10 Ibid., 384–403, at 386–7. In comparison with the Declaration of Arbroath, the Remonstrance has been described by Scottish historians as 'a rambling, loosely organised piece of writing' (Grant Simpson, 'The Declaration of Arbroath', 24), and 'a rambling tirade of invective' (Barrow, *Scotland and its Neighbours*, 14).

11 The process by which Geoffrey's *Historia Regum Britannie* came to be regarded as English History is discussed in R. William Leckie Jnr, *The Passage of Dominion: Geoffrey of Monmouth and the Periodization of Insular History in the Twelfth Century* (Toronto 1981). The results of how the British past was 'captured and possessed by the English' has recently been explored perceptively in R. R. Davies, *The First English Empire: Power and Identities in the British Isles 1093–1343* (Oxford 2000), 41–3.

12 *Annales Ryenses*, s.a. 1287 (Eirik's coronation). For the text of the chronicle, see *Danmarks Middelalderlige Annaler*, ed. E. Kroman (Copenhagen 1980), 150–76. Kroman's edition is from Hamburg Stadtbibliotek MS. 98 b, which he dates to c. 1300 (see ibid., 149). This is the only manuscript to which he refers. The chronicle is a fusion of annals and a king-list, and begins with the legendary origins of the Danes: the first annalistic item is *s.a.* 1028 (the martyrdom of King Ólafr of Norway), and the annalistic element only becomes frequent from the late eleventh century. The chronicle ends in 1288, and presumably assumed its surviving form sometime in that year or soon after. Hamburg Stadtbibliotek MS. 98 b is a copy (as can be seen, for example, in the appearance of Eirik as king no. '116' rather than 113, a simple mistake in copying minims: see ibid., 176, apparatus).

13 Saxo Grammaticus, *The History of the Danes*, i, Peter Fisher (trans), Hilda Ellis Davidson (ed.) (Cambridge 1979), 4 (preface). For the date of Saxo's work, see ibid., 1. For Archbishop Absalom, see ibid., ii, commentary by Hilda Ellis Davidson and Peter Fisher (Cambridge, 1980), 19. Absalom advised Knud IV (1182–1202) that he should refuse to repeat the homage which Danish kings in the twelfth century had hitherto made to the German emperor.

14 The origins of the legend are discussed in John Carey, *The Irish National Origin-Legend: Synthetic Pseudohistory*, Quiggin Pamphlet no. 1 (Cambridge 1994), 8–12.

15 Dauvit Broun, *The Irish Identity of the Kingdom of Scots in the Twelfth and Thirteenth Centuries* (Woodbridge, 1999), 48–9, for edition of this part of Fordun's chronicle.

16 *Scotichronicon* (Watt), i, xxviii–xxix. This included the 'Partholón' account of Scottish origins which can be identified in Fordun's chronicle: see Broun, *The Irish Identity*, 76–81 (where a *terminus ante quem* of 1301 is suggested). The earlier *terminus ante quem* is based on the suggestion that much of Fordun's chronicle is derived from an earlier work datable to sometime in or between February and April 1285: see most recently Dauvit Broun, 'The Picts' place in the kingship's past before John of Fordun', in *Scottish History: the Power of the Past*, Edward J. Cowan and Richard J. Finlay (eds) (Edinburgh 2002), 11–28, at 25–7.

17 *The Historia Brittonum*, 10 vols, David N. Dumville (ed.), iii, *The 'Vatican' Recension* (Cambridge 1985), 69–70. The other volumes are forthcoming: for the place of this section in other recensions see ibid., 56–7. Text, translation and commentary are given in Carey, *The Irish National Origin-Legend*, 5–7.
18 Broun, *The Irish Identity*, esp. 109–32.
19 Ibid., 120, 198; *Scotichronicon* (Watt) vi, 182–3.
20 *The Original Chronicle of Andrew of Wyntoun*, F. J. Amours (ed.), Scottish Text Society, 6 vols (1903–14). For the dating 1408 x 24 see Broun, *The Irish Identity*, 96 n. 40.
21 *Chron. Wyntoun* (Amours), ii, 202–7. For the passage in *Historia Brittonum*, see n. 17, above.
22 *Henry, Archdeacon of Huntingdon, Historia Anglorum. The History of the English People*, Diana Greenway (ed.) (Oxford 1996), 28–31.
23 For this paragraph, see Broun, 'The Picts' place in the kingship's past', 11–16.
24 For what follows, see Dauvit Broun, 'The birth of Scottish History', *SHR*, 76 (1997), 2–22, at 12–13.
25 This is archetype β (which included king-list and origin-legend), probably written sometime in the 1290s: Broun, *The Irish Identity*, 109, 198.
26 This is archetype γ (which included king-list and origin-legend), written sometime during the reign of King John (1292–1304): Broun, *The Irish Identity*, 109, 198. It survives translated into French in Thomas Grey's *Scalacronica*, begun sometime in or after 1355 and completed sometime in or after 1363. The king-list section of this text in *Scalacronica* (known by the siglum *K*) is edited in Marjorie O. Anderson, *Kings and Kingship in Early Scotland* (2nd edn; Edinburgh, 1980), 286–9.
27 *Liber Extravagans*, ed. Dauvit Broun with A. B. Scott, in *Scotichronicon* (Watt) ix, 54–127, at 78–9. For the date of the poem see ibid., 56–7 (where grounds for a tighter date-range of 1304 x 1306 are noted).
28 For what follows, see Broun, 'The Picts' place in the kingship's past', 17–19, 28.
29 The most influential of the various attempts to explain such assumptions are: Benedict Anderson, *Imagined Communities: Reflections on the Origin and Spread of Nationalism* (rev. edn; London 1991); Ernest Gellner, *Nations and Nationalism* (Oxford 1983); Eric Hobsbawn, *Nations and Nationalism since 1780: Programme, Myth and Reality* (Cambridge 1990); Anthony D. Smith, *National Identity* (Hardmondsworth 1991). For a critical assessment of these approaches, see Adrian Hastings, *The Construction of Nationhood: Ethnicity, Religion, and Nationalism* (Cambridge, 1997) and Anthony D. Smith, *The Nation in History. Historiographical Debates about Ethnicity and Nationalism* (Cambridge 2000).
30 F. M. Bernard, *Herder's Social and Political Thought. From Enlightenment to Nationalism* (Oxford 1965), 141–4.
31 Attempts in the late eighteenth and nineteenth centuries to create the cultural infrastructure for Celtic nations are discussed in David Greene, *Makers and Forgers*. The G. J. Williams Memorial Lecture 1975 (Cardiff 1975).
32 On this aspect of the Declaration, note also the similar observation made in Seán Duffy, 'The Anglo-Norman era in Scotland: convergence and divergence', in *Celebrating Columba. Colm Cille á Cheiliúradh. Irish-Scottish Connections 597–1997*, T. M. Devine and James F. McMillan (eds) (Edinburgh 1999), 15–34, at 17–18.
33 *. . . he was Inglisman yet then*: Barbour, *The Bruce*, Duncan (ed.), 509 (bk. XIII, line 560/556).
34 *. . . than/ Wes with the king as Scottisman*: ibid., 703 (bk. XIX, lines 73–4).
35 Dauvit Broun, 'Anglo-French acculturation and the Irish element in Scottish identity', in *Britain and Ireland 900–1300. Insular Responses to Medieval European Change*, Brendan Smith (ed.) (Cambridge 1999), 135–53, at 141–2. This point is discussed in more detail in *idem*, 'The

Attitude of *Gall* to *Gaedel* before John of Fordun' in *M`orun Mór nan Gall: the Great Ill-will of the Lowlander. Lowland Perceptions of the Highlands*, D. Broun and M. MacGregor (eds) (forthcoming).

36 Adam of Dryburgh, *De tripartito tabernaculo* in *Patrologiæ cursus completus . . . series Latina*, J.-P. Migne (ed.) (Paris 1841–), cxcviii, cols. 609–792, at col. 723: . . . *in terra Anglorum, et in regno Scotorum* . . .

37 Dauvit Broun, 'Defining Scotland and the Scots before the Wars of Independence', in *Image and Identity. The Making and Re-making of Scotland through the Ages*, Dauvit Broun, R. J. Finlay and Michael Lynch (eds) (Edinburgh 1998), 4–17, at 9, 15–16.

38 Susan Reynolds, *Kingdoms and Communities in Western Europe, 900–1300* (Oxford 1984).

I would like to thank the organisers of the original conference for the invitation to deliver this paper, and Dr Nerys Ann Jones for her continued support and encouragement.

DECLARING ARBROATH

Edward J. Cowan

It is a gratifying irony, representing as it does appropriate reciprocation, that Resolution 155 of the American Senate (March 1998) should assert that the American Declaration of Independence is modelled upon the papal letter of 1320 since that missive was dubbed the Scottish Declaration of Independence, very early in the twentieth century, in due homage to the emotive document of 1776. The uniqueness of the Arbroath letter is such that it does not require the reinforcement of American accolade. I have already attempted to explain something of this remarkable document, exploring the relevance of the deposition clause, hitherto largely doubted or ignored by academic criticism, and have sought to investigate the inspirational roots of the celebrated freedom passage, nowadays so often quoted if imperfectly understood.[1] The recognition of 6 April,[2] the anniversary of the Arbroath letter, as National Tartan Day in the US, although welcomed in that country by people from a wide range of backgrounds not exclusively Scottish, has proved highly controversial among the chattering classes in the Auld Country. Although the campaign to observe a 'Scottish Day' originated in Canada and has now impacted upon Australia and New Zealand as well (albeit on a different date), it would appear to be alleged American usurpation of the occasion, which has particularly stuck in critical craws. It thus seems appropriate to investigate something of the origins of Tartan Day and the remarkable blossoming of interest in what many of the celebrants worldwide would regard as an obscure document emanating from an unfamiliar period and a country, which only a minority have ever visited. Even if its name is all too frequently mispronounced,[3] the burgh of Arbroath is now enjoying wider global familiarity than at any time in its history while the document in which it is forever enshrined is attracting unprecedented interest. That there should apparently be a desire to deny that interest in the darker recesses of certain political factions, as well as in those of the media and academia, is almost beyond belief, if not entirely unpredictable.

Although 'Arbroath' (by which I intend to signify the letter rather than the burgh), was much better known in the medieval manuscript tradition than some scholars have allowed, having attained a near-legendary character by the fifteenth century,[4] the beginnings of the process by which its status became mythic may be traced to its first published translation into English in 1689, the year, of course, of the so-called 'Glorious Revolution'. The pamphlet is entitled *A Letter from the Nobility, Barons & Commons of*

Scotland wherein they *declare* (my italics) their adherence to King Robert 'as restorer of the Safety and Liberties of the People'. Furthermore they '*Declare*, that if the King should offer to subvert their Civil Liberties, they will disown him as an Enemy, and choose another to be King, for their own Defence'. Thus through a more-than-somewhat forced interpretation, the document is incorporated into the Whig tradition. No less significantly, it becomes a declaration, a politically motivated and anachronistic designation which confers upon the document a prestige and status that was certainly no part of its original intent, for the word 'declaration' has the technical sense of a statement subsequently issued to explain an act or action.

Declarations were known in the reign of James VI & I but they became increasingly common during the civil wars of the seventeenth century. It is well accepted that the various declarations issued in 1689 had a direct influence on those who deliberated upon independence at Philadelphia in 1776. Thomas Jefferson, for example, is thought to have drawn upon a draft of the English Declaration of Rights,[5] but it is much more likely that he was indebted to the Scottish Claim of Right, which mentioned James VII's forfeiture of his right to the crown, rather than the fiction of abdication adopted by the English document. George III clearly did not abdicate his rule of America. Rather, in the words of Jefferson's declaration, like James, he forfeited his right;[6] Scotland, or at least Scottish political propaganda, provided a more useful precedent than did England. I have already speculated, on no compellingly convincing grounds, that Bishop Gilbert Burnet may have been responsible for the 1689 translation of 'Arbroath'.[7] It may be further suggested, though at present not proven, that a copy of that pamphlet found its way to the American colonies. What is not in doubt is that 1689 represents a kind of defining moment in the history of the Arbroath letter for which the year serves as the crossroads of the centuries, looking back to the inspirational rhetoric and halcyon days of the Wars of Independence, providing present confirmation of the constitutional monarchy, and, fancifully perhaps, pointing forward, towards the mythic and parahistorical status, which would be conferred upon it by later generations of Scots.

James Anderson, the fierce opponent of Union in 1707, gleefully reported the observations of the English historian, Samuel Daniel, that Edward I's claims to the superiority of Scotland initiated the mortal dissension between the two nations, 'that consumed more Christian blood, wrought more spoil and destruction, and continued longer than ever quarrel we read did, between any two people of the world'. Daniel graciously conceded that the invaded country, though weaker and smaller, enjoyed the greater honour since it was never subdued though often overcome, 'continuing, notwithstanding of all their miseries, resolute to preserve their liberties'. Anderson proceeded to commend the Declaration of the Clergy (1309) and the Declaration of Arbroath as 'Manifestos of Independence'.

> Can there be a greater Evidence of the Independency and Freedom of a Nation, Than the Liberties which we find our Ancestors exerted. One remarkable Instance is in a plain and weighty Paragraph of these repeated solemn Declarations by the Clergy and Community of Scotland. In them it is said; *That the Right and Title of King Robert the Bruce to the Crown, was declared by the Judgement of the People, That he was assum'd to be King, by their Knowledg*

and Consent, for ends mention'd by them; That being Advanced by their Authority to the Crown, he was thereby Solemnly made King of Scotland. These appear to be Important and Comprehensive Sentences. How far they establish and confirm a revolution Settlement, as being agreeable to our ancient Constitution; Or how far they discover, That a Claim of Right is no novelty in Scotland, but was the principle and Practice of our Fathers: And how far the Title of King Robert Bruce and his Successors, who have sway'd our Scepter, for these four Hundred Years, is Settled and Founded in these Principles, I leave to every Man to Judge: But sure I am, These Declarations plainly evince, That any homages made by the People of Scotland, to Edward the first, were extorted Acknowledgements.

Like Burnet, Anderson made a transcript of the original at Tyninghame House and he later commissioned a magnificent engraving of the document from Isaac Basire. He reported that Robert owed his kingship to Divine Providence, right of succession and the consent of his people who fought not for glory, riches, nor honours (as he correctly translated the plural – the frequently rendered singular, 'honour', is a mistake), 'But only for Liberty which no good man loses but with his Life.'

> Being so zealous of their Liberties, they were not asham'd to acknowledge the small Bounds of their Countrey, but rather rejoiced and gloried in their being contented with their own, and that in so little a Spot of ground, they and their predecessors had maintained their Independency.[8]

Patrick Abercromby waxed eloquent over the 'bold, loyal, judicious & pious Letter' of 1320 though he strenuously contested the notion that the Scottish monarchy was purely elective.[9] Nonetheless, although 'Arbroath' was invoked by several Whig propagandists, and commented upon by such scholars as Lord Hailes, it was to be some time before it was incorporated into the mainstream Scottish historiographical tradition. Scott was not greatly impressed, content as he was to plagiarise Hailes, although John Galt was. The latter, in a note to *Ringan Gilhaize; or The Covenanters* (1823), in which novel he quoted the freedom passage, memorably noted English ignorance of the Scottish political character observing that, 'The English are a justice-loving people, according to charter and statute; the Scotch are a wrong-resenting race, according to right and feeling: and the character of liberty among them takes its aspect from that peculiarity'. He proceeded to quote the seventeenth-century translation of Arbroath *in extenso*.[10] Galt departed from the 1689 translation in only one place. Where the latter asserted that for so long as a hundred remained alive 'we will never give consent to subject our selves to the Dominion of the English', Galt was content with 'we will never Subject ourselves to the Dominion of the English'. His omission was a little odd since the idea of consent was as crucial to the Covenanters as it was to the propagandists of 1689, but his wording is identical to that of the 1703 pamphlet, which was obviously his source.[11] It is clear that Anderson, Abercromby and Galt all preferred Latin 'liberty' to Anglo-Saxon 'freedom', which latter word did not attain prominence in the translations until the end of the nineteenth century.

Hill Burton in his lengthy history of Scotland noted 'a solemn address . . . a great remonstrance', but William Burns in 1874 was truly the first to produce a substantial discussion of the 'Aberbrothoc manifesto' which he variously characterised as a 'declaration', and a combined pleading and remonstrance. The latter word did exist in the Middle Ages, recorded from 1477 in the sense of appeal or request, but in the course of the seventeenth century it came to mean a remonstrance or a statement of grievances, often acquiring overtones of 'declaration'. Burns was inspired to write his two bulky volumes by the general ignorance manifested by those pro and contra the movement to erect the Wallace Monument at Abbey Craig, Stirling. As well as discussing 'Arbroath' at some length, he also noted the Declaration of the Clergy in 1309 and the Irish Remonstrance of 1317. He was not a trained historian but he was a patriot who was convinced that a crucial period of Scottish history was in danger of serious distortion and downright dismissal at the hands of contemporary English and Scottish authorities. As such, his views, on a wide range of issues, including race and religion, deserve greater respect than they have so far received.[12] John Macintosh detected 'a spirited and constitutional address . . . of much historic and constitutional importance'.[13] Peter Hume Brown in his three-volume *History of Scotland* (1900) mentioned it briefly.

Local historians were less restrained. J. M. M'Bain believed that 'Arbroath' 'asserted for all time the independent nationality of the Scottish people'. He thought it one of the most remarkable documents in 'Scottish National History', questioning whether there was anything anywhere with which it might be compared 'in its stalwart assertion of national independence and the democratic spirit which inspires it'. In firmness and fervour, he opined, the declaration had not been surpassed in his own century. 'The Declaration of Arbroath breathes the spirit which never yet has been conquered, and it established for all time the nationality and independence of the Scottish kingdom, which never again was questioned, even in the darkest days of subsequent history'.[14] He was followed by another parish chauvinist, J. Brodie, who entitled his publication – little more than a pamphlet – *About Arbroath: (Fairport of Scott's "Antiquary") The Birthplace of the Declaration of Scottish Independence, 1320* (Arbroath 1904). His title said it all, for his discussion was exceedingly brief though it included a chunk of poesy by one A. T. Mathews:

> When William's Abbey, noble pile,
> Stood unsurpassed in Britain's isle,
> When vows were ta'en within her wa's
> To stand or fa' for freedom's cause –
> When Bruce wore Bonnie Scotland's croon
> And knights and nobles thronged the toon,
> 'Twas then Arbrothock led the van
> 'Gainst England's might – Rome's impious ban.

He was in no doubt that the man who defeated 'English pretensions to the suzerainty of Scotland' and papal diplomacy, was Abbot Bernard de Linton, who, for long identified, traditionally and erroneously, as the author of the Declaration, enjoys commemoration in the name of a local pub.[15] What is noticeable in both verse and prose is the implication that Bruce and the Scots not only established independence from England, but also from Rome. The preposterous idea that those involved in the Declaration somehow anticipated the Reformation was reiterated by Nigel Tranter in his 1971 novel, *Robert the Bruce, The Price of the King's Peace*, which sees 'Arbroath' as an antecedent of the National Covenant of 1638.[16]

Otherwise the mythologisation of 'Arbroath' has proceeded nicely, largely unaided by the *literati*. What should be noted, however, is the extent to which the significance of the document has been advanced and publicised by local advocates in Arbroath itself without much obvious input from professional historians who generally shied clear of any serious investigation of the letter until the lead-up to the 650th anniversary in 1970. It was the Burns Federation, not the Scottish Record Office, that, in 1949, initiated the idea of making a copy of 'Arbroath' available to every secondary school and training college in the country, two years after the launching of the annual Arbroath pageant.[17] It could thus be argued that the main interest in the Arbroath Declaration was populist, in the best sense of the word, or even democratic, until a new generation of more sympathetic historians emerged in the 1950s and 1960s.[18] Despite the efforts of the latter, many misunderstandings remain, most commonly that 'Arbroath' was an oath or covenant of some kind, signed, rather than sealed, by those involved, as a result of a great parliament or convention held at the abbey. It is often said, incorrectly, to have been sent to the pope at Rome, rather than to Avignon. If such is the case in the homeland it is hardly surprising that confusion about the document reigns in other parts of the world as well.

Tartan Day was actually a Canadian invention. In the late 1980s Mrs Jean Watson of Nova Scotia proposed that one day a year should be reserved to remember and honour the contribution of the Scots to the early history of Canada, securing the support of Scottish groups and politicians to that effect. Having succeeded in her own province she then tackled the rest of the country. Her suggestions were adopted by the Clans and Scottish Societies of Canada (CASSOC) which then prevailed with Ontario MPP Bill Murray to promote a Private Member's Bill in the Ontario Legislature. As a result the Ontario Parliament unanimously adopted the following resolution on 19 December, 1991:

> That in the opinion of the House, recognising the multi-cultural nature of Ontario and the contribution of the Scottish community to the economic, agricultural and cultural wellbeing of Ontario, and recognising that the 6th day of April is a day of historical significance to the Scottish community, as it marks the anniversary of the declaration of Scottish independence made in 1320, this House should proclaim the 6th of April as Tartan Day.

It was explained that the letter was directed to the pope by the nobles, barons and freeholders, 'together with the whole community of Scotland', requesting that the country's independence under the kingship of Robert Bruce be recognised. 'The document not only enunciated the principle of constitutional kingship'; it also included the inspirational lines, 'For so long as a hundred of us remain alive etc., a message as relevant today as it was in 1320'. The document concludes by stating that, 'Tartan Day commemorates all that is best in Scottish History and Culture as well as the massive contribution to the growth and development of Canada'.[19]

Given its origins, Tartan Day may be a grandchild of Premier Angus MacDonald's initiatives on the tartanisation of Nova Scotia beginning in the 1930s.[20] Most Scots blanch at the nomenclature even though younger Scottish males have taken back the kilt in recent years for graduations, weddings, and other special occasions such as football matches. In the minds of some, however, tartan sends out the wrong signals of a plastic Scott-land mired in a romantic past. The word 'tartan' is now at least five hundred years old having first been recorded about 1500. The postmodern dilemma is that many throughout the world seem intent upon adopting the national garb of which some Scots are ashamed and wish to discard, but with which their country is forever identified.[21]

Another supporter had been the Scottish Studies Foundation established by a number of Scots-Canadians, mostly in Ontario, in 1987. It was due to this body that notice was taken of the Declaration's deposition clause, euphemistically characterised as 'the principle of constitutional kingship'. Many of the Foundation's members worked tirelessly towards the establishment of Tartan Day. Meetings were held in Toronto – memorably at the Toronto Press Club under the auspices of 'Honest Ed Mirvisch', businessman extraordinaire and theatre impresario, who enjoyed making jokes about Rabbi Burns and who wore a kilt every 25 January. There were also gatherings at the University of Guelph which hosted the finest Scottish Studies programme on the North American continent. For several years the intention was to try to explain the significance of 'Arbroath', in any sympathetic venue to folk who, in the main, had never heard of it, as briefly and simply as possible. In support of the cause in British Columbia, a massive function was organised in Hotel Vancouver. It should be stressed that no one who worked on these projects was, in any sense, aware of any kind of political agenda. The point is important in view of charges frequently made that the event in the US was usurped by the American Right. There was no Canadian Declaration of Independence with the potential to warp or misrepresent 'Arbroath' in any way. It must be admitted that some Canadian Scots were supportive because they were, and are, suspicious of immigrants, convinced that the contribution of the Scots to Canada is further minimised and devalued with the passing of every year, but thankfully, for every one of such persuasions, there were numerous others who rejoiced in the multicultural nature of Canadian society, who were proud of their small piece in the Canadian mosaic, and who detected much in Scottish culture and history which was, and is, worthy of celebration. Much of the Scottish past, after all, represents the prehistory of a country such as Canada.[22] Party political allegiance was not at any time, even remotely a consideration. The gnomes of Bay Street sat down with members of the NDP, and recent conservatives with former commies. There was no room for political differences among folk who had some claim, or aspiration, to Scottish roots and who thus could never agree about anything! More than once we wondered how Bruce could organise a kingdom when consensus on some wretched committee or other remained so elusive. The Foundation, which had promoted earlier functions around 6 April, organised its first official Tartan Day dinner at Casa Loma, Toronto in 1993 on which occasion

Major-General Lewis Mackenzie, former Commanding Officer of the UN Forces in Sarajevo, was honoured with the newly established 'Scot of the Year Award'.

The year 1994 saw the adoption of Tartan Day in Manitoba, sponsored by Gerry McAlpine's bill in recognition of the role that 'Scottish Manitobans have played and continue to play in Manitoba's cultural heritage', a vote for, among others, Lord Selkirk and the Red River settlers. In fact, as in Ontario, the day had been recognised on an annual basis for several years. British Columbia and Saskatchewan had by now come on board. All of the Canadian provinces, together with the Yukon, now celebrate Tartan Day, with the exception of only Newfoundland and Quebec.[23]

In Australia and New Zealand – and other countries not specified – Tartan Day is celebrated on 1 July. Some American states designated 1 July as 'Migrants' Day', which included Scots, though in New Jersey Scottish heritage and traditions were recalled on 1 October. The Antipodeans favoured the July date because on that day in 1782 the Act of Proscription (1747), banning the wearing of tartan after the last Jacobite rising, was repealed. It is salutary to recall that the sentence for infringing the ban was seven years transportation, which might be thought a further consideration so far as Australia was concerned though the country did not receive its first convicts until 1788. Reasonably enough, 1 July was thus deemed more appropriate for the celebration of Tartan Day. In any case, with ongoing referenda in Australia on the monarchy/republic question, 'Arbroath' with its deposition clause could still be seen as a somewhat sensitive item. Aussie opportunism, however, allows them a further distinction, namely combining the event with the anniversary of the restoration of the Scottish parliament on 1 July 1999.[24] Lest the impression is given that the response 'Down Under' is somewhat tepid, it should be mentioned that in Hamilton, New Zealand, Tartan Day is billed as 'an Inter-Celtic event for Scots, Irish, Cornish, Welsh, Manx and other people who favour the wearing of the tartan, and who contribute to the overall continuance of the Celtic cultural legacy in New Zealand society'.[25] The Kiwis, commendably, are clearly intent on making the event more all-inclusive.

In March 1996, at the invitation of Miss Duncan Macdonald of the Caledonian Foundation, Neil Fraser, as Past Chairman of CASSOC, attended a meeting of what would shortly become 'The Coalition of US Scottish Organizations', in Sarasota, Florida. There the Americans were apparently captivated by the Canadian experience of Tartan Day, placed on the agenda by Miss MacDonald, and plans were made to adopt it. Oddly, there seems to have been some discussion about dates because Fraser had to explain that 1 July would not be suitable to Canadians since it was Canada Day and thus no more of an option than 4 July.[26] The point is of considerable interest because if the Americans had attempted to change the date – though Canadian agreement is inconceivable - the link with 'Arbroath' would have been lost. The whole stushie about the relationship between the two declarations would never have happened, and neither would National Tartan Day because without the Scots' 'momentous document' it is difficult to see how the American Senate, which is known to be rather reluctant to adopt any more 'national days' would, or could, have legislated 6 April as a date of 'special significance for all Americans'.

The following year (1997) Senator Trent Lott made an announcement from the floor of the Senate to the effect that Tartan Day was about to be observed throughout the country, the arrangements being made by members of The Coalition, a point of which they are somewhat proud because 'they took action on an issue important to them and did not wait for the government to specify the date'.[27] The event was apparently a great success, reported in one source with almost, we might think, a *frisson* of 1776;

> Around the country, a true grass-roots effort took place. Thousands of Scots-Americans found ways to observe the first tartan day: in churches, on village greens, at Scottish festivals, at social gatherings, and in the home. It would seem that at last the Scots in America had found a cause around which all could rally. Tartan Day was observed on April 6, 1997, for the first time in US history. And it is a day that will be observed so long as there are Scots who care about their heritage.[28]

The charming and energetic Joanne Phipps, of the Caledonian Foundation and the Clans of Scotland Inc., emerged to liaise with Trent Lott's staff, supplying information and materials such as Duncan Bruce's book, *The Mark of The Scots*, which was to prove hugely influential. She was to remain heavily involved until 2002. Her hard work paid off when Lott rose in the Senate on 20 March 1998 to present Senate Resolution 155, which stated that April 6 'has a special significance for all Americans, and especially those of Scottish descent, because the Declaration of Arbroath, the Scottish Declaration of Independence', was signed on that day and the American Declaration was modelled upon that inspirational document. The resolution honours the role that Scottish Americans played in the founding of the nation, in that 'almost half of the signers of the Declaration' were of Scottish descent. Duncan Bruce's assessment is that of the fifty-six signers, twenty-one 'or almost 38 per cent, have been identified as having Scottish ancestry'.[29] In the resolution Scottish Americans are acknowledged as having 'helped shape this country in its formative years and guide this nation through its most troubled times'. They have made 'monumental achievements and invaluable contributions' across most fields of human endeavour, contributions recognised by more than two hundred organisations such as clans [sic], societies, clubs, and fraternal organisations. In conclusion Senate designates 6 April as 'National Tartan Day'.[30] Thus it came to pass that the Arbroath letter of 1320 wound up on Capitol Hill, and literally thousands of Americans are clamouring to find out what it is all about.

The whole thing may be thought to have come about with indecent haste but whether that provides ammunition for Euan Hague's case is perhaps a matter of debate. His article has proved profoundly upsetting in certain Scottish-American quarters. Tartan Day is, for him, the invention of a tradition, but not as envisaged by Eric Hobsbawm, though since the latter wrote,[31] we have all wandered further into the wastelands of postmodernism.[32] For example, critics who have lined up to trash and ridicule American celebrations of 6 April have been remarkably silent about the shameless fabrications and ruthless plunderings associated with Edinburgh's Hogmanay celebrations, which have arisen, for crassly commercial purposes, during an even shorter time-span. Hague has written an interesting piece which really tells us more about the opinions of the recently disgraced Senator Trent Lott than it does about the myriads of decent people who wish to indulge in a day excursion into Scottish culture. Lott adheres to the familiar saga of the heroic formation of the United States, reinforced by a 'genealogical appeal to Scottish origins', which is in the main bogus. Further reinforcement is sought in assertions that the one declaration was modelled on the other, and that a continuum in declarations can be detected in Scottish bloodlines running in the signers of 1776. Hague also rightly takes issue with the assumption that places European males at the heart of America to the obvious detriment of women and other ethnic groups, not to mention blacks and native peoples.

There is no doubt whatsoever that much of Lott's history is sheer invention and that he is guilty of totally unsubstantiated claims, making unqualified assertions which others would wish to challenge or modify. The senator made it known when accepting the Wallace Prize[33] in Washington in 2000, that a major influence in his thinking was Mel Gibson's *Braveheart* movie. Indeed, he confided to his audience on the steps of the Capitol that having seen the film he wished to pass on the inspirational news to fellow senators from the South. In their absence he intoned the word 'Freedom' into their answering machines. Derisible though this may be, we should recall that in Scotland, where the same film was accepted quite uncritically throughout the nation, a certain political party attempted to sell memberships to patrons emerging from the cinema, thus presumably predicating a Scottish future upon a bogus past. In the US countless enthusiastic supporters of Tartan Day state that they have no time whatsoever for the Trent Lotts of this world, but that they were happy to exploit his interest in order to have the event officially recognised. Their attitude might be compared with that of the Scottish nobility at the start of the Great Cause. A point of which all too many Scottish critics seem oblivious is that 'Tartan Day has been specifically developed outside of Scotland to serve a diaspora community'.[34] Despite the Scottish politicians, businessmen, performers and academics who troop across the pond each April, the celebration is not, in a crucial sense, a Scottish event at all. Indeed, some Americans have been heard to mutter darkly about a Scottish monopolisation or takeover.

There has been no shortage of non-diasporeans more than willing to disburden themselves of their opinions about 'Brigadoon on the Potomac',[35] to preach that 'the 12 million US citizens who claim Scottish ancestry lack profile, political clout and any real sense of coherent identity', arguing that they 'should be trying to reconnect with modern Scotland', and suggesting by way of encouragement that Tartan Day is invented and spurious.[36] So, of course, are Christmas and St Patrick's Day which everyone is perfectly free to observe or ignore. That well-known enthusiast, former government minister Brian Wilson, who fulsomely welcomed Tartan Day in 1998, now protests that he always thought the event 'a pretty shallow waste of time'.[37] Neal Ascherson writes that Tartan Day is a 'heavenly junket' for Scots in the US, 'but is also a test of integrity; behind the day is a web of nonsense about the past of Scotland. Do Scots have to accept these fibs, in case we hurt our big host's feelings?'.[38] The immediate response is to reflect that there will be no such web of nonsense associated with the likes of 25 January or St Andrew's Day then? The second is to state that in over twenty years of lecturing in America, on virtually an annual basis, on numerous different subjects, I have never once felt the need to indulge in conscious untruths, or been aware of expectations on the part of either hosts or audiences that I should spare their feelings. Americans, for some reason, are educable in a way that Scots often are not; if told that their views are erroneous their attitude is to ask why, and weigh the evidence accordingly. Most of them exist in a culture of debate. All that is required is a hook. Many who have seen *Braveheart*, for example, are happy to reject it as history while using it as a launching pad for commencing some consideration of the deeper issues involved in the Scottish Wars of Independence.

On three separate occasions I have had the good fortune to participate in academic symposia associated with Tartan Day, in Washington DC, each time looking at the possible influence of 'Arbroath' upon Philadelphia and each time reaching negative conclusions though admittedly, of late, increasingly wondering, with Neal Ascherson, if Lott *et al.* 'are right for all the wrong reasons'.[39] Colleagues at these symposia have included both Scots and Americans who have spoken on a variety of topics. Nobody to my knowledge has been told what to say or has altered their material to suit the supposed prejudices or assumptions of the audience. The indefatigable Alison Duncan has been centrally involved in planning those events. It is well known that she is the SNP representative in Washington yet no-one has been scrutinised for party affiliation. Can we, in our wildest imaginings, envisage a scenario in which four foreign academics would be imported and funded to take part in an academic conference run in conjunction with a Scottish festival? When will our capital city pay for a group of specialists to present papers on 'Hogmanay: celebrating the Specious and the Spurious'?

A major sticking point is the assertion that the American Declaration is modelled upon the Arbroath letter. Duncan Bruce furnishes the most detailed case for such dependency through a comparison of the two documents.[40] Although the idea is not new, and Bruce's examples may be thought to be superficially persuasive, the American historical establishment is unlikely to be moved.[41] Yet he makes a more convincing *prima facie* case than exists, for example, for the influence of Magna Carta, which scholars have been more or less happy to accept for very many years. The sceptics, however, this writer included, will demand more evidence before the case is totally convincing, though it is far from closed; for us the jury is still out.

It is easy to be sceptical when contemplating Tartan Day websites. Reynoldsburg, Ohio, for example, offers a Bonnie Knees Contest.[42] The Dallas/Fort Worth site refers to Arbroath as a 'treaty', which, webbies are assured, will sound very familiar to Americans, since much of their declaration comes from that document.[43] Other places offer such delights as The Wicker Clan Kilted Balloon Team. At Chemainus, Vancouver Island, BC (formerly Scots Town), all visitors during Tartan Week will be greeted and given a tartan bow to wear. Fresno, California, mounts a Kilt and Celt Golf Tournament. Flagstaff, Arizona, promises 'fun for all who love tartans and anything else Scots'.[44]

On the other hand not all activities can by any means be dismissed as frivolous. The estimated number of Scots killed at the Alamo, where large heather wreaths are laid, varies between thirty and one hundred.[45] Schools in the Cincinnati area are offered educational websites, which invite students to become completely immersed in Scottish culture by visiting 'Electric Scotland'. 'For a wee bit a' music', the instruction is to click 'Scottish Songs'. 'Fortunately, the lyrics are included so you can read along. Unfortunately, they are written exactly the way they are sung'. The newspaper assignment for that week is to find a Scottish name in a current issue of the *Cincinnati Enquirer* and then read the 'clan' history.[46] In Ratton, New Mexico, and several other places, information sheets about Tartan Day and Scotland are distributed to schools and churches. The celebrations in Tidewater, Virginia, raise money for the Richard S. Baird scholarship fund for Scottish Studies.[47]

Potentially the academic and cultural spin-offs are enormous. In 2002 almost ten thousand pipers marched up Sixth Avenue in New York. It did not matter that most New Yorkers thought that the Scots were present to offer comfort after the on-going trauma of 9/11; no other nation on the planet had been offered the privilege of a friendly invasion, of such colour and such sound, on such a scale. Even the rocks in Central Park were singing. At a piping concert it had to be explained that the phenomenally successful pipe band, Scottish Power, was named after an energy company, and not (by implication) after some radical political group. On a somewhat sadder note it is perhaps only the Scots who still consider the pipes a uniquely Scottish possession. Michael Macdonald of New York and The Silver Fox Center for a Global Anthropology writes:

> For months after the horrific and tragic events of September 11th, the bittersweet laments of pipes and muffled drums echoed through a multitude of communities in and around New York City and along the Atlantic corridor. The notes of 'Amazing Grace' became the single, universal representation of national, if not international, mourning, felt by Americans and variously witnessed by people round the world . . . Music, musician and band transcended the fundamental role of transmitting ethnic tradition. Now embellished as one among few universally revered symbols representing an enormously complex, inter-ethnic American identity, pipes and drums have become the tools of continental ritual specialists as they did a century before in Canada, Australia, and the British Isles. They are today the druids of 'Nine-Eleven' instrumental in the making of sacred memory with the World Trade Center, The Pentagon, and a field in Pennsylvania.[48]

We must take care that when all of the world owns the Declaration of Arbroath, as hopefully it will, the Scots are not entirely dispossessed, as may be happening with the pipes. In future years Tartan Day will be observed across the whole of the US and Canada, in Australia and New Zealand and hopefully in other parts of the world, such as Iceland which planned an event at Seydisfjordur in 2001. Speakers will be required at all levels from universities to church halls, from official dinners and receptions to picnics, just to state in brief what it all means. At the very least we should make sure that every student attending history classes, whether at school or university, in Scotland, knows something about the Arbroath Declaration.

The ideas of 'Arbroath' are well worth exporting but we should not be overly complacent in assuming that they are completely familiar in the land that produced them. The document is important because it shows how one small country on the periphery of Europe responded to the unique situation in which the forces of history had placed it. By 1320 the Scots had been arguing the issues of sovereignty and freedom for some thirty years. During that period they sought support for their arguments wherever they could find them – in chronicles and histories, in the Bible, in canon law, and in the works of the ancients, as represented by a writer such as Sallust from whom the document's freedom passage was borrowed. 'Arbroath' not only articulated, for the first time in European history, the full-blown idea of the contractual theory of monarchy, which lies at the root of all modern constitutionalism, but it also appealed to such universals as freedom and human dignity, thus elevating the debate to one which far transcended the sometimes messy business of the Scottish Wars of Independence. In the process the Scots developed new notions of nationhood and of monarchy, and, drawing upon the works of contemporary theorists with whom young Scottish canon lawyers had studied on the Continent, they invoked what later became the doctrine of the sovereignty of the people. To dismiss Tartan Day as nonsense is to contemptuously offend hundreds of thousands of people who are far more interested in our history and our country than we have any reason to expect. Most of the folk who have worked to establish it have been motivated by nothing more than very good intentions.

The US has some particular reasons for adopting Tartan Day of which some of its early supporters may not have been completely aware. Two Scots signed the Declaration of Independence in 1776. One of these was a lawyer from Fife, named James Wilson, who is regarded by American authorities as the man who contributed the crucial concept of the sovereignty of the people to the American constitutional debates. He also, on one occasion, made reference to 'essential Liberty, which . . . we are determined not to lose, but with our lives'. His fellow countryman and co-signer was John Witherspoon, sometime minister of the Laigh Kirk, Paisley, who became president of Princeton. Nowhere in his available writings does he quote 'Arbroath' but it is surely significant that a contemporary who took part with them in the drafting of the American Declaration wrote of both Witherspoon and Wilson:

> Both strongly national & can't bear any thing in Congress which reflects [badly] on Scotland. [Witherspoon] says that Scotland has manifested the greatest Spirit for Liberty as a nation, in that their History is full of their calling kings to account & dethroning them when arbitrary and tyrannical.[49]

In this assertion may there lurk the shade of 'Arbroath'? The question is at least worthy of debate. It is not possible to go so far as to agree that the American Declaration of Independence was 'modelled' on that of Arbroath but the question of Scottish influence, if not exactly open, is deserving of further consideration. Scottish assumptions about freedom and independence helped mould the ideas and values of such great countries as New Zealand, Australia and Canada. In a way it would be surprising if the United States was somehow exempt.

A LETTER

From the NOBILITY, BARONS & COMMONS of SCOTLAND, in the Year 1320, yet extant under all the Seals of the NOBILITY:

DIRECTED TO

POPE IOHN:

Wherein they declare their firm Resolutions, to adhere to their King ROBERT the BRUCE, as the Restorer of the Safety, and Liberties of the People, and as having the true Right of Succession: But withall, They notwithstanding Declare, That if the King should offer to subvert their Civil Liberties, they will disown him as an Enemy, and choose another to be King, for their own Defence.

Translated from the Original, in *Latine*, as it is insert by Sr. George *Mckenzie* of *Rosehaugh*, in his Observations on Precedency, &c.

Edinburgh, Re-printed in the Year 1689.

FIGURE 1
The first published English translation of the Declaration of Arbroath.
(Reproduced courtesy of Glasgow University Library, Special Collections)

APPENDIX

Printed versions of the Declaration of Arbroath

The intention in Section A is to list printings which could have been sighted by Scots, or others, who emigrated to America before the Revolution. The listings in both sections are doubtless incomplete since it has not proved possible to return an exhaustive survey of all publications and translations. Apologies for any such omissions. In all cases except for B.8 only full texts and/or translations have been listed.

A. Before 1776

1 Sir George Mackenzie, *Observations upon the Laws and Customs of Nations as to Precedency* (Edinburgh 1680). Latin only.

2 *A letter from the nobility, barons & commons of Scotland, in the year 1320, yet extant under the seals of the nobility: directed to Pope Iohn: wherein they declare their firm resolutions, to adhere to their King Robert the Bruce, as the restorer of the safety, and liberties of the people, and as having the true right of succession: but withal, they notwithstanding declare, that if the king should offer to subvert their civil liberties, they will disown him as an enemy, and choose another to be king, for their own defence. Translated from the original, in Latine, as it is insert by Sr. George Mckenzie of Rosehaugh, in his Observations on precedency etc* (Edinburgh: reprinted in the year 1689). Latin and English.
   Note: 'reprinted' refers to 1, above, and does not imply that there was an earlier printing in 1689.

3 *A letter from the nobility, barons and commons of Scotland, in the year 1320 etc* Edinburgh, *Impressum juxta typum nuper Edinburgi excusum, anno* 1700. Latin and English.
   Note: title identifies Sir George M"kenzie (*sic*) as 'His Majesty's advocate'.

4 *A letter from the nobility, barons and commons of Scotland, in the year 1320 etc.* (Edinburgh: reprinted in the year 1703). Latin and English.
   Note: a cheap and ugly print throughout. After the line, 'God (who is ignorant of nothing) knows . . .' the text is reduced, and crammed into the last one and a half inches of the page.

5 James Anderson, *An historical essay, showing that the Crown and Kingdom of Scotland is imperial and independent* (Edinburgh 1705). Appendix No. 14. Latin and English.
   Note: an original, exuberant and impassioned translation.

6 *A Letter from the nobility, barons and commons of Scotland, in the year 1320 etc.* (Edinburgh: reprinted 1706). Latin and English.

7 *The Works of that Eminent and Learned Lawyer Sir George Mackenzie of Rosehaugh*, 2 vols (Edinburgh 1716), vol. 2, 145–6. Latin only.

8 *The Works of that Eminent and Learned Lawyer Sir George Mackenzie of Rosehaugh*, 2 vols (Edinburgh 1722), vol. 2, 526–8. Latin only.

9 George Crawfurd, *Lives and Characters of the Officers of the Crown and of the State in Scotland . . .* (Edinburgh 1726), 432–4. Latin only.
   Note: Mackenzie's text.

10 James Anderson, *Selectus diplomatum & numismatum Scotiae thesaurus, in duas partes distributus; prior syllogen complectitur veterum diplomatum sive chartarum regum et procerum Scotiae, una cum eorum sigillis, a Duncano II ad Jacobum I id est, ab anno 1094 ad 1412 etc.* (Edinburgh 1739), numbers LI, LII. Latin only.

11 *A Letter from the Nobility, Barons & Commons of Scotland, in the year 1320 . . . directed to Pope John etc* in *The Harleian miscellany: or, A Collection of scarce, curious, and entertaining pamphlets and tracts, as well in manuscript as in print, found in the late Earl of Oxford's library. Interspersed with historical,*

*political, and critical notes. With a table of contents, and an alphabetical inde*x, William Oldys (ed.), 9 vols (London 1744–6), vol. 4, 1745, 485–9. Latin and English.

12 *A letter in Latin and English, from the nobility, barons and commons of Scotland, in the year 1320, yet extant under all the seals of the nobility, directed to Pope John, who, and predecessors were most great and magnificent . . . and did many singular favours . . . to Scotland etc.* (Edinburgh 1745). Printed and sold in the Swan-Close. Latin and English.

   Note: the fulsome description of the pope may be due to the probable printer, Robert Drummond, a supporter of the Jacobite Rebellion in 1745.

13 Walter Goodall, *Joannis de Fordun Scotichronicon cum Supplementis ac Continuatione Walteri Boweri etc*, 2 vols (Edinburgh 1747–59), vol. 1, 275–7. Latin only.

14 *A Letter from the Nobility, Barons & Commons of Scotland in the year 1320 etc.* (Edinburgh 1745), in Baron John Somers, *The Somers Collection of Tracts. A Third Collection*, vol. 3 (London 1751). Latin and English.

B. Since 1776

1 *A Letter from the Nobility, Barons, and Commons of Scotland in the year 1320 etc.* (Edinburgh 1745) in *The Harleian miscellany*, 9 vols (London 1808–11), vol. 4, 1808, 511–14. Latin and English.

2 *A Letter from the Nobility, Barons & Commons of Scotland, in the year 1320 etc.* (Edinburgh 1745), *The Somers Collection of Tracts*, 2nd edn, revised, augmented and arranged, 13 vols (London 1809–15), vol. 11, (1815), 573–77. Latin and English.

   Note: the editor of the revised edition was Walter Scott. He added the following preface which typifies his generally tepid response to the document. 'This tract was published about the time of the Revolution, and again in Queen Anne's time. The manifesto was drawn up in the parliament at Aberbrothock. After a preamble, in which is enunciated every fable of early Scottish history, the Barons assume a more dignified and manly style'.

3 *A letter from the Nobility, Barons & Commons of Scotland, in the year 1320*, in *Miscellanea Scotica*, vol. 3 (Glasgow 1820), 123–8. Latin and English.

   Note: reprint of 1689 translation.

4 John Galt, *Ringan Gilhaize; or The Covenanters* (1823), *The Works of John Galt*, D. S. Meldrum and William Roughead (eds), 10 vols (Edinburgh 1936), vol. 8, 326–34.

5 *Acts of the Parliaments of Scotland*, vol. 1 (Edinburgh 1844), 474. Latin only.

   Note: includes Isaac Babire's engraving of 'Arbroath', originally commissioned by James Anderson and subsequently supplemented by the engraving of William Lizars.

6 C. A. Alvord, *A letter from the nobility, barons, and commons of Scotland, in the year 1320*. Privately printed (New York 1861).

   Note: this is the earliest American version of the declaration so far noted.

7 *National Manuscripts of Scotland*, 3 parts (Edinburgh 1870), Part 2 No. XXIV. Facsimile, Transcript and Translation. Latin and English.

8 *Liber Pluscardensis, The Book of Pluscarden*, Felix J. H. Skene (ed.), 2 vols, Historians of Scotland Series, vols 7 and 10 (Edinburgh 1877, 1880), vol. 1, 163–6, 189, vol. 2, 201–5, 252–4. Latin and English.

   Note: *Pluscarden*, which was written in 1461 and which survives in five manuscripts dating from before 1500, includes both a full and a partial text of 'Arbroath', see Cowan, '*Freedom Alone*', 89–91.

9 Herbert Maxwell, *Robert the Bruce and the Struggle for Scottish Independence* (London 1897), 272–4.

   Note: quotes most of the document omitting first two paragraphs.

10 R. L. Mackie, 'The Declaration of Arbroath', *Scots Magazine*, new series, xxi, no. 1, 1934, 9–18. Latin and English.

11 R. K. Hannay, *The Letter of the Barons of Scotland to Pope John XXII in 1320 being part of an Address to the Heriot-Watt College Literary Society on Friday 5th October 1934* (Edinburgh 1936). English only.

12 *Scotland's Declaration of Independence. The Historic letter known as the Declaration of Arbroath in 1320 from the Scottish Nation to the Pope as International Arbitrator*, United Scotland (Edinburgh 1943). English only.

   Note: 'Reprinted (with spelling modernised) from a translation printed along with the Latin original, in 1703, in Edinburgh, for circulation to the Scottish people when the incorporating Union was under discussion.'

13 *The Scottish Declaration of Independence*, Facsimile, Burns Federation, 1949.

   Note: a gesture as magnificent as the quality of the reproduction.

14 *Scottish Pageant*, Agnes Muir MacKenzie (ed.) (Edinburgh and London 1946); 2nd edn 1952, 189–93. English only.

15 T. M. Cooper, *Supra Crepidam* (London 1951), 62–71. Latin and English.

16 *A Source Book of Scottish History*, W. C. Dickinson, G. Donaldson and I. Milne (eds), 3 vols (Edinburgh 1952–4), vol. 1, 131–5. English only. The Latin text is supplied in the revised and enlarged edition (Edinburgh 1958), 151–8.

   Note: based on the Cooper version and the 1689 translation.

17 Moray McLaren, *The Wisdom of the Scots; A Choice and a Comment* (London 1961), 53–6.

   Note: reprint of Lord Cooper's translation in *Supra Crepidam* above.

18 *The Declaration of Arbroath*, Facsimile, Scottish Office (Edinburgh 1969). Latin and English.

19 A. A. M. Duncan, *The Nation of Scots and the Declaration of Arbroath*, Historical Association (London 1970). Latin and English.

20 James Fergusson, *The Declaration of Arbroath* (Edinburgh 1970). Latin and English.

21 Gordon Donaldson, *Scottish Historical Documents* (Edinburgh 1970), 55–8. English only.

22 Walter Bower, *Scotichronicon*, D. E. R. Watt (ed.), 9 vols (Edinburgh 1989–98), vol. 7 (1996), 5–10. Latin and English.

23 James S. Adam, *The Declaration of Arbroath* (Arbroath 1993). Latin, Gaelic, Lallans and English.

24 Bernard de Linton, *The Declaration of Arbroath* (Edinburgh 1995). Latin and English.

25 John Barbour, *The Bruce*, edited with translation and notes by A. A. M. Duncan (Edinburgh 1997), 779–82. English only.

26 Alex C. Murphy, *The Declaration of Arbroath – 1320* (Dalkeith c. 1998). Latin and English.

27 Duncan Glen, *The Declaration of Arbroath* (Kirkcaldy 2000).

28 *The Declaration of Arbroath*, Facsimile (National Archives of Scotland, Edinburgh 2002).

29 Edward J. Cowan, *'For Freedom Alone': The Declaration of Arbroath, 1320* (East Linton 2003), reprint, with kind permission, of Professor Duncan's translation in Barbour's *Bruce*, above, 144–7. English only.

NOTES

1 Edward J. Cowan, *'For Freedom Alone' The Declaration of Arbroath, 1320* (East Linton 2003). See also 'Identity, Freedom and the Declaration of Arbroath' in D. Broun, R. J. Finlay and M. Lynch (eds), *Image and Identity: The Making and Re-making of Scotland through the Ages* (Edinburgh 1998), 38–68.

2   In *'Freedom Alone'*, 119, it was noted that there is no information as to why the document was dated on 6 April. In 1320 Easter Sunday fell on 30 March. 6 April was thus Quasimodo, sometimes known as 'Low Sunday' and later, in Irish, Mioncháisc, 'Little Easter'. The name derived from the introit at Mass, *Quasi modo geniti*, 'as newborn babes' (1 Peter 2:2), which celebrated 'Sunday in taking off white robes'. Such robes were shed on that Sunday by those who had been baptised at Easter. By dating 'Arbroath' to 6 April the Scots may have been signifying that they were, so to speak, 'born again', or cleansed, having been for long the object of papal disapproval. The second chapter of Peter is greatly concerned with obedience and subservience, but is also a celebration: '9 But ye are a chosen generation, a royal priesthood, an holy nation, a peculiar people; that ye should shew forth praises of him who hath called you out of darkness into his marvellous light: 10 Which in time past were not a people, but are now the people of God: which had not obtained mercy, but have now obtained mercy'. Equally suggestive is '15 For so is the will of God, that with well doing ye may put to silence the ignorance of foolish men: 16 As free, and not using your liberty for a cloke of maliciousness, but as the servants of God . . . 25 For ye were as sheep going astray; but are now returned unto the Shepherd and bishop of your souls'. This suggestion may seem somewhat far-fetched and unprovable, but medieval people, especially clerics, wrote and thought in code, employing a discourse laden with symbology and analogy; it is unlikely that the significance of 6 April would have been missed, *A Handbook of Dates for Students of British History*, C. R. Cheney (ed.), rev. edn Michael Jones (Cambridge 2000), 172; Bonnie Blackburn and Leofranc Holford-Strevens, *The Oxford Companion to the Year* (Oxford 1999), 625–6.

3   Americans not quite familiar with the place-name tend to pronounce it something like 'Urbrot' though in examination scripts at the University of Guelph it metamorphosed into 'Our Broth', presumably just one medieval variety of Scotch broth.

4   In the *Liber Pluscardensis* see Cowan, 'Freedom Alone', 89–90.

5   Lois G. Schwoerer, *The Declaration of Rights, 1689* (Baltimore and London 1981), 3–29.

6   Pauline Maier, *American Scripture. Making the Declaration of Independence* (New York 1998), 56.

7   Cowan, 'Freedom Alone', 134. Burnet states that he had quite a hand in the English declaration and that he made some corrections, mainly with reference to the Church, in the Scottish one. When he was minister of Saltoun he made a transcript of the 'Arbroath' original at Tyninghame. He later appended it to his *History of the Reformation in England*, London 1683. We can only speculate as to whether Burnet showed his transcript to his pupil, Andrew Fletcher of Saltoun. It must be admitted that although Burnet cited Magna Carta on at least two occasions in 1688–9 he nowhere mentions 'Arbroath', Gilbert Burnet, *History of his Own Times* With Notes, etc., 6 vols (Oxford 1833), vol. 3, 300, 302, 380, 399–400.

8   James Anderson, *An historical essay, showing that the Crown and Kingdom of Scotland is imperial and independent* (Edinburgh 1705), 251–2. 257–8, 263.

9   Patrick Abercromby, *The Martial Atchievements (sic) of the Scots Nation*, 2 vols (Edinburgh 1711–15), vol. 1, 610–31, reprinted in 4 vols (Edinburgh 1762).

10 John Galt, *Ringan Gilhaize; or The Covenanters, The Works of John Galt*, Patricia J. Wilson (ed.), Association for Scottish Literary Studies (Edinburgh 1984), 244, 324–7.

11 Wilson's note in Galt, *Ringan Gilhaize*, 360, is misleading in suggesting that at one point 'the original is more orthodox than Galt's mistranscription'. She also errs in attributing the translation to Sir George Mackenzie. The mistake, however, is understandable because of misleading entries in library catalogues where the title page usually states, correctly 'Translated from the original, in Latine, as it is insert by Sr. George Mackenzie of Rosehaugh, in his *Observations on Precedency* etc', reduced in some catalogue entries to 'translated from the original, in Latine . . . by Sir George Mackenzie'.

12 William Burns, *The Scottish War of Independence. Its Antecedents and Effects*, 2 vols (Glasgow 1874), vol. 1, 1–21. On 'Arbroath' see vol. 1, 297–316; vol. 2, 113–15.
13 John Mackintosh, *History of Civilisation in Scotland*, 4 vols (Paisley and London 1892), vol. 1, 297–8.
14 J. M. M'Bain, *Eminent Arbroathians: Being Sketches Historical, Genealogical, and Biographical 1178–1894* (Arbroath 1897), 16–18.
15 Professor Duncan has convincingly demonstrated that Abbot Bernard of Arbroath was not the same man as Bernard de Linton, *Regesta Regum Scottorum V The Acts of Robert I*, A. A. M. Duncan (ed.) (Edinburgh 1988), 198–203.
16 Nigel Tranter, *Robert the Bruce, The Price of the King's Peace* (London), 254–66. This book concludes Tranter's trilogy on Bruce which afforded him an opportunity to prove his stature as a novelist, but unfortunately he did not rise to the challenge. It is truly surprising that Scottish creative writers have, in the main, completely avoided the subject of the Wars of Independence. Tranter was a prolific writer who can take the credit for interesting many thousands of readers in Scottish history. He also wrote *The Wallace* (London 1975).
17 A. I. Dunlop, 'Arbroath Declaration of Independence', *Burns Chronicle* (1950), 56–60.
18 For a discussion of scholarly interest see Cowan, '*Freedom Alone*', 4–12.
19 W. Neil Fraser, 'Tartan Day in Canada and the United States', *www.tartans.com*. Supplementary information kindly supplied by Miss Duncan MacDonald of The Caledonian Foundation USA. See also William S. Connery, 'Tartan Day. Modern Observances of Scottish Heritage', *The World & I*, April 2002, 170–7.
20 Ian McKay, 'Tartanism Triumphant: The Construction of Scottishness in Nova Scotia 1933–1954', *Acadiensis* 21 no. 2, 5–28.
21 The best account of tartan and its history is to be found in Hugh Cheape, *Tartan, The Highland Habit* (Edinburgh 1991).
22 Edward J. Cowan, 'The Myth of Scotch Canada' in *Myth, Migration and the Making of Memory. Scotia and Nova Scotia c.1700–1990*, Marjory Harper and Michael E. Vance (eds) (Halifax and Edinburgh 1999), 49–72.
23 *www.greatclanross.org*.
24 *www.electricscotland.com/tartanday-whatson*.
25 *www.rampantscotland.com/features/tartanday*.
26 Fraser, 'Canada Day'.
27 Pers. comm. Duncan MacDonald. 'Objection to National Tartan Day'. I am also indebted to Bob McWilliam of Whitefish Bay, Wisconsin, for information on the establishment of Tartan Day in the US.
28 *Caledonian News*, The Caledonian Foundation (Winter 1997), 3.
29 Duncan A. Bruce, *The Mark of the Scots. Their Astonishing Contributions to History, Science, Democracy, Literature, and the Arts* (Secaucus 1996), 32.
30 *Congressional Record, Proceedings and Debates of the 105th Congress, Second Session*, vol. 144, no. 32, Washington, Friday, 20 March 1998. The document together with the list of those senators who co-sponsored Resolution 155 is usefully reprinted in Euan Hague, 'National Tartan Day: Rewriting History in the United States', *Scottish Affairs*, no. 38, winter 2002, 100–01. The article appends a helpful bibliography which includes various Scottish newspaper contributions to the debate. On a further point The Coalition apparently disapproves of the epithet 'national' since it is not attached to Columbus Day or President's Day. The argument is that all such days are 'national' and hence the word is redundant (pers. comm.).
31 Eric Hobsbawm, 'Introduction: Inventing traditions' in Eric Hobsbawm and Terence Ranger (eds), *The Invention of Tradition* (Cambridge 1983).

32 Edward J. Cowan and Richard J. Finlay, 'Introduction' in Cowan and Finlay, *Scottish History: The Power of the Past* (Edinburgh 2002), 1–9.
33 The Wallace Award (which Sean Connery received in 2001) 'was created in 1970 by the founder-president of the American-Scottish Foundation, Lady Malcolm Douglas-Hamilton. The award has benefited by the establishment of Tartan Day as a national day of observance and is presented during the Tartan Day celebration and with a different venue, since it is now held in Washington DC rather than in New York City as in the past'. Information supplied by Miss Duncan MacDonald.
34 Hague, 'National Tartan Day', 95. See 97–8 for press and academic reactions to Tartan Day.
35 John McTernan, 'Why the true patriots don't wear plaid', *Scotland on Sunday*, 7 April 2002.
36 T. M. Devine reported in *The Herald*, 16 May 2002.
37 HREF = *www.scotland.gov.uk*; *The Herald*, 23 December 2002.
38 Neal Ascherson, 'Nothing to Declare', *Sunday Herald*, 30 June 2002. Ascherson is much more upbeat and 'primordialist' (his word) about 'Arbroath' in his *Stone Voices: The Search for Scotland* (London 2002), 262–74.
39 Ascherson, *Stone Voices*, 265.
40 Bruce, *Mark of the Scots*, 38–41.
41 Murray Forbes of the Navigator Foundation, in 1985, suggested that the 'Arbroath' document was a declaration on behalf of the entire Scottish people. 'Its claim of the irreducible identity of the Scottish people, and of their right to continue in that identity, constituted a fundamental principle of law which could also be found in the US Constitution', *The Influence of the Scottish Enlightenment on the U.S. Constitution*, The British Institute of the United States and The Mentor Group, 1986, 15–16. The same publication carries a version of a paper by Neil MacCormick on 'The Idea of Free Government', i.e. as distinguished in the writings of some Enlightenment Scots. Though he does not say so some of MacCormick's quotations could be interpreted as containing echoes of 'Arbroath'. What are of greater interest, however, are the dismissive comments of two heavyweight American historians, John Pocock and Jack P. Greene, united in their doubts about possible Scottish influence, 28–40. It is no wonder that Garry Wills, *Inventing America* (New York 1978) received such a dusty reception since it put forward powerful arguments for the influence of Scottish Enlightenment thought on the Founding Fathers, a viewpoint for which there is, at present, a much greater amount of sympathy. 'Arbroath', however, is always likely to remain far too remote a possibility for most historians.
42 HREF = *www.reynoldsburgtartan.com*.
43 HREF = *www.dfwtartanday.org*.
44 HREF = *www.rampantscotland.com/features/tartanday*.
45 HREF = *www.rampantscotland.com/features/tartanday*.
46 HREF = *www.cincinnati.com/nie/archive*.
47 HREF = *www.tidewaterscots.com*.
48 Michael Macdonald, 'Amazing Grace Without a Kilt: The Changing Dynamics in the Transmission of Tradition', 13–14. Typescript kindly supplied by Michael.
49 Cowan, '*Freedom Alone*', 131.

THE DECLARATIONS OF THE CLERGY, 1309–10

Archie Duncan

THE document of 6 April 1320 was known to Scots (if at all) as the Declaration of Arbroath, 'the popular name of the Letter of the Barons of Scotland to Pope John XXII';[1] sanctioned by long usage, sanctified by an initial capital letter, the name obscures the fact that this petition was a letter, a 'diplomatic document'[2] of a kind well enough known at the time, for which there was a recent precedent from the English barons to the pope in 1301, and from the Scottish barons to Philip IV of France, from a parliament at St Andrews on 16 March 1309. All these were prompted by communications to the ruler, as was apparently the case in other, and earlier, such letters. It would thus seem that the other document known from the 1309 parliament, a statement by the Scottish clergy which was generally addressed 'to all Christ's faithful' and for which no prompting communication has been identified, was of a different character and truly deserves to be described as a 'Declaration'.

That this statement of the Bruce right to kingship was a pastoral encyclical designed to be read out from Scottish pulpits some Sunday was the assumption exemplified by Tytler's view that 'these solemn transactions gave strength to the title of Bruce and increased a popularity which was already great'.[3] The applause must still have been audible in 1828, for no contemporary measure of 'popularity' survives, but it is also unlikely that domestic propaganda was prepared in Latin for the sermon. It is the argument of this paper that the clergy's Declaration was also another diplomatic letter prompted by circumstances foreign to Scotland.

Its assertion of massacres of innocent victims, fires unextinguished, a variety of terrors, and criminal minds, is paralleled in, for example, the 1320 letter, both suggesting that distortion was as important a rhetorical weapon then as now,[4] though then the West's aim was to expel Muslims from the Holy Places. To achieve that, the spiritual authority of the pope must bring secular powers, its idiosyncratic kings, to act together in the matter, a purpose for which he allowed them to tax churchmen, watching helplessly as the money was diverted to other purposes. The Scots were unimportant players on this European field, save when they stood in the way of the most sincere crusading monarch, Edward I of England. When he demanded their acknowledgment of his overlordship in May–June 1291, they suggested that the Roman church was *domina*, lady, of their kingdom, and later recalled vividly Edward's cutting dismissal: 'If that Roman priest wishes to say anything on behalf of the freedom of Scotland so far as it concerned him, he would have to come to London and put it forward there before' Edward.[5] They did not take up the challenge until 1294 when Pope Celestine V was prompted to rule their submission to Edward invalid because it had been extorted by fear.[6]

Some detail was added to this case in 1296 when King John's defiance of Edward I damned him by cataloguing his enormities (violence, slaughter, burnings) against the liberties of king and kingdom, God and justice, but kept silent on papal lordship or other papal interest. Boldness returned with Scottish successes in 1297, so that in June 1299 Boniface VIII, seizing the congenial arguments advanced by the Scots, for a time pushed Edward I into a tight corner by the bull *Scimus fili*. In sum, but with much detail, it claimed that Scotland belonged to the Roman see, not to the English king, and invited Edward to prove the contrary.[7] John Balliol was 'the unnamed man to whom you, [Edward], are said to have committed, although improperly, the rule of the kingdom',[8] the Scots presumably having hinted, or admitted, that Edward's 1292 judgment for King John had been *ultra vires* and of no effect.

In January 1301 Edward had the English barons respond to Boniface in a letter claiming Scotland as a possession of the English king and denying papal jurisdiction, which, they said, they would not let Edward accept.[9] In May of that year Edward sent a detailed answer to part of *Scimus fili*, a long pro-English historical survey, a quarter of it devoted to the choice of John Balliol and the latter's wicked rebellion, but all ignoring totally the papal claims.[10] In answer to this the Scots drafted two briefs in 1301–2, the first, the 'Instructions', making no reference to King John; the second, Baldred Bisset's *processus*, in what is clearly a change of approach, ended by describing him as rightfully king by inheritance, by custom approved by the kingdom's inhabitants, and forced by fear to confess (in his 1296 submission) to conspiracies against the English king. Both recount Edward's 1291 dismissal of the 'Roman priest'.[11]

Much was going in favour of the Scots. King John was released into the custody of Philip IV, and retired with a pension to Bailleul,[12] and by the end of 1301, when making a truce with Edward I, Philip insisted on provision for John's return to Scotland with a French force, while Edward admitted to Bruce the possibility that the papal curia would give judgment against his, Edward's, rights in Scotland.[13] The Scots at Scone promised King Philip to abide by the truce, in a letter bearing a new royal seal of King John, which can only have been made by the French government, so closely does it resemble French royal seals. It was presumably brought from France by Bishop Lamberton of St Andrews, who came with the truce and with Philip's letter 'asserting that there will be no peace between him and the king of England unless the Scots are included'; the people, we are told, were buoyed up by such firm words.[14]

But put not your trust in princes, lay or ecclesiastical. This house of cards collapsed when Philip, abandoning the Scots, made peace with Edward in May 1303, and turned on Boniface (who had also ditched the Scots),[15] sending agents to mug him so that he died within the week. From 1303, for twenty years, the kings of England and France preserved an uneasy peace, depriving the Scots of an active enmity to be exploited. But in 1305 the papacy passed to the Frenchman Clement V, the first pope to spend his pontificate within the French kingdom, free from the petty rivalries of central Italy, a dedicated champion of the Crusade. For that reason he was (reluctantly) subservient to Philip IV, who undertook to lead a western army to Palestine. Philip's interest was genuine, but it involved taking Constantinople to make his brother emperor there before turning to Palestine where, renouncing the French throne, he was to become king of Jerusalem. He wished the ineffectual Templar and Hospitaller Orders united under his command to achieve his mission of an eastern French hegemony – a project which Clement successfully resisted, though he condoned destruction of the Byzantine Empire. Both men needed money and an end to wars which troubled the major Christian realms.[16]

To resolve two of these matters, on 13 October 1307 the French government arrested, and seized the property of, some 15,000 persons associated with the order of Templars in France on grounds of heresy. Probably Philip believed the trumped-up charges, but much of the order's wealth came to him, and Clement could only wave parchments asserting papal protection of the Order to delay its final and horrible extinction.[17] To show he was doing something, in August 1308 he summoned a General Council of the Church to meet at Vienne in October 1310, later postponed by a year. It was to discuss the Crusade, the Templars and reform in the church.

By then the situation in Scotland had changed drastically. Robert Bruce had become complicit in a murder, then a king, then a hunted fugitive, and finally, in August 1308, master of the northern part of his kingdom, by the capture of Aberdeen.[18] As early as July 1308 someone at the curia (at Poitiers), possibly James Stewart, had secured Bruce's absolution from papal excommunication.[19] Towards the end of 1308 Philip sent an embassy to urge a truce between Edward II and Robert in the interests of the crusade, a truce concluded to last from 2 February to 1 November 1309, and later renewed till mid-1310.[20] Clement pressed that the bishops of St Andrews and Glasgow should face judges at the papal court, as Edward I had agreed but his son at first refused, and William Lamberton, bishop of St Andrews, having eaten humble pie, was released to live in Northamptonshire in May 1308, and was in the bishopric of Durham in August.[21] Robert Wishart, bishop of Glasgow, no less 'guilty', remained obdurate and was imprisoned until reluctantly handed over to the papal nuncio, the bishop of Poitiers, on 25 November 1308.[22]

As soon as the truce came into effect on 2 February 1309, Robert I must have sent out summons to parliament which was in session at St Andrews forty-three days later, on Sunday, 16 March 1309. On 4 March Edward II had given a safe-conduct to the envoy of Philip IV going to the bishop of St Andrews and Robert Bruce in Scotland.[23] Bishop Lamberton would certainly have had Edward's permission to go to Bruce, and had probably been with him since early February to influence the choice of St Andrews for parliament and to foretell the arrival of Philip's messenger. Edward's permission would be dictated by bulls of Clement V summoning Lamberton and the bishops of Glasgow and Whithorn to Vienne (for Clement had reduced those called to a selection of bishops partly drawn up by Philip IV),[24] and ordering Lamberton to enquire into the lives of the Templars and to report the outcome to an assembly where he would 'gather all in one', the equivalent of a Scottish provincial council.[25] Arranging this enquiry probably explains the 1309 assembly at his see, but parliament rather than a church council was required as the setting to answer Philip IV's pleas.[26] Pope Clement had retained the practice of summoning the laity in the persons of all kings in papal obedience[27] – save the kings of Ireland and Scotland. We know this from the register of Clement's bulls, but contemporaries in Britain had no such evidence, and Bruce would fear that the former king at Bailleul might receive a summons to a king of Scotland, directed to him by the influence of his patron, Philip IV.

This is the context for the documents produced at St Andrews on 16 and 17 March 1309, which older scholarship treated ill.[28] The Declaration of the clergy, dated 17 March, existed in two originals, now known only in seventeenth-century copies made by Sir James Balfour; despite the claim of the official printed record to have included one of these, they remain unprinted.[29] Balfour noted at the end of the second version that he found it in Cotton's collection, his first version in Edinburgh castle, and this statement is misplaced in the official edition as applying to 'This deed', the barons' reply to Philip IV.[30] In his study, D. W. Hunter Marshall listed four versions of the Declaration (I shall come to the remaining two), giving them the *sigla* A–D;[31] his C and D, I shall call 1309/1 and 1309/2, the order in which they occur in Balfour's transcript. 1309/1 he found in Scotland, where it had been kept; it was from unnamed prelates and the rest of the clergy appointed in Scotland. 1309/2 had been preserved in London, probably in the royal archives where Cotton would find it; it added two words to the *intitulatio*: the senders included the rest of the clergy *and community*. The addressees are not any person or any obvious group, but all Christ's faithful.

But the Declaration is a response to Edward I's letter to Boniface VIII in 1301. It begins (c. 2 in my appended translation) by admitting that John Balliol had been *de facto* made king by the English king but that 'the faithful people' always held Bruce (the Claimant) as true heir, picking up on Edward's 1301 claim that John had the kingdom *de facto* when resigning it in 1296, and denying his claim that when John had been found true heir to the kingdom, this was approved 'by the prelates, earls, barons, communities and other important inhabitants of the kingdom'.[32] There is no word of blame for John in the declaration; rather he is a pawn and a victim, whom (c. 4) the people and commons (*populus et plebs*) saw deprived and imprisoned 'on various pretexts' by the king of England, by whom the kingdom suffered servitude, with a catalogue of wrongs breathtaking in its rhetorical force, both longer and fiercer than anything earlier or the equivalent passage in the Arbroath Declaration. This, too, is probably a response to Edward I's 1301 catalogue of horrors committed by the Scots in 1296,[33] and is considerably more forceful than the 'Instructions' of 1301, which condemns the atrocities at Berwick in 1296 but finds it 'too wearisome to write down' other acts of savagery.[34] After the horrors of servitude under the king of England, the clergy's Declaration tells (end of c. 4) of the need for restoration and government, *reparatio et regimen*, whence the accession of Robert I, who, by divine grace and successful war, restored the ruined kingdom, as had happened before and as Picts expelled Britons and were expelled by Scots 'as were many others' (c. 6).

In the rhetoric of the Declaration, and especially in explaining Bruce's kingship, the 'people' play a key role. So far as I know, 'faithful people' is unique to this text, where they occur twice and in the context of the Bruce right (cc. 2, 6); there may be deliberate ambiguity here, of fidelity to the Bruces and to Christ, whose faithful are addressed in c. 1. 'People' *simpliciter* occurs twice in c. 4, apparently with the meaning 'populace' but something more is implied by *populus et plebs* who in c. 4–5 agreed on Bruce as heir to the kingdom and who might be cited (falsely) as against him in c. 7. This matter could not have arisen before 1306, but an account of the same acceptance in a 1321 version which seems to reuse earlier materials, the Bamburgh memorandum, gives a variant – it is the 'magnates (*proceres*) and nobles by unanimous consent of the whole people' who recognised Bruce as true heir.[35] We may recognise the *populus* and *plebs* of the Declaration as the *nobiles* and *populus* respectively of the memorandum.

More securely, the 1309/2 Declaration, issued by prelates and the rest of the clergy *and community*, records their fealty to King Robert as by prelates 'and the rest of the clergy *and people*' (c. 8).[36] This last word echoes the earlier text (cc. 4, 5, 7), which probably explains this cumbrous addition of 'the rest of' of laity in an otherwise ecclesiastical context. With the other addition, 'community' (c. 1), it enhances the significant role of the people in the narration by adding them to the authorship of the Declaration, and must have been thought to strengthen its message. But I know of no other instance in which 'community' was introduced without a qualification, 'of the kingdom of Scotland'; as found here, 'the rest of' something whose whole or other part had not been defined is vague and unsatisfactory, and it is not surprising that it is found in no other version of the Declaration. But the unique (so far as I know) lexical equation of 'community' and 'people' throws an interesting light upon the use of both words to imply universality where only an influential minority can have acted.

In fact *populus* and *gens* are rare before 1309. In the 1290s and in the 'Instructions' and *processus* of 1301–2 'inhabitants' of the kingdom is used,[37] but in the 'Instructions' 'people' are only the wandering and mythical Scots; in the *processus*, *gens* occurs once, in the conclusion.[38] There is clearly much semantic flexibility in the rhetoric of these and later documents, in which the magnates or prelates were presented as the only or leading authors. After 1306 they made freer claims to universality, in which the demands of the *cursus* would influence the choice of words (e.g. *gens* or *populus*) used; but that 'people' meant the people who mattered had long been accepted by the church, demanding election by clergy and people; in this as in other respects, the church could not speak very differently from contemporary lay society.[39] Domestically or abroad, the social significance of 'people' would be understood by readers of the Declaration.

For this reason, no revolution was implied when it came close to asserting that the people's election of Robert I made him king. While he had inherited a right, it was the people who judged he had done so, who agreed on him, who consented in his elevation to kingship and by whose authority he was advanced in the kingdom (cc. 4, 5); this quadruple authorisation led to his 'solemn king-making' (c. 6); indeed the Latin of the last phrase may better translate 'and by their authority he, having been advanced in the kingdom, was solemnly made king'.[40] But this striking emphasis was probably forced upon the Declaration's author. It was impossible to deny that John had been king and although he had the status only *de facto*, and was promoted and deprived by the English king (who is never named), it was still a challenge to Bruce to explain how the claimed better right of his grandfather and himself came to be acknowledged, which alone would eliminate Balliol's title. Bruce had enjoyed no victory to show divine judgement in his favour, and so must make do with acknowledgment by the people, well suited since their sufferings showed constancy of belief, yet they were anonymous and therefore unchallengeable.

And once king, Robert showed himself worthy of the name, since 'by the Saviour's grace' he had restored the kingdom, following many precedents for such restoration after ruin. Chosen by the people, he had given the restoration which they sought.

By 1320 the story had changed; the secular lords, senders of the Declaration of Arbroath, ignored the deceased Balliol save in one hint: Bruce would not be allowed to subject them to the dominion of the English. They insisted upon uninterrupted royal succession (without previous ruins),[41] so that Edward I had attacked a headless kingdom (a gross misrepresentation of 1296), which suffered great miseries (but not desolation). Robert it was who suffered 'toil and fatigue, hunger and peril' to set his people and heritage free (reversing the subject and object in the 1309 narrative), becoming king by divine providence, heritable right and the due consent of all (only thirdly and 'due'); the people are but passive participants.[42] Apart from 1309/2, the clergy's Declaration does not speak of the 'community', but it broadcast as remarkable a doctrine as anything said in 1320, the people as source of royal authority.

Of course, Robert's grandfather had been first to urge Edward I to subject Scotland to his dominion and in 1309 Robert had not 'restored the kingdom', half of which was in English occupation. These are but two obvious distortions among the many omissions and commissions of the Declaration. But it also has curious vagaries of construction, for example, the anonymity of those who oppressed Scotland after ending the wrongful kingship of John, or the abrupt shift from the mythical history of peoples expelled (end of c. 6), possibly derived from Bisset's *processus*,[43] into c. 7 where an anonymous 'anybody in opposition' might claim right to the kingdom by virtue of sealed letters containing the consent of 'people and commons'; this is to be rejected because it had been extorted by fear and force, extorted, that is, from the people.

The identity of 'anybody' and the exact purport of the sealed letters are not obvious, but the former must be either John Balliol or Edward I. Balliol had no letters consenting to his kingship from prelates and magnates, but he twice recorded his fealty to Edward with a group of witnesses,[44] and these letters would support Edward's claim to the kingdom as overlord. But the ragman documents sealed in 1296 by some 1,500 Scots, promising fealty to Edward I as overlord of Scotland, fit the description of 'containing the people's consent'[45] in a way that Balliol's submission does not; these had been transcribed into a notarial instrument in triplicate between 1300 and 1306 for diplomatic use,[46] and recent knowledge of this, perhaps derived from Lamberton or from the French envoy, may explain why c. 7 reads like an afterthought to the Declaration. It is a leap in the argument after the Britons, Picts and Scots of c. 6. C. 8, beginning *Nos igitur* . . . ,

'Therefore we', the clergy, knowing the truth of the foregoing, had sworn fealty to Bruce, follows well after c. 6, but awkwardly after c. 7. But, afterthought or not, c. 7 does not continue the theme of restoration by the sword (c. 6), but records a concern that someone, some tribunal or higher authority, might misguidedly recognise an opponent's claim to the kingdom; the authority is indicated by the canonical defence, that the letters relied on by 'someone' were extorted by fear – a defence intended for an ecclesiastical audience.

The Declaration is a sustained justification of the right and title of Bruce against John by name and Edward II by implication, in part a riposte to those English claims sent to the pope in 1301 relating to recent events, but ignoring most of the English case, including the myth and history justifying overlordship. It is an anticipation of part of the 1320 Declaration, yet different from it in many details and in emphasis and purpose. In 1320 Bruce sought to have the Pope write to Edward II to cease his war against the Scots; there is no hint of that in the 1309 Declaration, which has but one message: Robert Bruce is on all counts our rightful king. And the sub-text is that he should be recognised as king by all Christ's faithful.

The different rhetorics of the 1309 and 1320 Declarations are exemplified by one word: freedom. In 1309 it was said that the English king imposed servitude upon the Scots, in 1320 barbarities, yet in 1309 the remedy was 'restoration and government', a job description for a new chief executive, but not the cry of a people's cause; and Robert's achievement was, somewhat flatly, that he had restored the kingdom. If servitude called for any remedy, it was surely freedom, as in the equivalent passage in 1320 when: we were freed, freed from the hands of our enemies, protect our freedom, fight for freedom alone, all in the space of a few lines. The 1320 rhetoric of the freedom which no good man loses came from Sallust, but I cannot believe that the author who in 1309 wrote of servitude, did not mention freedom because he had not read Sallust.

Indeed 'freedom' was invoked in 1309, when two letters from the nobles to Philip IV of France emerged from parliament, one dated 16 March. This responded to the letters of credence brought by the French envoy, letters which do not survive but which pressed the need for peace so that the Holy Land might be recovered. The nobles commended Philip for his devotion to this cause, thanking him for the expression in the credence of his 'outstanding and special regard' towards King Robert, 'whom right and true [*decayed section*] and the justice and grace of the King of Kings raised up as our leader and prince'. The letter thanks the king for his regard towards 'our king and us' in restoring the rights and liberties (*freedoms*) of the kingdom, and speaks of raising 'the standing of our king' and restoring the kingdom to its pristine freedom.[47] The message to Philip is that recovery of the freedom of the kingdom comes before recovery of the Holy Land, but there is a sub-text: help to raise the standing of our king; that is, secure external recognition of his title – twist the arm of Clement V somewhat harder. There is little or nothing here to suggest that Philip himself had denied Robert the title of king.

That must have been the reason for a second letter from the barons to Philip, known only from an eighteenth-century summary, a 'declaration of the nobles of Scotland to

Philip . . . of the right and title of Robert to the crown of the kingdom of Scotland and that Robert I is the true and undoubted and nearer heir to Alexander III'. Professor Barrow rightly suggests that the text of this cannot have been far removed from that of the Declaration of the clergy, which does indeed describe Robert as 'true heir . . . to be preferred to all others', and accepted by the people 'without doubt' (c. 2). But why two letters to Philip?

In August 1309 another French messenger was at London on his way to Scotland with Philip's letter to Robert, earl of Carrick, in a box, but stitched to his belt the same letter addressed to Robert, king of Scotland, both in the envoy's handwriting.[48] If a similar device of double letters had been used in February–March, then the extant letter, welcoming Philip's expressions of affection, replied to that addressed to King Robert, while the lost letter akin to the clergy's Declaration replied to that withholding the royal style – and a London chronicler (not noted for accuracy, it must be admitted) asserts that there was a letter from Philip to Robert, addressed '*amico carissimo et comiti de Karrik . . . salutem*'.[49] Why the Scots should have responded to this we cannot know for sure, but I make a tentative suggestion below.

It was possible for barons to assert to Philip the claim to pristine freedom in 1309, and to urge it on the pope in 1320, but this was avoided, and I think deliberately, in the clergy's Declaration, though it would surely have gone down well if expounded from the pulpit in Scotland. I can find only one possible explanation: that in 1299 and 1301 the Scots had allowed freedom to be identified with papal overlordship. Recall and revival of this fiction by its beneficiary, the papacy, was almost the last thing Robert wanted in 1309, so freedom had no place in the clergy's rhetoric; and this rhetoric was intended for the wider church, where the papacy might recall its role as overlord, which the Scots had been anxious to promote in 1299–1302.

The reflections of earlier documents in the Declaration and its selective use of events which would be fully known in Scotland show that it was not intended for domestic ears, but for an international forum proposed in 1309. An ecclesiastical audience is indicated by the ecclesiastical senders, and sealing by the bishops – who would on precedent attend, or have access to, an ecumenical council of the church – points unmistakably to the Council of Vienne as the intended recipient. Indeed the self-description of the clergy as *in regno Scocie constituti* is exactly how they were addressed by Clement V in bulls of August 1308 calling for investigation of the Templars.[50] The Declaration said nothing derogatory about past tergiversations of papal policy for, despite being in effect an appeal from pope to Council, Robert had no need to add Clement to his enemies. It pulled punches on the responsibility of the English for oppression of Scotland, for there would be English prelates and envoys of Edward II at the Council, where Bruce would have only the uncertain friendship of Philip IV's envoys. The clergy's Declaration was meant for the Council, representing the whole church, all Christ's faithful, lest John Balliol should come knocking for admittance as king of Scotland.

Now for the difficulties. First, the lost letter from the nobles to Philip IV, dated according to Anderson's summary, at St Andrews in '1308', before 25 March 1309. It must surely belong to 16 or 17 March 1309, and if of the same date as the extant letter to Philip, to 16 March, the day before the clergy's Declaration. It is possible therefore that the text was first drafted as the letter of the barons and then revised for the clergy. The extant letter to Philip and the Declarations all use the rhythms of the papal cursus, however, suggesting that both letters to Philip were intended to be seen by, and to influence, ecclesiastics – French ecclesiastics – at the Council. It would be tactful to give these letters, whatever their true date, an earlier one than the generally addressed Declarations.[51] Secondly, our sources and the sealing, first addressed by D. W. Hunter Marshall in 1926.[52] Sir James Balfour noted for 1309/1 the attachment of episcopal seals, St Andrews and Dunkeld, with six unnamed detached, and for 1309/2 six green seals of unnamed bishops attached. Of the twelve Scottish bishops, Glasgow, Galloway, Argyll and Sodor cannot or would not have been present, and it is most unlikely that Caithness could have been.[53] The tally of episcopal seals was surely short unless some were obtained without consent or were substituted by the seals of others, for example, chapter seals.[54]

More certain is the fate of the original documents. None of them is likely to have been found by Balfour outside Britain, but 1309/2, the version with 'community' among the authors, had been preserved by Cotton from the English archives, and had certainly reached Edward II, from the hand of either the 'neutral' Lamberton, or of a French envoy. The significance of the difference between this and 1309/1, retained in Scotland, must remain uncertain. The clumsy 1309/2 must surely be a revision of the version represented by 1309/1, and it is just possible that it was deliberately amended to be allowed to fall into English hands; if not, it would be intended for the papal bureaucracy at the Council, and its variation from 1309/1, kept in Scotland, has a bearing on the relationship of the original 1320 Declaration kept in Scotland and the version sent to John XXII.[55]

In fact, the Scots must have discovered that their Declaration had not reached its intended destination, for eleven months later a version identical to 1309/1 (save for the date) was engrossed and sealed by at least some bishops. Bishop Lamberton had done exactly what he had been ordered to do about the Templars. On 3 October 1309 Edward II gave a safe-conduct to the papal inquisitor-depute appointed for Scotland, so that in November 1309, with Lamberton, he held an inquisition into the Order in Scotland at Holyrood abbey, in English-held territory. Every witness, and there were forty, exonerated the members of misdoing.[56] In the following February, 1310, a council of the Scottish church was held at Dundee, which would absolve them and report this to Clement. The postponement of the Council of Vienne to 1311 had still not been announced, so time would seem short if the Declaration was again to be sent to it. To the Dundee council are attributed two more versions of the Declaration of the clergy, which do survive in the original, significantly in our national archives.[57] One of them, 1310/1, follows the 1309/1 text save for the date, 'a Scottish General Council celebrated' (a word used for ecclesiastical meetings) at the Friars minor of Dundee, 24 February, 1309/10 'and the fourth year of the reign of the same king'.[58] Significant royal input is suggested by the regnal year, not found in 1309/1 and /2, and, as we shall see, by the handwriting. The impossibility of meeting at a Dundee friary, outside the town ditch, inside which the English garrisoned the castle, is a frequently repeated but mistaken

FIGURE 1

Declaration of the clergy, dated Dundee, 24 February 1309/10. National Archives of Scotland, SP13/4. The original parchment (without seal tags) is 541mm (top) x 228mm (r.h. side). [Referred to as 1310/1 in this discussion.] (Reproduced by permission of the National Archives of Scotland) objection to this document's authenticity, for a truce was in force. Bishop Lamberton, trusted by both sides, was evidently there, an ecclesiastical council would almost certainly have been cleared with the English warden, and the townsfolk were famously patriotic.[59]

The fourth and last Declaration 1310/2 varies significantly from the other three in that its *intitulatio* lists the senders as twelve Scottish bishops, each individually named, and without any mention of the rest of the clergy.[60] Now this presents its own problems, for in 1310 Robert Wishart, bishop of Glasgow, was in papal custody, and William Sinclair, 'bishop of Dunkeld', was at best elect of Dunkeld until 1312, when he was consecrated at Vienne.[61] These difficulties have led scholars to place this version, 1310/2, later than 1314 and earlier than 1316 (when Wishart died),[62] for it is, indeed, undated. Comparison of the originals of the two Declarations 1310/1 and /2, or of the photographs provided here, reveals that the text of 1310/1 is finished with a series of dashes, to preclude any additions, and that it would not be possible to write another line below its text (Fig. 1). But 1310/2 finishes the sealing clause in mid-line, has no dashes, but has a space fourteen millimetres deep to add another written line; the intention here was to add a date (Fig. 2). A scribe who had earlier accompanied Bruce in the north, writing a charter at 'Lochbren', near Urray in Easter Ross on 8 August 1309, wrote both 1310/1 and /2, so they are very likely to be contemporaneous with each other and, more loosely, with the charter.[63] The suggested later date assumes a domestic audience, for there was neither pope nor council in 1314–16, but at this time few in Scotland were likely to question the right of Robert I openly. I can find nothing to suggest that the Declaration might have been sent to cheer up the English. It is, however, possible that the original of 1310/1 in Edinburgh is the only exemplar thereof and that none was sent furth of Scotland because it was soon decided that a version naming the bishops, that is, 1310/2, would secure a better hearing at Vienne. As with the 1309 Declaration, there is no evidence that any 1310 version reached the Council of Vienne.

We must assume that in 1310 the king somehow had use of seals of, or representing, bishops who opposed him (as in 1309), and that he expected an early papal confirmation of Sinclair and release of Wishart, and so ventured to use their names in 1310/2, to which a date would be added. Neither expectation was fulfilled and 1310/2 remained unfinished in the royal archive. For 1310/1, the reliable James Anderson had reported in 1705 some vestiges of seals, though in a 1926 survey of sealing of the original documents, R. K. Hannay could see no unambiguous traces,[64] and I can see no traces at all. There are still three seals on 1310/2. Both 1310/1 and /2, then, probably had some seals attached; we do not know how many, nor, with a few exceptions, exactly whose – nor, indeed, how genuine they are. But this does not invalidate the Declarations' importance as key documents in the war of historiography to secure the throne of Scotland for Robert Bruce.

They show the shifting political situation in which the Scots fought English pretensions. The freedom of the kingdom may engage our sympathies today, but in 1299 to the Scots it meant papal suzerainty, and a detailed rejection of the English historiography. After the revolution of 1306 the musty deeds of Arthur and Giric, hashed and rehashed in 1301, were ignored; freedom from English lordship was not argued by legal brief,

FIGURE 2

Declaration of the bishops, undated. National Archives of Scotland, SP13/5. The original parchment (without seal tags and seal, omitted here) is 411mm (top) x 250mm (r.h. side). [Referred to as 1310/2 in this discussion.] (Reproduced by permission of the National Archives of Scotland) because it was never to go to court. It appeared as fact, not debate, in the letter to Philip IV, but still was carefully excluded from the clergy's Declaration lest it recall concomitant papal suzerainty. On the contrary, in 1309 and 1310 Robert's aim was to assert his right by inheritance, by acceptance by the people confirmed by battle. But the recipients of his rhetoric, Philip and the Council, show that he wrote because of the danger that the case made in 1301 for John Balliol, who still enjoyed Philip's pension, would bring John back on to the international stage as king of Scots.

Ten years later John was dead, the war still continued despite heavy defeat of the English in battle, which brought them closer to recognising Robert Bruce as king, but unable to swallow loss of overlordship. This shift of context explains the very different emphasis in the 1320 Declaration, which touches only briefly on Robert's right to be king, but hammers home ancient freedom, ancient conversion to Christianity, subversion by Edward I, achievement of freedom by Robert, who must not compromise independence. In short, not Robert's kingship restored, but our freedom.

Translation of the Declaration of the clergy in texts 1309/1, 1309/2 and 1310/2. St Andrews, 17 March 1309 and Dundee, 24 February 1310

(The division into paragraphs and their numbering are editorial.)

1. To all Christ's faithful to whose knowledge the present writing shall come, the bishops, abbots, priors and the rest of the clergy [1309/2: and community] appointed in the kingdom of Scotland, greeting in the Author of salvation.

2. Be it known to all of you that when a ground of dispute had arisen between the lord John Balliol, lately in fact raised to be king of Scotland by the king of England, and the late lord Robert Bruce of worthy memory, grandfather of the lord Robert, the king who now is, namely as to which of them was nearer by right of blood to inherit and reign over the Scottish people, the faithful people always held without doubting, as they had always understood from their ancestors and predecessors, and believed to be true, that the said lord Robert, the grandfather, was true heir after the death of King Alexander and of his grand-daughter, daughter of the king of Norway, and was to be preferred over all others for the government of the kingdom,

3. although, [by] the enemy of humankind sowing weeds, by various machinations and plots of rivals which it would be tedious to tell at length, the matter was turned to the contrary, on account of which reversal and the lack of royal dignity, heavy calamities thereafter befell the kingdom of Scotland and its inhabitants, as experience of the fact, the mistress of events previously often repeated, has openly declared,

4. the people and commons of the aforesaid kingdom of Scotland, therefore, worn out by the stings of many tribulations, [seeing] the said lord John on various pretexts taken, imprisoned and deprived of kingdom and people by the king of England, and the kingdom of Scotland also lost by him and reduced to servitude, laid waste by a huge spoliation,[65] overwhelmed by the bitterness of frequent grief, desolate for the lack of right government, exposed to every danger and given up to the occupier, and the people robbed of their goods, tortured by wars, made captive, chained and imprisoned, oppressed, subjugated and enslaved by immense slaughters of innocents and ceaseless conflagrations, and on the

THE DECLARATIONS OF THE CLERGY, 1309–10

edge of total ruin unless there be speedy action, with Divine guidance, for the restoration of the kingdom thus marred and desolate and for its government,

5. by the providence of the Highest King, under whose empire kings reign and princes have authority, unable to bear any longer so many and such great heavy losses, more bitter than death, of goods and persons, for lack of a captain and faithful leader, by Divine instigation, agreed on the said lord Robert, the king who now is, in whom the rights of his father and grandfather to the aforesaid kingdom, in the judgment of the people still reside and flourish incorrupt, and with their concurrence and consent he was raised to be king, to reform the deformities, correct what needed correction and direct what needed direction,

6. and by their authority having been advanced in the kingdom, he was solemnly made king of Scots, with whom the faithful people will live and die, as with the one who, gifted with the right of blood and other cardinal virtues is fit to rule and worthy of the name of king and honour of kingship, since, by the grace of the Saviour, by repulsing wrong he has by the sword restored the kingdom thus deformed and ruined, as many former leaders and kings of Scots had restored, acquired and held the said kingdom when often ruined in past times, as is more fully contained in the magnificent ancient deeds of the Scots and as the war-struggles of Picts against Britons and Scots against Picts, expelled from the kingdom, with many others routed, subdued and expelled by the sword, clearly bear witness.

7. And if anyone in opposition claims right to the foresaid kingdom by letters sealed in the past and containing the consent of the people and commons, know that all this took place by force and violence which could not then be resisted, by multiple fears, bodily tortures and a variety of terrors which can confound the senses and fall on the steadfast.[66]

8. Therefore we, the bishops abbots priors and rest of the clergy [1309/2: and people] aforesaid, knowing that the foregoing is based on truth and warmly approving the same, have made due fealties to the said lord Robert, our illustrious king of Scotland, and we acknowledge and by the tenour of this present document publicly declare that the same ought to be done to him and his heirs by our successors in future.

9. And in sign of witness and approval of all the aforesaid, we, not compelled by force, induced by fraud nor stumbling in error, but of pure and lasting and spontaneous free will, have caused our seals to be affixed to this writing.

10. [1309/1 and /2] Given in the parliament held at St Andrews in Scotland on the 17th of March in the year of grace 1308 [=1309].

[1310/1] Given in the Scottish General Council celebrated in the church of the Friars Minor of Dundee on the 24th day of the month of February in the year of the Lord 1309 [=1310] and the fourth year of the reign of the same [king].

NOTES

1 Sir James Fergusson, *The Declaration of Arbroath* (Edinburgh 1970), 1. G. G. Simpson, 'The Declaration of Arbroath revitalised', *Scottish Historical Review*, lvi (1977), 11–33 is a perceptive critique of earlier studies of the 1320 letter. Like these two writers I have not researched the earliest occasion on which it was called a 'Declaration'; to the few medieval writers who knew of it, it was always 'a letter'.

2 Simpson, 'The Declaration . . . revitalised', 18.
3 P. F. Tytler, *History of Scotland* (new edn; Edinburgh 1879), i, 107; Tytler knew only the reissue of the letter in 1310, of which anon.
4 I have looked in vain for 'destruction of peoples' (mass destruction) to perfect the continuum.
5 *Scotichronicon by Walter Bower* [*Scotichr.*], General Editor, D. E. R. Watt, vi (Aberdeen 1991), 158, 161, 176–7.
6 *Chronicle of Pierre de Langtoft*, T. Wright (ed.) (Rolls Series 1866–8), ii, 220–3; *Chronicle of Walter of Guisborough*, H. Rothwell (ed.) (Camden Series 1957), 270.
7 *Anglo-Scottish Relations, 1174–1328, Some Selected Documents*, E. L. G. Stones (ed.) (Oxford 1970), nos 23, 28.
8 *Anglo-Scottish Relations*, 169 translates *licet indebite* as 'and in this you acted without regard for what was fitting'. The word *indebite* means more than 'improperly' and less than 'illegally'; perhaps 'without due process'. That Balliol was meant is supported by Edward I's insistence that he had promoted Balliol to be king *debite*; *Anglo-Scottish Relations*, 210 and n. 3.
9 *Foedera*, i, 926–7; *Scotichr.*, vi, 110–13.
10 *Anglo-Scottish Relations*, no. 30; *Scotichr.*, vi, 110–13.
11 'Instructions' in *Chronicles of the Picts, Chronicles of the Scots*, W. F. Skene (ed.) (Edinburgh 1867), 232–271; *Scotichr.*, vi, 135–65. *Processus in Chron. Picts-Scots*, 271–84; *Scotichr.*, vi, 169–88. I shall refer to the *Scotichr.* edition.
12 G. W. S. Barrow, *Robert Bruce and the Community of the Realm of Scotland*, third edition (Edinburgh 1988) [Barrow, *Bruce*], 95, 344 n. 28.
13 M. Prestwich, *Edward I* (London 1988) 486; *Foedera*, i, 937; F. Palgrave, *Documents and Records Illustrating the History of Scotland*, i (all published), (London 1837), 241–7; *Treaty Rolls*, i, P. Chaplais (ed.) (London 1955), 149–52; for Edward's agreement with Bruce, *Anglo-Scottish Relations*, no. 32.
14 *Acts of the Parliaments of Scotland* [*APS*], i (Edinburgh 1844), 454b. For John's seal, J. H. Stevenson and M. Wood, *Scottish Heraldic Seals* (Glasgow 1940), i, 6, no. 22. For a photograph, R.-H. Bautier, 'Échanges d'influences dans les chancelleries souveraines . . .' in his *Chartes, Sceaux et Chancelleries*, ii (Paris 1990), 209, no. 18; *Cal. Docs. Scot.*, ii, no. 1431; Barrow, *Bruce*, 349 n. 61 for the date.
15 *Foedera*, i, 942, two bulls of Boniface VIII (13 August 1302) one blaming the bishop of Glasgow for troubling Edward I, the other urging the Scots to make peace with him.
16 S. Schein, *Fideles Crucis* (Oxford 1991), ch. 6, especially 198–9; A. Leopold, *How to Recover the Holy Land* (Aldershot 2000), 26–37 gives a good summary of the fantasies dreamed in the west in 1305–14.
17 Schein, *Fideles Crucis*, 243; for a full account, M. Barber, *The Trial of the Templars* (Cambridge 1978).
18 John Barbour, *The Bruce*, A. A. M. Duncan (ed.), 360, note on 9.
19 *Scotichr.* vi, 318–21, 431.
20 *Chronicle of Lanercost*, J. Stevenson (ed.) (Bannatyne Club 1839), 213.
21 *Foedera*, ii, 41–2, 44, 45; Watt, *Biographical Dictionary*, 322.
22 *Foedera*, ii, 64. In my previous discussion of this subject, 'The War of the Scots', *Transactions of the Royal Historical Society*, sixth series, ii (1992), 132, I carelessly dated this release 'November, 1309'.
23 *Foedera*, ii, 68.
24 *Registrum Clementis V*, ed. monachi Ordinis S. Benedicti, iii (1886), no. 3631. E. Müller, *Das Konzil von Vienne, 1311–12*, (Münster-i-W. 1934), 22–3, lists on 663–70, Scotland at 669. The French list did not have Glasgow, who was added by the papacy.

25 *Reg. Clementis V*, iii, no. 3511, *congregatis in unum*.
26 Perth and Dundee, and possibly nearby Cupar, were still in English hands, but there is no hint of a garrison at St Andrews itself. It was accessible by sea from the coastal lands to the north and the English-held south.
27 *Reg. Clementis V*, iii, nos. 3626–7.
28 For important modern discussions, Barrow, *Bruce*, 184–5; D. E. R. Watt, *Medieval Church Councils in Scotland*, (Edinburgh 2000), 104–10.
29 *Acts of the Parliaments of Scotland*, i (1843), i, 289, col. b. The error of the claim was pointed out by D. W. Hunter Marshall, 'A Supposed Provincial Council at Dundee, 1310', *SHR*, xxiii (1926), 280–93 at 281–3. It must be said that variants from the printed 1310 version are few and usually explicable as Balfour's misreadings. Sir James Balfour of Denmylne, Lyon King of Arms (?1598–1657), was an active transcriber of medieval documents, but his scholarship was not always above reproach.
30 British Library, Harleian MS. 4694, fos. 5r–6r, 35r–36r with Balfour's explanation of his sources on 36r. This is printed in full in *APS*, i, 289, col. a (the passage 'This declaratione . . . ane vther in England') and thus applied (wrongly) to the nobles' letter, which is not copied in Harleian 4694. The error has misled G. G. Simpson, 'The Declaration revitalised', 28: 'Two duplicate originals of this letter . . .'
31 Hunter Marshall, 'Council at Dundee, 1310', 281–3.
32 *Anglo-Scottish Relations*, no. 30, 210, 217; *Scotichr.* vi, 122, 126; further on this relationship, Barrow, *Bruce*, 185.
33 *Anglo-Scottish Relations*, no. 30, 212–14; *Scotichr.* vi, 125
34 *Scotichr.* vi, 164; there is no such passage in Baldred's *processus*, nor in the Bamburgh memorandum (referred to below). There is a one-line charge against Edward I in John's *diffidatio*; *Anglo-Scottish Relations*, no. 23, 142.
35 P. A. Linehan, 'A Fourteenth-century History of Anglo-Scottish Relations in a Spanish Manuscript', *Bulletin of the Institute of Historical Research*, xlvii (1975), 106–22.
36 Hunter Marshall, 'Council at Dundee, 1310', 281, is wrong in claiming that *et communitate* 'is continued throughout the document'. In Harleian MS. 4694 fo. 36r the reading *populo* is clear and could scarcely be confusion by Balfour.
37 In his bull of 13 August 1302, telling the Scottish bishops to have their flocks keep the peace with Edward I, the phrase *populus Scoticanus* is used.
38 *Scotichr.* vi, 140 line 19; 142 ll. 35, 44, 62; 146 l. 59; for *populus* (and see 148 l. 31). Ibid., 142 ll. 27, 29, 55; 146 l. 28 for *gens*. In the *processus*, see ibid., 188 line 31, fearing annihilation of the 'blood, people (*gens*) and name of Scots'.
39 In the Declaration of Arbroath, the noble senders could ring the changes on *gens, populus* and *nacio*; these covered adequately the merits of the magnates.
40 *et ipsorum auctoritate regno prefectus rex Scottorum solempniter est effectus.*
41 The kings seem to have been summated between 1292 and 1296 at 112, whence the 113 in the Declaration of Arbroath, probably in ignorance that 112 was John Balliol; D. Broun, 'The Birth of Scottish History', *SHR*, lxxvi (1997), 4–22 at 13–15.
42 R. James Goldstein, *The Matter of Scotland* (Lincoln: Nebraska 1993), 87–101 is a stimulating discussion.
43 *Scotichr.*, vi, 180–3; cf. 140–7.
44 E. L. G. Stones and G. G. Simpson, *Edward I and the Throne of Scotland* (Oxford 1978) [*Throne of Scotland*], ii, 258–9 (20 November 1292); 262–3 (26 December 1292).
45 The use of 'containing' may avoid the awkward fact that the letters record fealty, not consent.

46 Cf. the note in *Anglo-Scottish Relations*, 284, n. 2 which is misleading; Barrow, *Bruce*, 364 n. 102, would include the homages to Edward of 1291 and 1304, but these were not recorded in sealed letters. Edward I claimed only that in 1296 prelates, magnates and communities did him homage and fealty (*Scotichr.*, vi, 126–7; *Anglo-Scottish Relations*, 217) and there is no mention of the submission in 'Instructions' or *processus*. For the notarial instruments, Stones and Simpson, *Throne of Scotland*, i, 92–7, 209–10; ii, 376–7; *Instrumenta Publica* (Bannatyne Club 1834).

47 Original, National Archives of Scotland, SP13/3; *APS*, i, 459, with facsimile. The original is defective in places; translation in W. C. Dickinson, G. Donaldson and I. A. Milne, *Source Book of Scottish History* (Edinburgh 1958), 142–3 (to be used with caution).

48 *Foedera*, ii, 79; *Treaty Rolls*, i, no. 472.

49 *Annales Paulini*; *Chronicles of the Reigns of Edward I and Edward II*, W. Stubbs (ed.) (Rolls Series 1882), i, 266, under 1308, i.e. before 25 March 1309. Philip is said to have summoned both Edward II and Robert to his parliament.

50 *Reg. Clementis V*, iii, nos 3401, 3511.

51 On the cursus, *Regesta Regum Scottorum*, v, A. A. M. Duncan (ed.) (Edinburgh 1988), 164–6. The damage to the letter of the barons to Philip makes it impossible to identify all examples of the cursus there.

52 Hunter Marshall, 'Council at Dundee, 1310', 281–3, correcting *APS*, i, 289.

53 Hunter Marshall, 'Council at Dundee, 1310', 281 notes the sealing of 1309/1 and discusses the bishops 285–93; for 1309/2 Harleian MS. 4694, fo. 36r.

54 It is not impossible that for some bishops a seal matrix may have been forged from an impression of a genuine seal.

55 Simpson, 'The Declaration . . . revitalised', 12–16 is the only earlier exposition of these problems.

56 *Foedera*, ii, 94; *Records of Antony Bek* (Surtees Soc. 1953), no. 144, p. 155; *The Spottiswoode Miscellany*, ii (1845), 7–16. The inquest was however abandoned because of the dangers of war, and there was indeed an interval between truces in November 1309; *Chron. Lanercost*, 213.

57 Original, National Archives of Scotland, SP 3/4 and 3/5; figures 1 and 2.

58 Original, National Archives of Scotland, SP 13/4; facsimile, text and translation, *National Manuscripts of Scotland*, ii (Edinburgh 1870), no. xvii; text, *APS*, i, 460; text and translation, *Anglo-Scottish Relations*, no. 36.

59 Hunter Marshall, 'Council at Dundee', 283–5; map in E. P. D. Torrie, *Medieval Dundee* (Dundee 1990), 40; *Scotichr.*, vi, 84–7.

60 Original, National Archives of Scotland, SP 13/5; *APS*, i, 460–1. Apart from the *intitulatio*, the text has only minor variants from 1309/1 and 1310/1.

61 Watt, *Biographical Dictionary*, 496b. On 2 February 1313 Edward II still referred to him as 'elect of Dunkeld'; *Cal. Docs. Scot*. iii, no. 301.

62 Hunter Marshall, 'Council at Dundee, 1310', 293; Watt *Biographical Dictionary*, e.g. 25a, 323b, 496b.

63 *RRS*, v, 177, 297. The identification of Lochbren as Loch Broom, though put forward by W. J. Watson (*Place Names of Ross and Cromarty* (Inverness 1976, reprint), 241) and accepted by me in *RRS*, v, has been persuasively queried by Professor Barrow, who, in a letter, points to its occurrence linked with Dingwall ('Innerasfran') in Bagimond's Roll (*Miscellany of the Scottish History Society*, vi (1939), 50); see also the *persona de Loch Bron* (*Registrum Episcopatus Moraviensis* (Bannatyne Club 1837) no. 75). It occurs as *ecclesiam de Bron* in the constitution of the cathedral of Ross, where it is the sub-chanter's prebend (*Vetera Monumenta Hibernorum et Scotorum Historiam Illustrantia*, A. Theiner (ed.) (Rome 1864), no. CLXXXII) showing that it is to be identified with the parish of Urray near Dingwall in Easter Ross (*Origines Parochiales Scotiae* (Bannatyne Club 1851–5), ii, part 2, 518).

64 Hunter Marshall, 'Council at Dundee, 1310', 282–3.
65 *ingenti populacione*, translated in *Anglo-Scottish Relations*, 283 as 'great slaughter'.
66 On this phrase see 'A Thirteenth-century Phrase', in *The Collected Papers of T. F. Tout*, (Manchester, 1932–4), ii, 285–7; more briefly it is found in *Scimus fili*; *Anglo-Scottish Relations*, 168–9.

ARBROATH ABBEY

A NOTE ON ITS ARCHITECTURE AND EARLY CONSERVATION HISTORY

Richard Fawcett

ARBROATH ABBEY is most commonly thought of as the place where the Declaration of Arbroath originated in 1320, as a consequence of the accident of history that the chancellor of the kingdom was its abbot at the time. This is entirely understandable, but it should not be allowed to eclipse the significance of the abbey as one of the outstanding ecclesiastical buildings to have been produced within the architectural province that comprised lowland Scotland and northern England in the decades on either side of 1200. The short essay offered here on the architecture and modern conservation history of the abbey is intended to provide some background to the papers on the Declaration itself. Serendipitously, the abbatial residence, within which the Declaration may have been signed, is one of the best preserved parts of the abbey, though only the core of the surviving structure would have been in place during Bernard's abbacy.

The dating evidence

The church, which was the principal building of the Tironensian abbey of Arbroath, was one of the largest ecclesiastical structures ever raised in Scotland (Fig. 1). As completed in the early decades of the thirteenth century, it had a total length of some ninety metres, a size which, together with the outstandingly high quality of its architecture, reflected its status as a major royal foundation and as the intended burial place of its founder, King William the Lion. It continued to meet the needs of the community it housed up to the Reformation with only relatively minor structural changes and additions, though it must be assumed that the liturgical arrangements within the fixed architectural framework would have been modified periodically to meet changing views on what was most appropriate. The main complex of conventual buildings, of which very little now remains, was arranged around a cloister on the south side of the church, with the abbot's house off its south-west corner, while a stretch of precinct wall, with the principal gate into the precinct at its centre, extends to the south-west of the church.

There are a number of documentary references, or pieces of information of other kinds, that may have a bearing on the dating of the abbey's construction and of the later alterations to it. Presumably the first building operations were associated with the foundation of 1178 (*Arb. Lib.*, i no. 1), with the possibility that work was instigated before the formal act of foundation. By 4 December 1214 enough of the church was

Figure 1
Arbroath Abbey, from the east. The east gable of the church is to the right and the sacristy to the left.
(© Crown copyright, reproduced courtesy of Historic Scotland)

complete for the patron to be buried within it (*Scotichronicon*, v, 3), even if that need have been no more than the eastern arm, since his place of burial was before the high altar. From what we can understand of the architecture, it is likely that the main body of the church was largely complete by the date of its dedication on 8 May 1233 (*Chron. Melrose*, 143). The first recorded structural damage was caused by a storm in January 1272, which led to a great fire, and which probably necessitated some rebuilding (*Scotichronicon*, v, 385).[1] Further damage was caused by the actions of English enemies in the fourteenth century, to which there are references on 11 May 1350 and 11 February 1378/9 (*Arb. Lib.*, ii, nos. 23 and 36). Soon after the latter, in 1380, the church was struck by lightning, and the community had to be housed elsewhere for a period (*Scotichronicon*, vii, 381; *Cal. Scot. Supp.* i, 92). A contract of 16 February 1384 with William Plumer for re-leading the choir roof may indicate that one phase of repairs was nearing completion (Salzman 1952, 471). The sacristy and treasury block was added during the abbacy of Walter Paniter (1410–49), to judge by heraldic evidence.[2] Later in that century, in 1474, the signing of a contract with the wright Stephen Liel of St Andrews for maintenance and repairs suggests that the abbey was continuing to take its structural responsibilities seriously (*Arb. Lib.*, ii, no 192).

The Abbey Church

The layout of the church

The church was set out with an aisle-less presbytery of two bays, as the location for the high altar, and there was an aisled choir of three bays to its west, although it is possible that the monastic choir and the screens that enclosed it would have extended below the crossing (Fig. 2). Projecting laterally outwards from the crossing were transepts of three bays, with a chapel aisle on the east side of each. The aisled nave was nine bays long. There were three towers, one over the crossing of the four arms, and two over the western bays of the nave aisles, the latter flanking the great processional entrance at the centre of the west front. The other entrances into the church that are known to have existed were: one in the south transept at the foot of the night stair which led down

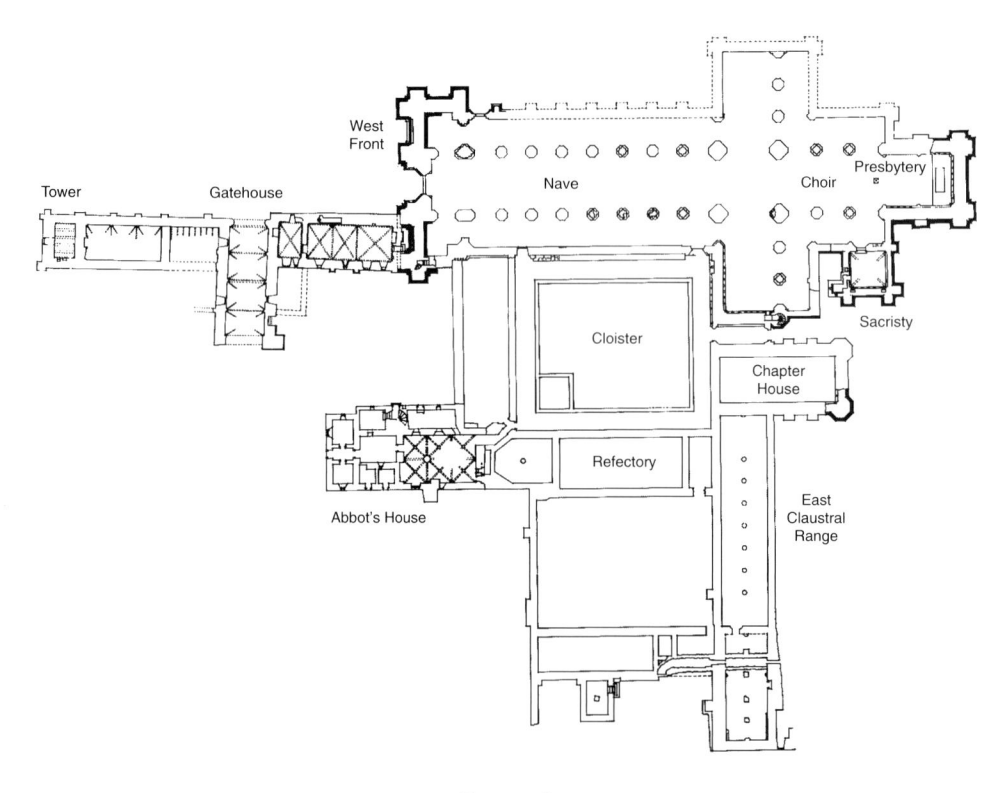

FIGURE 2
Arbroath Abbey, the plan of the surviving buildings and excavated foundations.
(© Crown copyright, reproduced courtesy of Historic Scotland)

from the monks' dormitory in the east conventual range; two into the south nave aisle, which aligned with the east and west cloister walks, and gave daytime access to the church for the monks; one in the second bay from the east in the north aisle, which would have been the principal entrance for layfolk. A sixth doorway was cut when a sacristy and treasury block was added against the south side of the choir around the mid-fifteenth century. There may also have been a doorway in the north transept to give access to the burial ground on that side.

Despite the extremely fragmentary state of the church, clear pointers to the original relative height of the various parts are provided by the thickness of the surviving walls. Thus the outer walls of the south choir aisle, of the south transept chapel aisle and of the south nave aisle are relatively thin, since they rose through no more than a single stage. By contrast the walls of the unaisled presbytery and the main body of the south transept, which rose to about twice the height of the aisles, are very much thicker, as are the surviving parts of the west towers, which rose yet higher. The only parts of the church known to have been covered with stone vaulting were the aisles and the later sacristy, all of which had four-part ribbed vaults, though the aisle vaulting did not continue into the base of the west towers.

From a description written by Canon James Coutts of Glasgow in 1517 (Theiner, *Vet. Mon.*, no DCCCCXXV), we can add a little more to our understanding of what survives. The high spaces of the church had wooden ceilings (possibly of arched profile in view of the height to which the circular west window must have reached); the roofs were mainly lead-covered, though parts had shingles. The high altar, which was set a little way in from the east wall (as is still to be seen from its excavated base), had a gilt timber retable with representations of Christ as Salvator Mundi, the Virgin and Child, St Thomas Becket, and King William the Lion as donor. Two or three sung masses were celebrated at that altar daily. There were twelve other altars within the church (two of these would have been at the choir aisle ends, four in the transept chapels, and at least one against the rood screen; the positions of the other five are uncertain, but they may have been against the nave arcade piers). The choir stalls, which were in two tiers, were of timber, and there was a large organ. Within the sacristy were stored a silver cross, many chalices and other vessels, silver images, a large number of sets of vestments of cloth of gold and silk, and the abbot's pastoral staff and mitre. A further clue to the liturgical arrangements is a socket stone set at the junction of the choir and presbytery, which may have been for the principal lectern, while the location of the altar at the east end of the south choir aisle is indicated by the survival of an arched recess for a double piscina and an aumbry (see Fig. 14).

In general, the church was constructed of carefully cut red or pink sandstone ashlar, with a strikingly high level of surface enrichment throughout. The exception to this is the lower part of the south nave aisle wall below the level of the windows, which is built of roughly coursed rubble from a short way west of the south-east processional doorway to its junction with the west wall of the west claustral range (Fig. 3). Is it a possibility that this wall is the relic of a first building campaign aimed at providing a smaller first church and adjacent conventual buildings than those which were eventually

FIGURE 3
Arbroath Abbey, the south wall of the nave, showing the change of masonry between the lower and upper parts of the wall. The south transept is to the left.
(© Crown copyright, reproduced courtesy of Historic Scotland)

built, albeit they may have been superseded even before they were completed? The architectural evidence, as seen particularly in the foliage carving of a number of capitals in the presbytery and south transept, suggests that the building campaign which created the present church was only initiated around the last years of the twelfth century, a decade or more after the foundation. However, once started, it was clearly pressed ahead rapidly, and most of the building, with the possible exception of the upper parts of the towers, is likely to have been completed by the dedication of 1233. Assuming that the lower part of the south wall is indeed earlier, its retention appears to have caused some difficulty when the south-west tower was eventually laid out. At the junction of the south nave wall and the west side of the west range, a rather awkward dog-leg section of walling had to be embodied within the base of the tower, although modern

FIGURE 4
Arbroath Abbey, the south wall of the presbytery and the south choir chapel on the left, with the sacristy on the right.
(© Crown copyright, reproduced courtesy of Historic Scotland)

rebuilding has confused the evidence. It is also a possibility that the west doorway was a part of the first building campaign, perhaps being relocated to its present position at a late stage of building operations (see Fig. 9).

The design of the church

The presbytery is likely to have had three tiers of triplet single-light windows to its east wall, the lower one and a half tiers of which survive (see Fig. 1), and there was perhaps a circular window in the gable on analogy with what still survives in the south transept. There were tiers of single single-light windows to the two bays of the aisle-less presbytery flanks, although much of what is now seen there is nineteenth-century rebuilding. Internally, below the windows of the presbytery there was a decorative blind arcade rising from a bench, and there were evidently wall shafts to articulate the bays. The presbytery and choir aisles had triplets of arches framing the single-light windows, the arches flanking the windows being blind, and the bays of the choir aisles were defined by wall shafts rising from the floor (Fig. 4). By contrast, in the south aisle of the nave the wall shafts only began at corbels above the lower walling, perhaps providing further support for the idea that the lower wall was retained from an earlier building campaign (see Fig. 3).

The richness of effect sought in the presbytery is perhaps even more evident in the gable wall of the south transept (Fig. 5), which has two lower tiers of decorative blind arcading with pointed arches of different forms, and there is a third tier of round-headed arcading opening on to a mural passage off the night stair. Above this is a pair of tall single-light windows, the lower part of the western one being blocked because of the presence of the dormitory behind; in the gable is a large oculus.

Apart from the end walls of the four limbs of the building, which terminated the views down and across the building, the main internal impact would have been created by the internal elevations of the high central spaces. These can now only be reconstructed from the incomplete surviving evidence in the south-east corner of the south transept and at the north-west corner of the nave (Figs 5 and 6). Except below the towers, where the piers had to be very much more substantial, the arcades were carried on clustered-shaft piers of eight keeled shafts, while each bay of the gallery had a single round-arched opening, subdivided by a pair of pointed arches. At clearstorey level it seems there were two single-light windows in each bay, with a pair of arches on the inner face of the mural passage corresponding to the windows. The best evidence for the upper storeys is now on the inner face of the north-west tower, but there they cannot have been altogether typical, since they were treated as flying screens in front of the unfloored space of the tower, and there was no clearstorey passage.

The greatest external architectural emphasis of the abbey was concentrated on the twin-towered west front, which must have been one of the last parts to be completed (Fig. 7). The central part of the front, corresponding to the main space of the nave, has the great round-arched processional doorway at its base, surmounted by a deep vault-like arch which carried a triple-gabled gallery of most unusual form and of uncertain function. Above this gallery was a band of blind arcading, and rising into the gable was

FIGURE 5
Arbroath Abbey, the south transept.
(© Crown copyright, reproduced courtesy of Historic Scotland)

FIGURE 6
Arbroath Abbey, the north-west corner of the nave, with the west front to the left.
(© Crown copyright, reproduced courtesy of Historic Scotland)

FIGURE 7
Arbroath Abbey, the west front, with the precinct wall to the right.
(© Crown copyright, reproduced courtesy of Historic Scotland)

a great circular window, which is likely to have been originally filled with plate tracery. The two towers have massive angle buttresses. At their lowest level, corresponding to the central doorway between them, is a band of syncopated blind arcading, the outer plane of arches set at a higher level than the inner plane (Fig. 8). The upper parts of the towers as first built were largely occupied by two tiers of paired single-light windows, with a band of diagonally-set masonry between that appears to have been inspired by Roman *opus reticulatum*; there was an arched corbel table at the wall-head. It may be suspected that the towers were originally intended to be capped by lead-sheathed spires with pinnacles at the angles, but the northern tower is known from early views to have had an added upper storey, possibly placed there after the storm damage of either 1272 or 1380 (see Figs 25 and 26).

The round-arched west doorway had six orders of arches designed to be carried on free-standing shafts against an angled face, the arches being decorated with chevron and bobbin (Fig. 9). This doorway was rather different in spirit from the two other major doorways into the nave, both of which have pointed arches cut with delicately formed mouldings. The north nave doorway has arches that were carried on shafts alternating with engaged rolls, and had a gabled and arcaded superstructure (Fig. 10). The eastern doorway from the cloister, which was probably a little earlier than the north doorway, had three orders carried on shafts, and was flanked on each side by a blind arch. Unlike the very simple western doorway from the cloister, which rather oddly had its door towards the church rather than towards the cloister, the eastern doorway would appear to have been built beyond the stretch of wall that it has been suggested might be earlier than the rest of the church.

The sources for the design of the church

The master mason who designed this great church was clearly well acquainted with most of the important buildings under construction in lowland Scotland and northern England in the later decades of the twelfth century. This is not the place to attempt a detailed discussion of the range of ideas that may have conditioned the design,[3] though it should be mentioned that the architecture of the abbey's own mother house of Kelso appears to have been of relatively little influence. A major initial source of inspiration must have been the cathedral of St Andrews, the mother church of the diocese within which Arbroath was located, and which was itself under construction during the whole of the time that it took to build Arbroath. The plan of Arbroath can be understood as a truncated version of that of St Andrews though with the addition of two western towers.[4] The design of the triple tiers of windows in the eastern gable may also have drawn some inspiration from St Andrews (Fig. 11), even if the Arbroath master mason has shown an awareness of later developments on the approach taken at St Andrews, developments that are now reflected more completely at Brinkburn Priory, Northumberland (Fig. 12). So far as the internal elevations are concerned, it may be suspected that St Andrews was again an important source, though the design likely to have existed in the choir there had been given later interpretations in the nave of Jedburgh Abbey, and in the choirs of the priories at Hexham, Northumberland, and

FIGURE 8
Arbroath Abbey, the syncopated arcading along the lower walls of the west towers; there would originally have been shafts running between the arches and bases.
(© Crown copyright, reproduced courtesy of Historic Scotland)

FIGURE 9
Arbroath Abbey, the great west doorway.
(© Crown copyright, reproduced courtesy of Historic Scotland)

FIGURE 10
Arbroath Abbey, the north nave doorway.
(© Crown copyright, reproduced courtesy of Historic Scotland)

FIGURE 11
St Andrews Cathedral, the east gable of the church. The two upper tiers of three round-headed windows were replaced by a single traceried window in the first half of the fifteenth century.
(© Crown copyright, reproduced courtesy of Historic Scotland)

FIGURE 12
Brinkburn Priory, Northumberland, the choir and south transept. Although Arbroath's east gable would probably have been one storey taller, this gives some idea of its original appearance.
(Source: author)

Lanercost, Cumberland. Arbroath can only be understood within that wider context, and the parallels with Hexham are particularly close (Fig. 13).

Turning to the great showpiece of Arbroath's exterior, the west front (see Fig. 7), its impact must have been almost overwhelmingly impressive, and the master mason's ability to create a synthesis which went beyond the buildings from which he drew his ideas is particularly clearly demonstrated here. For its twin towers there were many precedents in England, and there was at least one in Scotland, at Dunfermline, which was still the principal Scottish royal mausoleum, even if William the Lion might have been hoping that Arbroath would replace it. The triple gables above the doorway had been foreshadowed at Jedburgh Abbey, although without the gallery, while the great circular window could reflect designs at some of the northern English Cistercian abbeys, such as Byland and Fountains (both in Yorkshire). However, it was the combination of all these elements that made Arbroath so impressive, and in this there may have been an

FIGURE 13
Hexham Priory, Northumberland, the interior of the choir. Apart from differences at clearstorey level, the interior of Arbroath Abbey would have shown many similarities with this.
(Source: author)

FIGURE 14
Arbroath Abbey, the sacristy seen from the north.
(© Crown copyright, reproduced courtesy of Historic Scotland)

awareness of the latest ideas on façade design in continental Europe, as seen at Laon Cathedral in France, for example.

The sacristy

Apart from the heightening of the north-west tower, of which virtually nothing now remains, the only significant addition to the completed church was the two-storeyed block set against the east bay of the south choir aisle, with a sacristy at the lower level and a treasury above (Fig. 14). This can be dated to between 1410 and 1449 from the presence of heraldry attributed to Abbot Walter Paniter on the arch of an aumbry in the west wall and on one of the wall shaft caps. The chamber of the sacristy rises to about the same height as the adjacent aisle, and is covered by a four-part vault. Its lower walls, except on the north side, which was the original external wall of the church, have

FIGURE 15
Arbroath Abbey, the interior of the sacristy. The doorway to the strong room is at the centre, and the aumbry with the arms of Abbot Walter Paniter is to the right.
(© Crown copyright, reproduced courtesy of Historic Scotland)

decorative blind arcading, the tympana of which have a strongly emphasised vertical groove which appears to have taken its lead from the decorative arcading of the west front (Fig. 15, and see Fig. 8). Along the east wall most of the arches of this arcading are carried on corbels rather than shafts, presumably because an altar was located here. The main lighting for the chamber comes from a pair of single-light windows in the east wall (see Fig. 1), and a large window with renewed tracery in the south wall.

Within the buttress at the south end of the west face is a small mural closet, perhaps intended to serve as a strong room, but the upper levels of this buttress contain a stair capped by a pinnacle, which gave access to the treasury on the first floor. This stair can be entered from either of two elevated doorways, one within the sacristy, and the other outside, both of which must have been reached by removable steps of some form. There was also a doorway to the treasury from the adjacent aisle roof space. Rather curiously, on the west face of the treasury there are the corbels for what appears to have been a latrine, though the treasury itself is now so incomplete that it is difficult to be certain why one was needed there.

The Conventual Buildings

The cloister and claustral ranges

Very little of the cloister now stands above ground level, but from what we know of its excavated plan it is not quite what might be expected at such a well endowed foundation.[5] In the first place, it is rather smaller than might have been thought appropriate, and whereas most cloisters are square in plan, Arbroath's is oblong, being longer from west to east than from north to south (Fig. 16, and see Fig. 2). This raises the possibility that a small square first cloister was extended eastwards, but that expansion to the south and west was prevented by the existence of other buildings which it was felt expedient to retain. Significantly, if the length of the cloister from north to south is measured out along the south wall of the nave from the west side of the cloister, the internal intake to the west of the south-east doorway is reached. This could provide further support for the possibility suggested above that the lower south nave wall, which is also the north wall of the cloister, is the relic of a project to provide a smaller first church and cloister around the time of the initial foundation, and perhaps before the founder's ambitions for his new abbey had expanded to the scale reflected in the church as finally laid out.[6]

The main structural relic of the east claustral range is the extensively refaced south-east corner of the chapter house,[7] which is likely to have been built in the early thirteenth century on the architectural evidence. Following on from what has been said about the south nave wall, could the range of which it forms a part have replaced an earlier range set a little further west? From the little of the chapter house that survives, it can be seen to have had polygonal buttresses at its eastern angles, and closely spaced buttresses along the parts of its flanks that projected clear of the range. It was covered with four-part vaulting, and its windows were embraced by arches carried on free-standing shafts both internally and externally. The rest of the ground floor of the east range would have

FIGURE 16
Arbroath Abbey, the site of the cloister. The south wall of the nave is to the left, the south transept at the centre, and the chapter house to the right.
(© Crown copyright, reproduced courtesy of Historic Scotland)

contained a parlour and warming room amongst other spaces, while there would have been the dormitory and necessary house or latrine on the floor above. From what has been found through excavation, it is known that the east range ran well beyond the cloister, and even extended beyond a second courtyard to the south of the cloister itself, bridging the great drain towards its outer end. It would seem that the scale of the abbey as represented by the east range was considerably greater than the scale of any complex likely to be planned in association with such a cloister.

The south range would have been largely occupied by the refectory, which was probably elevated above an undercroft. By the time of the description of 1517 there were said to be two refectories, one perhaps being a misericord where meat could be eaten without infringing the monastic prohibition of eating flesh within the refectory. West of the refectory was the kitchen, which evidently had three fireplaces ranged around the polygonal west end of the room.

The abbot's house

The most important off-shoot of the claustral ranges was the abbot's house, which projected from the west end of the south range, adjacent to the kitchen that served the refectory (Fig. 17). Like the chapter house in the east range, the architectural details of the earliest portion suggest that it was part of a major rebuilding operation of the early thirteenth century. Though there is likely to have been further accommodation for the abbot within the body of the west range, the principal room of the surviving part appears to have been a handsomely proportioned hall or outer chamber, which had lancet windows in the three walls that projected free of the claustral ranges. It was elevated to first-floor level above a vaulted undercroft that later served as a kitchen (Fig. 18); however, the large fireplace in that undercroft is clearly an insertion, and the adjacent remains of a two-light window, later converted into a doorway, suggest that the space once served a less utilitarian purpose. It was presumably within this residence that Abbot Bernard presided over the dating and issue of the Declaration of Arbroath in 1320.

FIGURE 17
Arbroath Abbey, the abbot's house viewed from the south. The cross-wall and buttress in this view are post-medieval, and the hall originally extended across the platform to the right.
(© Crown copyright, reproduced courtesy of Historic Scotland)

FIGURE 18
Arbroath Abbey, the vaulted undercroft of the abbot's house.
(© Crown copyright, reproduced courtesy of Historic Scotland)

In the later middle ages the house was greatly expanded. This was probably an operation carried out in more than one phase, with the building taking final shape in the early years of the sixteenth century on the evidence of the restored mullioned and transomed windows and the type of coped crowsteps employed for the gables. A two-storeyed extension with a new chamber and gallery on each floor was added to the west of the hall, together with a two-storeyed lean-to range along the north flank, which included an entrance vestibule, a spiral stair to the other floors and a closet and latrine off the abbot's chamber (Fig. 19). There are traces of painted decoration on the walls of the first-floor chamber, which give some hint of the fine qualities of the accommodation this house contained. The gallery at the west end of the building is a particularly intriguing survival, and may be a representative of the type of structure that building accounts suggest was more often constructed of timber. Despite some loss of authenticity when it was heavily restored in the 1920s, the abbot's house is one of the most complete

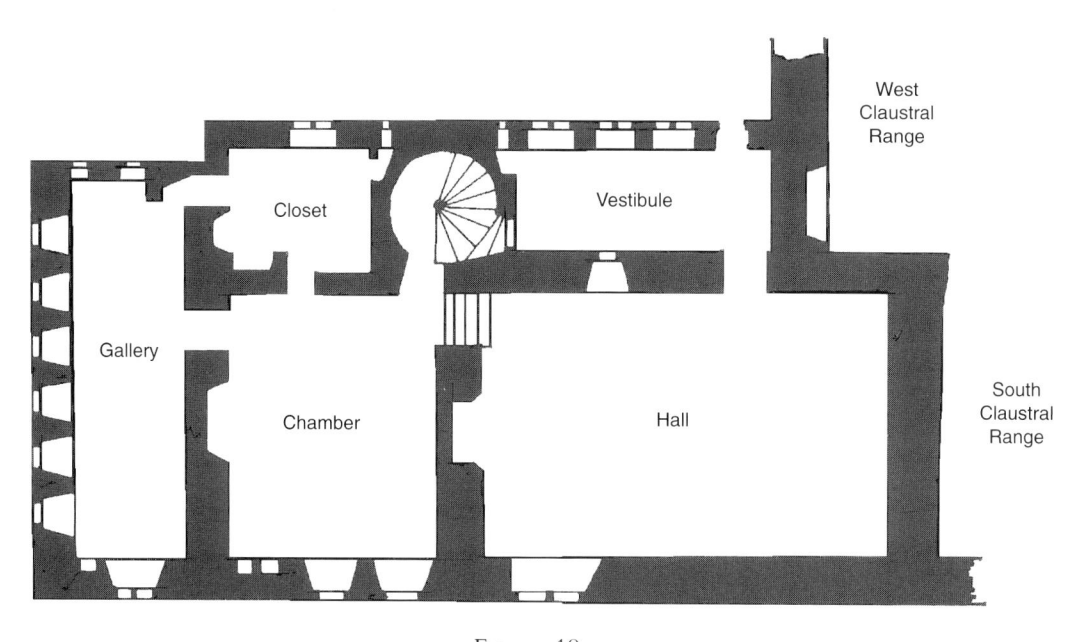

FIGURE 19
Arbroath Abbey, the plan of the principal floor of the abbot's house as it is thought to have been in its final medieval state. There are likely to have been more windows to the hall than are shown here, however.
(Source: author)

examples in Scotland of a late medieval high status unfortified residence. It must be remembered, however, that it was not meant to stand in isolation, but was designed as an off-shoot of the cloister, in a position where lip service could be paid to the idea that the abbot lived in common with his monks (see Fig. 2). Nevertheless, Canon Coutts' account of 1517 makes clear that the abbot's house was essentially separate from the living quarters of the monks.

The gatehouse range

The precinct of a major abbey was usually surrounded by substantial walls. This was partly to emphasise the sense of enclosure of the monks whose life was meant to be apart from the world, but also to defend the 'headquarters' of a body that, in the case of Arbroath, had become a great land-holding corporation. Apart from the many buildings that would have been required within the precinct, and of which so little now remains, the description of 1517 makes reference to the many wide and fair gardens of the monks, and even the cemetery to the north of the church is likely to have been treated as a garden. In laying out the precinct, it had to be positioned so that the west front of the abbey church and the entrance for lay folk in the north flank of the church were relatively freely accessible at one end of an area less strictly enclosed as an outer courtyard. There would have been several gateways into the precinct itself, and excavation has

FIGURE 20
Arbroath Abbey, the precinct wall, gatehouse and angle tower, with the west front of the church to the left.
(© Crown copyright, reproduced courtesy of Historic Scotland)

suggested there was one to the north of the church, though the main gate was to the south-west of the abbey church, on the south side of the outer courtyard. That gateway is at the centre of a stretch of high wall that runs down from the north-west corner of the church's south-west tower; however, since the wall obscures the base of the tower, it is hardly likely to be contemporary with it (Fig. 20). The wall now ends at another tower, at the angle where the boundary turned towards the south.

There are several phases of work in this stretch of precinct wall, with its gatehouse and angle tower. The buttresses of the wall to the west of the gatehouse have lateral intakes that could point to a mid-thirteenth-century date for that part, while the details of the upper storey of the gatehouse, which has blind arcading on each side of a large and presumably originally traceried window, indicate an initial date of construction for that part around the later thirteenth century (Fig. 21). However, the massive corbels for machicolated wall-walks on the gatehouse and angle tower are unlikely to be earlier than the fifteenth century, and the details of the crow-stepped gable of the gatehouse could be as late as the early sixteenth century. The unusually long gatehouse passage was covered by four bays of four-part vaulting, and there was provision for a portcullis

FIGURE 21
Arbroath Abbey, the outer face of the precinct gate.
(© Crown copyright, reproduced courtesy of Historic Scotland)

FIGURE 22
Arbroath Abbey, the tower at the north-west angle of the precinct wall.
(© Crown copyright, reproduced courtesy of Historic Scotland)

at the outer end, and for doors in the middle. The angle tower at the west end of this stretch of wall rose through four storeys and a garret (Fig. 22), the two lower storeys having ribbed barrel vaulting. The chambers on the upper storeys, to which there must have been separate access from an external forestair on the south side, appear to have

ARBROATH ABBEY: ARCHITECTURE & CONSERVATION

FIGURE 23
Arbroath Abbey, the range against the precinct wall between the abbey church and the gate, which may have been a guest house.
(© Crown copyright, reproduced courtesy of Historic Scotland)

formed a well-appointed lodging, presumably for a principal obedientiary or secular officer of the abbey. The form of the fireplaces suggest this lodging was last fitted out in the years around 1500.

There were two-storeyed ranges of buildings set against the precinct wall on each side of the gatehouse. To the east is a heavily restored range which has a lower storey with two rooms: the larger, which is of three vaulted bays, has a fireplace, while the other is of one vaulted bay (Figs 23 and 24, and see Fig. 2). The arrangement of the upper floor is now too far modified to be fully understandable. However, with such an arrangement of rooms, and in view of its close relationship with the outer courtyard on one side and the abbot's house on the other, it seems likely that this range could have served as a guest house for high-status visitors. A major abbey such as Arbroath would probably have had several guest houses, with varying provisions to meet the gamut of social standing of the abbey's visitors. It may be suspected that an inn known to have

FIGURE 24
Arbroath Abbey, the interior of the range between the church and the precinct gate.
(© Crown copyright, reproduced courtesy of Historic Scotland)

stood within the outer courtyard in the eighteenth century could have perpetuated another guest house (Fig. 25).

The range on the west side of the gatehouse was also divided by a cross wall into two parts. The eastern part, which was accessible from within the gatehouse passage, was covered at the lower level by an oddly asymmetrical ribbed barrel vault; the ground floor of the western part, which had a fireplace, was covered by three bays of four-part

FIGURE 25
Arbroath Abbey, the abbey church and precinct wall in 1790. It is at least a possibility that the building to the left of this view, now demolished, incorporated one of the monastic buildings. Fragments of the superstructure added to the north-west tower of the church after 1272 or 1380 are still to be seen in this view.
(Source: Francis Grose, *The antiquities of Scotland*, ii, London 1791)

vaulting. This range is traditionally believed to have housed the offices associated with the regality of the abbey, from where its estates were administered.

The Earlier Conservation History of the Abbey

The process of loss, decay and alienation

Over a quarter of a century after the Reformation, the passing of an Act of Annexation in 1587 (*Acts Parl. Scot.*, ix, 104) meant that both the abbey and abbacy of Arbroath, in common with those of many other religious houses, came to be technically vested in the crown. By that time, however, the estates were effectively in the possession of successive members of the Hamilton family, who had held the commendatorship since

1551. Eventually in 1606 and 1608, probably some years after the last members of the old community had died out, the abbacy was erected into a temporal lordship for James, marquess of Hamilton (*Acts Parl. Scot.*, iv, 321–2; *Reg. Mag. Sig.*, vi, no 2075). Subsequently, in 1642, the estates were granted to Patrick, earl of Panmure, whose descendants continued to regard themselves as owners well into the nineteenth century, though with an interlude between 1715 and 1764, when the earl was forfeited for his part in the rising of 1715.[8]

In all this time, it is doubtful if there were individuals or groups with any great interest in preserving the buildings of the abbey for their architectural qualities, and they were quickly seized upon as candidates for alternative use or, more frequently, as a quarry for building materials. It was only when interest in the medieval history and buildings of the abbey became more widespread, around the turn of the eighteenth and nineteenth centuries, that the crown began to restate its claim to the buildings. At this time it began to be asserted that the buildings themselves could not have been included in any grants of the abbacy, and efforts were made to determine who had any claims on them, and if those claims could be substantiated. This was in many ways to be a test case for other monastic sites. But, just as significantly, Arbroath was also to be a testing ground for the development of approaches to the conservation of important historic ruins, and it provides a fascinating insight into the emergence of methodologies, which can only be touched upon briefly here.

The process of destruction had begun as early as 1580, when the magistrates of the burgh successfully applied to the commendator for stone and timber to build a new parish church (Hay 1876, 91). In this case it seems that it was the east range that was being pillaged. But the robbing of materials from the church must have begun soon afterwards, and by the time that Slezer published his view of it in 1693, it was almost as completely ruined as it is now (Fig. 26). Orders were apparently given in 1702 that there should be no further theft of materials, but even if this had been effective it could not prevent the natural processes of decay, and there were partial collapses of the north-west tower in 1739, and of the south-west tower in 1772 and 1799. Fears for public safety led to the removal of the roof and perhaps the vault of the gatehouse in 1771 (Hay 1876, 96–7).

The only parts of the complex which appear to have remained in any sort of use were the abbot's house, the sacristy and the range to the east of the gatehouse, and although these uses were not ideal, they did at least ensure those buildings were kept in some sort of repair. The abbot's house had been leased out as a manse from 1701, but was being used as a thread factory from 1745, and by the end of the nineteenth century was being occupied as a house and school. The sacristy had been reduced to use as a carpenter's wood store by 1808, while the gatehouse range was being let out to various tradesmen, later being used by the burgh when it was referred to as the 'Civil Apartments'. In all this time the precinct was being progressively built over, while the abbey church became essentially a more select extension of the burial ground to the north, with the presbytery being appropriated as a burial ground for the Ochterlony of Guynd family from perhaps as early as 1769.

FIGURE 26
Arbroath Abbey, a late-seventeenth-century view of the abbey church from the north-east.
(Source: John Slezer, *Theatrum Scotiae*, London 1693)

The first works of conservation

A turning point in the fortunes of the abbey came in 1799 when, perhaps prompted by the further collapse of the south-west tower, the burgh magistrates petitioned the Barons of the Exchequer for a grant to repair the abbey. This was refused. But the momentum for preservation was clearly gathering strength, and when the lighthouse engineer Robert Stevenson was in Arbroath in 1809,[9] at the time that the Bell Rock Light was being built, the burgh commissioned him to rebuild the upper part of the circular window in the south transept gable. The main reason for this was quite simply that a stone from the window had fallen through the roof of a house adjacent to the transept, though it also seems that the gable was looked to as an aid to navigation. Further action followed some years later, which seems to have been prompted by a petition of 1814 from William Maule, descendant of the forfeited earls of Panmure, and later Baron Panmure, to be appointed Keeper of the Fabric. But by this stage the crown was beginning to perceive that it had some responsibility towards Scotland's monastic remains, and in the following year the Barons of the Exchequer instituted proceedings in the Court of Session to determine who might have any rights in the abbey. A judgment was given in favour of the crown in 1821, but appeals were then lodged, and the case dragged on for many years with no final resolution.

Nevertheless, in 1816 the Barons decided to carry out works themselves on the abbey church. This involved clearance of parts of the overburden, in the course of which the Frosterley effigy – which may be a posthumous memorial of William the Lion – was found.[10] Simultaneously, major works were carried out in an attempt to stabilise the fabric. At a period when there was little appreciation of the importance of preserving the authenticity of historic structures, the principal effort was directed at replacing decayed masonry with new stonework, and a great deal of rebuilding was carried out. The chief relics of this campaign are probably now to be seen in the presbytery area, where the extent of rebuilding is at least partly apparent in the colour and tooling of the stone, and in the way in which the decorative blind arcading of the lower wall of the south flank has been indicated. But the work was not confined to the presbytery, and it seems that much must have been done to the south transept and the north-west tower. Unfortunately, although this work was carried out with the best of intentions, the new masonry placed an intolerable level of stress on the historic fabric of the north-west tower, and in 1902, following a partial collapse, much of the masonry added in 1816 to the top of the tower had to be dismantled.[11]

A second, and probably rather less heavy-handed campaign of works was instigated in the 1830s, following a request to Robert Reid, who had been appointed head of a separate Scottish Office of Works in 1827. His recommendations were for consolidation of the wall-heads, underbuilding of some of the walls at the east end and lowering ground levels, all at a cost of £194. 5s, and this work was carried out in 1834–5.[12] In the approach taken by Reid we can probably see the beginnings of modern attitudes to the consolidation of ruined structures, in which the guiding aim is to preserve what has come down to us with a minimum of changes or additions. Further consolidation works were required towards the end of the century, in 1896, at an estimated cost of £170.[13]

The acquisition of the monastic buildings by the state

The works discussed above were concentrated on the abbey church, but from the start it was considered that every effort should be made to acquire the surviving monastic buildings and to remove post-medieval buildings that encroached upon the main area of the precinct. In 1834 Robert Reid said that consideration had already been given to having some of the encroachments removed, presumably in 1816, and in 1838 he sought guidance from the government's law officer on what might be done. It was left to Reid's successor William Nixon, Clerk of Works, to start the process, however. In 1840 he had advised that the property adjacent to the south transept should be acquired, and this was done two years later, after which it was demolished in 1843.[14]

Acquisition of a number of the remaining monastic structures followed in 1905, after the town offered all of the buildings that were deemed to be in its ownership through a grant that had been made in 1753.[15] The main structures affected by this were those associated with the precinct wall and the gatehouse. The abbot's house had to be excluded, since it was still occupied by tenants, and it was only in 1924 that it eventually passed into state care,[16] and was subsequently restored to what was thought to be its late medieval state.[17] The final significant addition to the state's holding was made in 1929 when an area of land around the site of the cloister was acquired.[18]

Approaches to conservation

It has to be accepted that, judged against current internationally accepted principles of conservation, some fairly invasive works have been carried out on Arbroath Abbey. The extent of rebuilding in 1816 has already been mentioned, and while Robert Reid's limited consolidation appears to have been more conservatively based, some of the works carried out since then might also be considered rather heavy-handed in retrospect. There might now, for example, be greater caution in removing later buildings, both because they could be regarded as part of the developing history of the site, and because of the possibility that they embodied medieval fabric.

Even well into the twentieth century it seems that the appearance of the monument was more important than the protection of its authenticity as a reflection of the intentions of those who had built and used it. This is seen in the decision to remove later partitions and to rebuild two bays of vaulting in the range against the eastern stretch of the precinct wall in 1938–9. But perhaps it is most apparent in the treatment of the abbot's house following its acquisition in 1924. It is clear from correspondence and early photographs that the house was in a poor state by then (Fig. 27). Nevertheless, it is unlikely that it would now be acceptable to remove eighteenth- and nineteenth-century works that were in themselves of some quality, in an attempt to reconstruct medieval details on the basis of evidence that was less than complete. It would be interesting to know how our successors will judge what has been done. It hardly needs stating that each generation has earnestly striven to do what it regards as best for the monument. But is it even possible that, as the pendulum continues to swing, future generations might surprise us by preferring the aesthetic approach taken in the 1920s and 1930s to what has been carried out in recent decades, where the attempt to ensure that nothing is done to compromise the authenticity of the historic fabric has resulted in an approach that some might consider over-purist?

It should never be doubted that there are enormous problems in conserving fragmentary fabric of great antiquity, especially when that fabric is built of a particularly friable stone, and in determining the best course of action much depends on what it is that we are hoping to conserve. For earlier generations it was perhaps mainly the inherent beauty and historic associations of the monument that were paramount; for ourselves, while the aesthetics remain important, the information that can be drawn from the fabric is perhaps even more significant, and it is therefore essential that there is no contamination of the evidence on which we have to depend. One of the great fascinations of Arbroath is that it is possible to see better than almost anywhere else how the difficulties of maintaining a complex monument have been tackled over a period of almost two centuries, from the time when the need to take active measures to retain what had come down to us was first fully recognised. As a result, there is now an additional onus upon us, and that is not just to ensure the conservation of the historic fabric, but to make every effort to preserve the evidence of the ways its conservation has been tackled

FIGURE 27
Arbroath Abbey, the abbot's house before restoration in the 1920s.
(© Crown copyright, reproduced courtesy of Historic Scotland)

in the past. If we are to have a true perspective on what it is that we want from the abbey ourselves, we must also try to understand what it was that our predecessors wanted from it.

NOTES

1. This was probably the same storm that resulted in the collapse of the unfinished west gable of St Andrews Cathedral.
2. On a fess between three stars as many roundels.
3. A slightly fuller discussion of the sources of the design will be found in R. Fawcett, 'Arbroath Abbey', and J. P. McAleer, 'The west front of Arbroath Abbey: its place in the evolution of the twin-tower façade', both in *Medieval art and architecture in the diocese of St Andrews*, J. Higgit (ed.) (British Archaeological Association Conference Transactions, xiv, Leeds, 1994), 61–83.
4. There is a possibility that St Andrews Cathedral had been planned to have two western towers, and that these were abandoned after the west front was built further east after the collapse of *c.* 1272(?).

5   The excavation of the claustral ranges after 1843 and 1929 was essentially a clearance operation, of which few records were made, and it is doubtful if much was registered beyond the main lines of the walls in their latest form.
6   This intake was evidently re-dressed and squared off when the doorway was built, but nevertheless clearly represents a break in construction. In view of the frequently found relationship between the length of naves and the diagonal of adjoining cloisters, there is an additionally significant relationship at Arbroath. The length of the wall represented by the early masonry, as measured from the west side of the west claustral range to the intake to the west of the south-east nave doorway, is equivalent to what would be the diagonal of a cloister that had its west wall on the line that it is known to have followed throughout the greater part of the middle ages, and an east wall aligned with the intake. This would result in a square cloister with sides of about 25.6 metres.
7   Early views show that the lower facing of the polygonal buttress was extensively robbed, which led to its being known as the 'Pint Stoup'.
8   Much of the known information on the later history of ownership and occupation of the abbey is summarised in a report of 22 August 1834 by R. Mackenzie on National Archives of Scotland file MW/1/468, and a report of 19 April 1911 by T. Carmichael on NAS file MW/1/472.
9   NAS file MW/1/463.
10 Report of 22 August 1834 by R. Mackenzie on NAS file MW/1/468.
11 Minute of 22 November 1902 on NAS file MW/1/464. See also Richard Fawcett, 'Robert Reid and the early involvement of the state in the care of Scottish ecclesiastical buildings and sites', *Antiquaries Journal*, 82 (2002), 269–84.
12 Report by Robert Reid of 26 July 1834 on NAS file MW/1/464.
13 Letter of 1 April 1896 on NAS file MW/1/464.
14 Minutes of 21 May 1842 and 13 May 1843 on NAS file MW/1/470.
15 Correspondence on NAS file MW/1/473.
16 Correspondence on NAS file MW/1/473.
17 On the evidence of drawings held in Historic Scotland's collections, the main work of restoration was carried out between 1925 and 1929.
18 Correspondence on NAS file MW/1/469.

REFERENCES

Acts Parl. Scot.	*Acts of the Parliaments of Scotland*, T. Thomson and C. Innes (eds) (Edinburgh, 1814–75)
Arb. Lib.	*Liber S. Thome de Aberbrothoc*, C. Innes (ed.) (Bannatyne Club, Edinburgh, 1848–56)
Cal. Scot Supp. i	*Calender of Scottish Supplications to Rome, 1418–22*, E. R. Lindsay and A. I. Cameron (eds) (Scottish History Society, Edinburgh, 1934)
Chron. Melrose	*Chronicle of Melrose*, A. O. Anderson (ed.) (London, 1936)
Hay 1876	G. Hay, *History of Arbroath* (Arbroath, 1876)
Salzman 1952	L. F. Salzman, *Building in England down to 1540* (Oxford, 1952)
Reg. Mag. Sig.	*Registrum Magni Sigilli Regum Scotorum*, J. M. Thomson *et al.* (eds) (Edinburgh, 1882–1914)
Scotichronicon	*Scotichronicon by Walter Bower*, D. E. R. Watt *et al.* (eds)
Theiner, *Vet. Mon.*	*Vetera Monumenta Hibernorum et Scotorum Historiam Illustrantia*, A. Theiner (ed.) (Rome, 1864)

IMAGES OF THE DECLARATION
THE ARBROATH PAGEANT

J. N. Graham Ritchie

In introducing the conference on the Declaration of Arbroath as President of the Society of Antiquaries of Scotland, my position was that of a former Arbroath schoolboy whose historical interests had been aroused by the colourful pageants commemorating the Declaration witnessed in my youth. My contribution was thus designed to introduce the conference and explore recent events, and the present paper retains something of the personal approach of the original presentation. Arbroath has a long and well-researched history. Archaeology is now beginning to add practical detail to the historical dimensions of the town's past, and in 'A new look at old Arbroath' David Perry brought the evidence of some twenty-seven excavations into a most interesting paper in 1998.[1] A very distinguished archaeological Fellow of the Society of Antiquaries of Scotland was born in Arbroath in 1832, namely Joseph Anderson, Keeper of the National Museum of Antiquities of Scotland for many years. He, in 1880, first drew attention to the Reliquary, possibly of St Columba, then held at Monymusk, that had formerly been a possession of the abbots of Arbroath, and a copy of which is part of the Abbot's Pageant costume.[2]

The main part of the conference considered the Declaration in a historical context, but the impact in the 1920s, later 1940s, early 1950s and again today, of bringing the past to a broad audience in visual form is equally important. I also intend to explore the way that the Scottish Office deliberated on how to commemorate the event in 1970 – the 650th anniversary of the Declaration – based on documents only recently in the public domain, and to say a little about the image that was prepared as a postage stamp. But I shall not venture beyond 1970, into the most recent Pageants. I wish to think about the timing of events and of the perceptions of those involved. But I hope that this introductory contribution can be seen as linking the events of 1320 with their recreation from 1920 and in more recent years.

600th anniversary celebration of the Declaration of Arbroath

The notion of pageants as a means of recreating history is an aspect of English social history of the first decade of the twentieth century. In Scotland, memorable pageants are rather later, with the Glasgow Art School Pageant in 1909 and Craigmillar, Edinburgh, 1927, and *The Story of the West* in Glasgow in 1928.[3] The great exhibitions of 1911 and

1938 in Glasgow involved pageants and tableaux in order to instil patriotic feeling and an interest in the past with both movement and colour; such re-enactments were equivalents of the videos and screen presentations of today's heritage centres. Local commemorations might also be the occasion for a pageant, for example, the celebration of the foundation of St Magnus Cathedral, Kirkwall, Orkney, in 1937.[4]

The first suggestions of a Pageant in Arbroath were made in readiness for the 600th anniversary of the Declaration in 1920. A little volume prepared at that time by Alan Inglis, Art Master at Arbroath High School, and a Fellow of the Society of Antiquaries of Scotland, on the *Costumes for the Forthcoming Pageant* provided the foundation for costumes created by seamstresses.[5] His interesting foreword sets the approach that may be found in several writings on the Pageant. His illustration shows a shadowy restored Abbey above a forbidding foreground of mill chimneys, a visual symbolism that would not characterise the town today (Fig. 1). Inglis sets the spirit of a future Arbroath Pageant and not only for the costumes:

> The selection of a character [to appear in the Pageant] is neither a question of social status nor of intellectual capacity, but simply a question of whoever can look the part best.
>
> The burly ploughman or hardy fisherman may be found to be the exact replica of what is commonly regarded as the bold, bad Baron, while the brilliant scion of an ancient house may look the part of a varlet to perfection.
>
> Democracy and enthusiasm, I trust, will go hand in hand.

The illustrations of costume are carefully thought out, and I can offer only one example (Fig. 2).

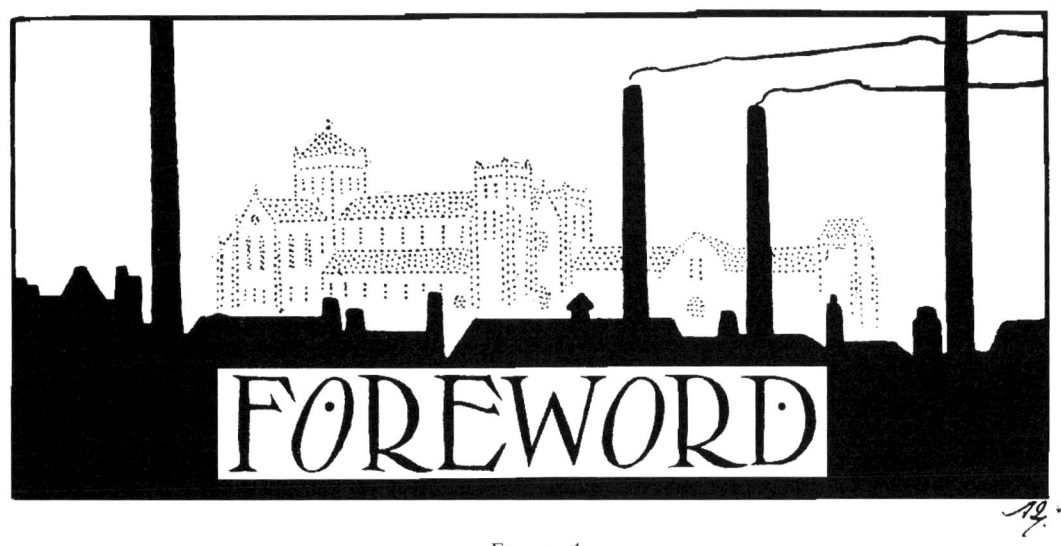

FIGURE 1
Foreword illustration to A. Inglis, Costumes for the Forthcoming Pageant *(1920).*

Figure 2
Religious vestments and utensils from A. Inglis, Costumes for the Forthcoming Pageant *(1920).*

The celebration of the event was held on Saturday, 11 September 1920, and full accounts were published in the two local newspapers, the *Arbroath Guide* of 11 September 1920 and the *Arbroath Herald* of 17 September 1920. The *Guide* outlines the vision of the Arbroath Town Improvement Association (at a time when the First World War was still raging) that the Declaration of Arbroath should be commemorated in 1920. The original idea had been one of 'a protracted celebration, with much spectacular accompaniment', but in the end the practicalities of the arrangements were handed over to the Town Council. We should consider more fully the reporting of the events as it underlines the local and national feeling of the importance of the celebration of the anniversary. There was a patriotic service in the Abbey with the Provost, Magistrates and members of the Town Council driving 'in open carriages to the ruins within whose crumbling walls the famous document was signed and sealed'. On the platform the Provost was accompanied by the Duke of Atholl, the Moderators of the General Assembly of the Church of Scotland and of the United Free Church of Scotland, the Earl of Strathmore, Lord Lieutenant of the county, and the MPs for the Montrose Burghs and for Forfarshire, as well as many other dignitaries. There is a photograph of the platform party in the collections of Arbroath Museum (Fig. 3). The Moderator of the General Assembly of the Church of Scotland gave a patriotic address punctuated by applause. The hymn 'Lord, while for all mankind we pray' was sung. This was followed by a rousing and witty address by the Duke of Atholl, for which moments of laughter are reported. The Moderator of the General Assembly of the United Free Church gave a final stirring address. 'A strikingly appropriate termination to an exceedingly impressive service was found in "Scots wha hae" which was rendered with fine feeling and expression

Figure 3
Platform party at the 600th anniversary celebration of the Declaration of Arbroath within the Abbey, 11 September 1920.
(Arbroath Museum collection, PA 1985 775; Copyright Angus Council)

by the large choir.' The accompanying photographs in the newspapers show the great throng in the Abbey. After the service the official party was conveyed to the Town House and from there repaired to the Webster Memorial Hall where the guests were entertained at luncheon. Both the Order of Proceedings and the Luncheon Menu are preserved in Arbroath Library.

The account in the *Guide* continues with an account of events later in the day:

THE CHILDREN'S PART
HISTORY IN MINIATURE

> It will be a matter of life-long regret to some that the project of an historic reconstruction of the great event was abandoned by the promoters from motives of expediency. Nevertheless, through the devotion to an idea on the part of two ladies of the Committee, the celebrations in the afternoon partook somewhat of the nature of a surprise pageant.

This was advertised as a 'Miniature Pageant and Grand Display of Dancing by Children in Costume' on the Abbey Green. The children's pageant included William the Lion, Thomas Becket, 'the notorious pirate' Sir Ralph the Rover, figures from Sir Walter Scott's novel *The Antiquary*, set round Arbroath, followed by dancing, as well as military displays by the Black Watch.

The sense of social responsibility is underlined by the *Herald*'s final paragraph: 'In order to avoid any expenditure of the community's resources a guarantee fund was raised for the purpose of defraying expenses and entertaining the distinguished guests, to which the manufacturers, solicitors, bankers, and merchants in the town liberally subscribed.'

A souvenir volume was published following the celebrations containing a translation of the Declaration, description and illustrations of the Abbey as it was in 1320, a section on Modern Arbroath, and photographs of prominent citizens. The souvenir volume is important in the present context, as it set out the historical background to the Declaration as it was understood in popular terms at that time from an Arbroath standpoint. In terms of visual symbolism it is interesting that the cover, by Alan Inglis, shows a single monk with his staff looking across to the 'Round O' of the Abbey; it is low-key in today's terms. Here are three separate sections from the volume.[6]

> If proof were needed of the importance of the Abbey of Aberbrothock in the height of its fame it would be found in the part played by its Abbots to secure the independence of the country from the galling yoke of the English. It seems, in fact, that more than any other Scottish town or city Aberbrothock lays claim to being the cradle of the Scottish nation, and it is with feelings of deep pride that today the representatives of the men who lived and worked under the shadow of the great red church of St Thomas celebrate the six-hundredth anniversary of the signing of that wonderful letter, which Scotland's great novelist, Sir Walter Scott, makes one of his characters say, 'should have been written in letters of gold'.
>
> [King Robert] summoned the Scottish Parliament to meet at Aberbrothock, and in the Regality Chamber of the Abbey, on the 6th day of April, 1320, a memorable Convention

of the Estates of Scotland was held under the presidency of the King himself, with his valiant Chancellor at his side there can be no doubt.

If the celebration at Arbroath in 1920 of the Declaration of Independence made in 1320 is local in scope, it is national in spirit – more truly national than a celebration would be with either the victory of Bannockburn or the Treaty of Northampton for its occasion. The victory made Freedom a fact. Liberty was won, however disturbed by strife and loss, division and treachery the following years were. The Treaty eight years later was the enemy's recognition of the fact. But in the Declaration drawn up in the Regality Chamber of the Abbey of Arbroath and addressed to His Holiness the Pope there is heard the calm, determined voice of a people's conscience – the passionless, deeply religious declaration of Right, for which our forebears were determined to fight to the end, however sore the fight and however far off the end.

It might be suggested that it is wrong to quote accounts of these 'events' and interpretations because modern historians have been at pains to give less colourful accounts of the preparation of the letter and to set it in the political context of the times. Popular interpretations are, however, very difficult to change. Allusion to Sir Walter Scott adds confirmation to the interpretation. Perceptions once formed can often only be reinforced. The contrast is very great between the interpretations of Agnes Mure Mackenzie's *The Kingdom of Scotland: a short history*,[7] presented to the writer as a school prize on the Webster Theatre stage in 1960, and historical considerations today. The language of the letter has been interpreted in several different ways. The celebration and re-enactment of its creation may produce an indelible 'historical' impression rather in the way that a film may influence its audience.

The Arbroath Pageant

In August 1947 the first Pageant was organised with a great many folk coming together at short notice. One assessment records: 'Time was short, but a number of enthusiasts worked hard and a most creditable performance was given, the success of which surprised even the organizers.'[8] A more formal body was created with the institution of the Arbroath Pageant Society in 1948 under the Honorary Presidencies of the Earl of Airlie and the Provost of Arbroath. Many people could be mentioned over the years, but I can list only a few, the then Chairman, A. Linton Robertson, a stately Robert the Bruce, Baillie Frank Thornton (a Fellow of the Society of Antiquaries of Scotland), George Shepherd, Editor of the *Arbroath Herald*, and from the early days too, Dr Agnes Mure Mackenzie, the patriotic historian and a loyal friend to the Pageant (although her views might not be endorsed by mainstream historians then or now). It is her translation of the document that is used in the Pageant programmes. The commitment of Frank Thornton and George Shepherd to the many ideals that are bound up with the presentation of the Pageant cannot be underestimated. The resonant sound of the Arbroath Male Voice Choir, as a Choir of Monks, within the Abbey was something never to be forgotten.

What had a small royal burgh to offer to the post-war feeling of relief at the end of hostilities, and the ending of constraints to civilian life under the restrictions of wartime?

How might this be presented? A unique aspect was the interpretation of a historical event in a particular way, and it is important to stress that it was an event that embodied some of the ideals of the time – national pride, freedom from tyranny.

What could be more impressive than the cover of the Programme of the 1948 Pageant, 'within the Abbey of Arbroath where, on 6th April 1320, there was signed the Declaration of Scotland's Independence as a Nation, by the Three Estates of Scotland, in Parliament assembled under the Presidency of King Robert the Bruce' (Fig. 4). I have quoted this in full for reasons that will become apparent later.

Figure 4
Cover of the Programme of the Arbroath Abbey Historical Pageant, 1948.

But there was much more to Pageant Week than the Pageant itself. To take 1948, as a representative early programme: on Monday there was Scottish country dancing in the Drill Hall; Tuesday, an amateur sports meeting; Wednesday, a full dress rehearsal in the Abbey for children; Thursday and Friday, the Pageant within the Abbey, with the Address given by Tom Johnston, a former Secretary of State for Scotland, and the Earl of Airlie. On Saturday the chairman was J. Wilson Patterson, a senior architect with the Office of Works, the predecessor of Historic Scotland, and the speaker was Lewis Spence, one of the founder members of the Scottish National Party, and the first nationalist to contest a parliamentary seat. And, of course, the whole community took part as actors or as members of the many tableaux that formed the procession. Here are but four: Rob Roy, 1717 – 3rd Arbroath Company Boy's Brigade; John Wesley receiving Freedom of Arbroath, 1772 – Methodist Church, Arbroath; Fisherwomen at Work – Arbroath Fisherwomen's Social Club; Women – Then and Now – Arbroath Business and Professional Women's Club. The sense of civic identity sings through the events of the later 1940s and early 1950s. One must remember that television did not come to Arbroath until the Coronation, and that for many years thereafter the Webster Theatre would resound to locally produced performances of Gilbert and Sullivan or *White Horse Inn*. Also, it is important to remember that the scenes of the Pageant were enjoyed by the many holidaymakers in the town. In 1953 there were 40,000 visitors, and although not all were there at Pageant time, a knowledge of the event was being taken to many parts of Scotland in those years.

The cover of the *Arbroath Official Guide Book* of 1950, drawn by Colin Gibson, illus-

Figure 5
Cover of the Arbroath Official Guide Book of 1950, drawn by Colin Gibson.

FIGURE 6
Study for Abbot and Bishop *by Colin Gibson*.
(Reproduced by kind permission of Mrs Gillian Zealand)

FIGURE 7
Provost D. A. Gardner with Arbroath's wedding presents for HRH Princess Margaret and Anthony Armstrong-Jones in 1960. The picture is by Colin Gibson.

trates the sense of civic and patriotic pride in the event (Fig. 5). Gibson's illustrations are very much part of the Pageant of these early years, and that for the programme of 1950 – the heading for the introductory play *The Laurel Crown* about the trial of William Wallace – shows great defiance. Gibson prepared a sensitive study for Abbot and Bishop at about the same time (Fig. 6), prepared in red chalk, as was the striking cover of the *Arbroath Official Guide Book* of 1950 mentioned above. Arbroath's pride in the Pageant is tellingly illustrated in its gift to HRH Princess Margaret on the occasion of her marriage to Anthony Armstrong-Jones in 1960. Colin Gibson was commissioned to create a picture of the Abbey and the Pageant procession, and the firm of Douglas Fraser & Sons Ltd of Friockheim made two candlewick bedspreads (*Arbroath Herald*, 29 April 1960) (Fig. 7). The importance of such illustrations is that they took knowledge of the Pageant and the 'modern' notion of the Declaration of Independence to many parts of the world, indeed wherever Arbroathians sent the annual volume prepared by the local newspaper. After World War II Colin Gibson gave up teaching to concentrate on writing and illustrating. If one were to believe that illustrations have an effect on the subconscious attitude to events, the stately evocations of the Pageant processions have had a profound effect on several generations in Angus. His *Nature Diary* in the *Dundee Courier and Advertiser* from October 1954 confirmed the individual nature of Angus, particularly with its wonderful scraperboard illustrations.

The order of the processions from the programme of the Pageant of 1949 is an example of the impressive display, with the Herald leading Lords Douglas and Randolph, with King Robert the Bruce leading the Barons of Scotland, and a Crossbearer and Acolytes heading that of Bernard de Linton and the Bishops of St Andrews, Dunkeld and Aberdeen (Fig. 8). Anyone who saw the Pageant in those days, particularly if they were young, was impressed by the horses (Fig. 9). The processions through the town were stately and serious (Fig. 10). The photograph of the group of bishops in 1951 shows the great care taken with the various costumes (Fig. 11).

The formats varied a little, but after the national anthem and an introduction, perhaps by the Provost, an address was given by a national figure. On 12 August 1950, for example, it was given by Sir Andrew Murray, Lord Provost of the City of Edinburgh, and he was supported by three other Lord Provosts and ten Provosts. A fanfare followed with the prologue spoken by Frank Thornton, after which came a short play, *The Laurel Crown*, with Sir William Wallace in Westminster Hall in 1305. The processions in the Abbey culminated with the arrival of the King and the signing of the Declaration. Finally, an epilogue.

Andy Stewart's rousing postscript to James Adam's volume on *The Declaration of Arbroath* strikes many a chord:[9]

> I am ashamed to confess that I had to be content with the English and the Scots versions as my Gaelic is confined to a few songs in that great and noble language and my schoolboy learned Latin is mainly long forgotten.
>
> In August of 1951 and then again a year later I was lucky enough to be asked to take part in the Arbroath Abbey Pageant when the signing of the Declaration of Independence was re-enacted, splendidly, within the precincts of the ruined Abbey of Aberbrothock. In

The Procession of Bernard de Linton Abbot of Aberbrothock

The Procession of Robert the Bruce King of Scotland

Cast

King Robert the Bruce	A. Linton Robertson
Lord Douglas	S. E. S. Burnett
Lord Randolph	Walter Burnett
and Barons of the Realm of Scotland	
Crossbearer	Ian Spalding
Abbot of Aberbrothock	George S. Shepherd
Bishop of St Andrews	Tom Matheson
Bishop of Dunkeld	D. L. Gardiner
Bishop of Aberdeen	Alexander Cargill
Bearer of the Banner of St Columba	Douglas B. Lowe
A Choir of Monks	Arbroath Male Voice Choir
and Acolytes, Monks and Door-keepers	
Commentator, F. W. A. Thornton	

FIGURE 8

Order of the Processions of Bernard de Linton, Abbot of Aberbrothock and of Robert the Bruce, King of Scots from the Souvenir Programme of 1949.

FIGURE 9
The procession of King Robert the Bruce, Herald and Barons of Scotland.
(Arbroath Museum collection PA 1981, 407; copyright Angus Council)

1952, I spoke both the prologue and the epilogue to these 'impressive scenes' as they were justifiably called by the *Arbroath Herald*. The epilogue summed up the whole spirit of the Pageant and incorporated the inspiring words of the ancient poet, John Barbour, on Freedom, a cry that came from the heart of a king who was the living soul of a nation.

I have never considered this occasion to be merely a theatrical experience, the whole Pageant had stirred its audience deeply in its simple and sincere enactment . . .

You can dip into the Programmes of the Pageants and find people of many different political persuasions commenting positively on their association with the event:

When rehearsals start, the cast is recruited, and year after year the same enthusiasts form the core of the members. The cast is truly representative of the entire community: Robert the Bruce is played by a veterinary surgeon; his principal barons by a riding school proprietor

FIGURE 10
The procession of the Bishops following the Cross-bearer, F. W. A. Thornton, 1952.
(Arbroath Museum collection PA 1981, 424; copyright Angus Council)

and a farmer. The Bishops are a jeweller, a master painter and a civil servant. There are engineers and merchants, schoolmasters, printers, salesmen and others from all branches of the town's commercial and industrial life filling many roles.[10]

A stirring assessment of the event is given by Agnes Mure Mackenzie:

No more than a couple of years ago, one Nor'-East burgh had an inspiration. Arbroath recalled that within the walls of its Abbey, six hundred years back, was read one of the noblest statements of human right, of the fundamental right, the right to freedom, that has never been worse menaced than to-day; and a group of folk set themselves to re-enact the scene of its sealing, there where it was sealed, by the King and Lords and Commons of this kingdom. Bruce rode again with Douglas and with Randolph and the blazons of all our Scottish chivalry, and the Round O sent forth the great words like a trumpet to echo across the sea to the lands of the world.

It could have been – such recoveries are too often – a mere self-conscious sham of dressing up. It was not. The town took it precisely in the spirit in which the people of the old Nor'-East had greeted 'the auld lovabill consuetud' – the grave commemoration of great issues, events past in time, immortally present in eternity, commingled with human 'gladnes and blythnes', things not incongruous to the great Declaration, but proof that the town has seen it as part of life, not a highbrow plisky to edify the bairns and give solemn folk a chance of incongruous braws.[11] [I had to look up 'plisky'; it means 'escapade'.]

As a coda to this section it is interesting to note a recent assessment of Scottish historical writing before and after World War II. The formation of the Saltire Society in 1936 may be noted as an indication that Scottish cultural traditions should be preserved and developed. Yet 'The Second World War and the enhanced sense of Britishness this engendered further diluted the importance of the subject (Scottish history), as did new ideological trends. The rise of historical materialism and its intellectual counterweights as a primary means of explaining the past marginalised the subject even further until the growth of Scottish nationalism in the late 1960s.'[12] Perhaps it should come as no surprise that the collection of documents on Scottish history prepared by Agnes Mure Mackenzie for the Saltire Society, the first part of which was published in 1946, was entitled *Scottish*

FIGURE 11
Three bishops, 1951; left to right, David Goodwillie, Tom Matheson and D. L. Gardiner.
(Arbroath Museum collection, PA 1981 430; copyright Angus Council)

Pageant. The volume contained a translation of the Declaration of Arbroath. In the preface to the *Scottish Pageant* Agnes Mure Mackenzie sets the tone:

> Our grandfathers liked entertainment combined with instruction. For a generation, they have been mocked for it: but the values of that inter-war generation have nowadays undergone a sizeable slump, and the writer who returns to an older idea needs no great courage for an innovation which, like most such, is no more than a renovation.
> This book is, in the main, quite frankly entertainment.[13]

Dr Mure Mackenzie also prepared a pamphlet on the Declaration, which was published in 1951.[14] The Arbroath Pageant as an occasion and pageants as books played a part in a growing popular interest in Scottish history.

650th anniversary celebration of the Declaration of Arbroath

For reasons one can perhaps imagine, the timing of the 650th anniversary celebration of the Declaration of Arbroath to fall in 1970 caused Scottish Office officials some unease. The Secretary of State for Scotland, William Ross (1964–70 and again 1974–6) was very Scottish in approach, but much against separatism.[15] The relevant files of the Scottish Education Department and the Scottish Home and Health Department came into the public domain in 2001 under the thirty-year rule.[16] The Scottish Home and Health File is entitled 'Commemorative Celebration of the Declaration of Arbroath' and has further index headings – Scottish Nationalism, Celebration, and Declaration of Arbroath. The sensitivity had apparently been compounded by offence taken in 1965 at the national celebrations for the signing of Magna Carta, and of the Simon de Montfort Parliament, which were considered by some to be local English events, and should not be accorded special significance in history teaching in Scotland as had been suggested. As I explored the files, I was amazed at how much hard copy had survived. I have tried to be circumspect. Nor must you think that I am contrasting local enthusiasms with central detachment and caution. Perceptions of the importance of the forthcoming anniversary were being formed from very different standpoints. Perceptions about the significance of documents and events form part of the fascination that surrounds the Declaration.

In 1965 the Scottish National Party had written to remind government of the important anniversary of 1970 and the files open: 'It would not I think be inappropriate for official celebration of this event in a more positive way than the mere issue of a commemorative postage stamp and, since the SNP will expect something more than an ackn. [to their letter], I would suggest that a PS [Private Secretary] letter, encouraging but not very informative, should be sent to them' (9 November 1965).[17] Later that month: 'I think it would appropriately spoil SNP's chances of making some political capital out of the correspondence if S of S [Secretary of State] were to sign a short letter himself, admitting that the letter had been shown to him and that it was his view that the 650th anniversary of the Declaration of Arbroath should be appropriately celebrated' (24 November 1965).[17]

By 1968 the memos are becoming firmer: 'You will remember that the SNP first raised this question two years ago and that, with our encouragement, the Secretary of

State committed himself to the view that the 650th anniversary of the Declaration of Arbroath be accorded "due public commemoration" in 1970 . . . As regards Government participation, I doubt myself we need do more than keep up pressure on the PMG [Postmaster General] and ensure that, whatever else, the Arbroath celebrations receive appropriate Ministerial recognition. The anniversary of the Declaration is certainly worth a stamp; but I doubt whether it warrants a more elaborate form of Government recognition' (11 January 1968).[17]

The Scottish Education Department's History Panel made the most measured and positive recommendations. [The following is not verbatim.][18]

1. Professor Archie Duncan of Glasgow University might be approached to see whether he could produce through the Scottish Branch of the Historical Association a booklet putting the Declaration into context. (As non specialists we are uncertain as to its importance in its own period.) [The pamphlet was indeed published.][19]

2. Perhaps a Jackdaw Series of Documents might be produced, which might inform Scottish Sixth Year Pupils?

3. The Saltire Society might be encouraged to embark on a project?

4. The BBC should be encouraged to produce programmes on the Declaration.

This was dated 27 April 1968.

The various memos cast doubt on the importance of the Declaration in historical terms, the relevance of 650 as an anniversary, even the fine language cannot really be assessed – well, it was in Latin. In discussion of a Draft Circular it was suggested that the words 'couched in fine prose' be omitted on the grounds that it was not possible to judge the merits of Latin of that period (5 December 1969).[17]

The final submission of both Departments to the Secretary of State is dated 17 April 1969.[16] The agonising over the design of the commemorative stamp by the Post Office is summarised. Following a letter from the Town Clerk in 1967 to the Postmaster General and to all Scottish MPs a Question was tabled by David Steel; in response, the Postmaster General indicated that he had added the Declaration to the list of subjects from which the 1970 stamps might be chosen and that advice on the design of the stamp would be appreciated. Memoranda by the Historiographer Royal for Scotland, Dr Mackie, and his predecessor Principal Rait, were reproduced to show that there was doubt among historians as to whether the Declaration was in fact sealed at a meeting convened at Arbroath, although it is headed 'apud monasterium de Abirbrothoc'; one view was that it was circulated for signature among leading Scottish nobles in the manner of a round robin. 'Although, therefore, Arbroath Abbey may not have been the scene of a formal assembly (still less a Scottish parliament) in 1320, the Abbey ruins would seem to be the most appropriate emblem for a commemorative stamp.'[17]

The Scottish Record Office intended to prepare an exhibition including their copy of the Declaration during 1970. A facsimile edition of the Declaration was published together with a translation and historical note. It was also noted that Sir James Fergusson, formerly Keeper of the Records of Scotland, had written a book about the Declaration which would shortly be published.

It was noted that 'The Education Committee of the Saltire Society, which was founded in 1936 to stimulate interest in Scottish traditions, history and culture and which, since 1963, has organised a projects competition for secondary schools, has decided to offer "The Declaration of Arbroath" as an option among the projects for primary schools in 1970'.

A national celebration, perhaps a service in St Giles, was considered, but it was felt that such a ceremony would not be meaningful to anyone unfamiliar with Scottish history. A national ceremony might merely serve as a focus for political activity. Indeed

> as successive Historiographers Royal have pointed out the Declaration was in no sense a Declaration of Independence analogous to that of the American Colonies in 1776; and for most Scotsmen Bannockburn, fought six years earlier, has a more obvious appeal as a milestone in the nation's history. There is the further consideration that any national ceremony might serve merely as a focus for political activity by the SNP. For these reasons we feel that there is no call for the Secretary of State to take the initiative in organising any commemoration of this kind.[17]

Although the ruins of the Abbey might form an appropriate emblem for the stamp, no sense of 'formal assembly' should appear. Several obvious words were off limits, too. '[I]t would be as well to avoid the use of words which would imply any form of assembly to draw up or ratify the Declaration' was the tenor of the letter to the Post Office.[18]

Of course, in the way of things, none of this background information was relayed to the actual designer of the stamp, and the Post Office had to admit that they had lost any Scottish Office communications; indeed, when contact was again made, the Scottish Office were told that the designs had been chosen and that printing was already underway. The designer, Fritz Wegner, complained in the 'London Letter' in the *Glasgow Herald* on 18 February 1970 that he had had a Dickens of a job achieving any kind of historical accuracy commemorating the Declaration of Arbroath. He wrote to Arbroath, researched in the British Museum on costumes of the period, but admits to 'making up' the table with its decoration of Celtic whorls and a St Andrews cross at which the Abbot of Arbroath sits surrounded by the nobles. Wegner was convinced that all the experts were going to emerge from hiding and denounce his design (Fig. 12).

Although the ruins of the Abbey are not there, equally there are not too many people present to worry the Scottish Office of the day.

The *Glasgow Herald* 'London Letter' is also revealing about the series of stamps issued at that time: the 'Mayflower' issue (350th anniversary) (1s 6d) was air mail to America where it was hoped it may be specially appreciated; 'Florence Nightingale' (150th anniversary of her birth) (9d), illustrated beside a hospital bed at Scutari, was mail to Europe including Turkey and Russia, though surely a little oblique for many recipients there; while the 'Declaration of Arbroath' (5d) was for domestic use. We should take

FIGURE 12
Commemorative postage stamp showing the Declaration of Arbroath in a series of Anniversaries issued on 1 April 1970 to a design by Fritz Wegner.
(Reproduced by kind permission of Royal Mail)

this further in numerical terms as the *Glasgow Herald* saw it: 'As 76,200,000 of the fivepenny issue are being printed, as opposed to 13,800,000 of the ninepenny, and 9,800,000 of the others, no one should be left in ignorance of the first-ever assertion of nationalism.' For those of you who will have forgotten the stamp it was a vibrant red, and the one thing that the Scottish Office neglected to suggest to the Post Office was colour. What the Scottish Office thought about the *Glasgow Herald* piece is not on record. From a philatelic point of view, the officials of 1970 might have reacted to the Robert Burns commemorative issue of 25 January 1996 with frissons of disbelief, for the 41p denomination has an illustration of William Wallace and large capital letters 'Scots, wha hae wi' Wallace bled', and indeed to the grimly victorious Robert the Bruce at Bannockburn in the Millennium Series *The Soldier's Tale*, a 19p issue of 1999.

A major local celebration was the interdenominational service held in the Abbey on 6 April in the presence of the leaders of the churches in Scotland and a representative gathering of the people of the Scottish Nation (Fig. 13), an occasion that was very much in the spirit of the service of 1920. The Pageant in 1970 was particularly impressive.

Perhaps the most lasting memorials to the 650th anniversary celebrations are Sir James Fergusson's book, which has a facsimile of the document in an end pocket,[20] and the

To commemorate the Six Hundred and Fiftieth anniversary of the Declaration of Arbroath sent forth from the Abbey Kirk of Saint Thomas a' Becket at Aberbrothock on 6th April, 1320, an Interdenominational Church Service will be held within the ruins of the Abbey of Arbroath on 6th April, 1970, at 2.30 p.m., in the presence of the leaders of the Churches in Scotland and a representative gathering of the people of the Scottish Nation.

The Provost, Magistrates and Town Councillors of the Royal and Ancient Burgh of Arbroath warmly greet

Mr. & Mrs. W. F. Ritchie.

whose presence on this historic occasion they would value and esteem, and to whom they now address this invitation to attend.

FIGURE 13
Invitation to the Interdenominational Church Service held within the ruins of the Abbey to commemorate the 650th anniversary of the Declaration of Arbroath.
(Source: author)

Scottish Record Office facsimile edition of the document, now published as a fine poster in an edition to celebrate the 675th anniversary. Fergusson's introduction is written in a very positive manner about the importance of the Declaration and its relevance. Appropriately in the present context Fergusson notes that the 'people of Arbroath have long taken a justifiable pride in their town's association with the famous Letter to the Pope'. The published facsimiles have meant that not only the spirit of prose but also the physical appearance of the document with its splendid array of seals, wherever appended, are now firmly within our national consciousness. It is interesting to remember that the seals had clearly made an impression on Sir Walter Scott.[6] The hand-out that accompanied the Scottish Record Office exhibition of 1970 takes a very different view to the Scottish Office considerations outlined above, and it is interesting that it appears that there was little contact between the Scottish Office and Scottish Record Office over the context of the document and the content of the proposed exhibition.

> The object of this exhibition is to set what is probably the best known historical document in Scotland in its historical context as part of a series of records produced during a crucial period in Anglo-Scottish relations between 1291 and 1328. Viewing it thus, as an instrument of medieval diplomacy, is in no way to detract either from its historical value as a statement of national independence unique in its time or from its literary value as a fine example of medieval Latin prose.

There are several other sub-plots, including a possible royal visit and a possible SNP celebration in the Abbey, that cannot appropriately be explored in a short essay that has been a celebration of local and popular approaches to the past and to the Declaration. Angus now has marvellous museums; its heritage has never been more successfully displayed. I submit as an observer of the last half century in the county that the themes of relationships, perceptions, sense of place and history, are of importance both for the recent and the further distant past, and that a respect for both local and national aspirations is vital. For any commemoration in 2020 for the 700th anniversary the interested parties should be much more fully informed.

NOTES

1 D. Perry, 'A new look at old Arbroath', *Tayside and Fife Archaeological Journal* 4 (1998), 260–77.
2 A. Graham, 'The archaeology of Joseph Anderson', *Proceedings of the Society of Antiquaries of Scotland* 107 (1975–6), 279–98.
3 J. Kinchen, 'Art and history into life: pageantry revived in Scotland', *Scottish Society for Art History* 2 (1997), 42–51.
4 A. Ritchie, *Viking Scotland* (London 1993), 132–3.
5 A. Inglis, *Costumes for the Forthcoming Pageant* (Arbroath 1920).
6 *Royal Burgh of Arbroath, 1320–1920, Declaration of Scottish Independence. Sex-Centenary Celebrations, Souvenir Volume* (Arbroath 1920), quotations from pages 7, 9 and 17. The quotation from Sir Walter Scott is from *The Fair Maid of Perth* (1828, vol. 3, ch. 2; in the Edinburgh Edition of the *Waverley Novels* (1999) 269). Simon Glover, father of the Fair Maid, Catherine, talks about government of the land:

> Our privileges have been often defended against the Pope himself, by our good monarchs of yore, and when he pretended to interfere with the temporal government of the kingdom, there wanted not a Scottish Parliament, who told him his duty in a letter that should have been written in letters of gold. I have seen the epistle myself, and though I could not read it, the very sight of the seals of the reverend prelates, and noble and true barons, which hung at it, made my heart leap for joy.

7 A. Mure Mackenzie, *The Kingdom of Scotland: A Short History* (Edinburgh and London 1957), 92. See also Eadem, *Robert Bruce, King of Scots* (London 1935), 307–9.
8 W. A. Illsley (ed.), *Third Statistical Account for the County of Angus* (Arbroath 1977), 525.
9 J. Adam (ed.), *The Declaration of Arbroath* (Arbroath 1993), 31.
10 Arbroath Abbey Pageant Society, The Seventh Arbroath Abbey Illuminated Pageant of the Declaration of Scottish Independence, *Souvenir Programme* (Arbroath 1953).
11 Arbroath Abbey Pageant Society, Pageant of the Declaration of Independence, *Souvenir Programme* (Arbroath 1949), 14.
12 M. Lynch (ed.), *The Oxford Companion to Scottish History* (2001), entry on Historians, 308.
13 A. Mure Mackenzie (ed.), *Scottish Pageant* (Edinburgh and London 1946).
14 A. Mure Mackenzie, *On the Declaration of Arbroath*, Saltire Society (Edinburgh 1951).
15 M. Lynch (ed.), *The Oxford Companion to Scottish History* (2001), entry on William Ross, 350–1.
16 National Archives of Scotland ED48/2095 and HH41/1883.
17 National Archives of Scotland HH41/1883.
18 National Archives of Scotland ED48/2095.
19 A. A. M. Duncan, *The Nation of Scots and the Declaration of Arbroath* (1320), Historical Association (London 1970).
20 Sir J. Fergusson, *The Declaration of Arbroath* (Edinburgh 1970).

ACKNOWLEDGEMENTS

I have greatly benefited from discussion with Anita Walker (President), and Bill Shaw (Producer), of the Arbroath Abbey Pageant Society, and I am grateful to Anita Walker for lending me a copy of *Costumes for the Forthcoming Pageant* and for helping to identify the participants illustrated in the photographs. The Arbroath Abbey Pageant Society has permitted publication of illustrations from their programmes. Mrs Gillian Zealand generously made available material from her personal archive of illustrations of the Pageant by her father, Colin Gibson. The Royal Mail has kindly allowed the postage stamp of 1970 to be reproduced and I am grateful to Peter Speller for making this possible (Signing The Declaration Of Arbroath Stamp © Royal Mail Group plc 1970. Reproduced by kind permission of Royal Mail. All Rights Reserved.) Norman Atkinson, Fiona Guest, Janice Lorimer and Fiona Sharlau of Angus Council, Cultural Services, helped to provide illustrations and photocopies, and Angus Council has permitted use of illustrations from their collections. The assistance of Janice Lorimer, Arbroath Library, in tracking down material relating to the 1920 celebrations has been particularly important. John Ellis kindly identified the quotation from *The Fair Maid of Perth*. Jane Brown, Senior Inspecting Officer, Government Records Branch, National Archives of Scotland, identified the relevant files relating to the 650th anniversary of the Declaration and Susan Corrigall permitted publication of this Crown Copyright material. The staff of Arbroath Library made the files on the Pageant instantly available. I am grateful to Ted Cowan and Alan Saville for advice. Anna Ritchie assisted in the preparation of the paper. Geoffrey Barrow's encouragement has been important in bringing this introductory presentation to publication.

THE DECLARATION OF ARBROATH

WHAT SIGNIFICANCE WHEN?

Grant G. Simpson

'CAN anything new conceivably be said about a document apparently so well known in Scotland as the Declaration of Arbroath?' I apologise for beginning this short commentary by quoting myself. I wrote these words just over twenty-five years ago as the first sentence of an article on the Declaration, published in 1977.[1] I repeat them now not only because the question remains apposite, but also because I feel a need to express regret for their tone, which is sardonic, perhaps even sarcastic. I certainly thought that more could be said and I proceeded to say some of it. Within the last thirty years or so many others have spoken also and I need only touch briefly on some names in an impressive array of commentators:[2] Archibald Duncan, Geoffrey Barrow and Donald Watt lead the field; Roger Mason has tackled relevant aspects of political thought; Fiona Watson has developed new angles of view on the Wars of Independence; and James Goldstein has contributed a transatlantic approach. Bruce Webster has produced a thoughtful survey article; and Edward Cowan has usefully looked into some of the political ideas which lie at the roots of the Declaration. Most recently, two of my Aberdeen colleagues, David Ditchburn and Terry Brotherstone, have presented the penetratingly conjoined thoughts of a distinguished Scottish medievalist and a widely knowledgeable historian of modern politics.[3]

I want now to try to home in on one crucial, central issue: what do we see as the significance of this well-produced and now widely known piece of medieval Latin composition? As we look across the centuries, we must consider not only its significance at the time, but also its importance in later periods down to the present. I am reliably informed that at least six copies of the document, in facsimile and translation, are to be found on the walls of Scottish public houses. And research into this phenomenon is being actively pursued. The text has also been presented in at least twelve sites on the internet. Clearly, there is considerable interest in it among a Scottish and wider public today.

To clear the ground, it will be helpful to ask first what elements of the topic have been clarified by the research of recent times. What can we be fairly sure of, which was not known to our predecessors, the scholars of some fifty years ago?

First, it is generally accepted that the document must be seen as essentially a product of the royal administration. The script of the duplicate original which remained in the royal archives in 1320 is that of the most prolific of the twelve or so visible royal clerks listed by Archibald Duncan as active in Robert I's loosely structured writing-office.[4] The drafting is most likely to have taken place principally within the royal secretariat. The text is not merely the result of discussion in some committee of Scottish barons, although it runs in their names. The Declaration reflects the ideas of Robert Bruce and his closest advisers, though it represents opinions with which the baronage was expected to be in general agreement.

The document is dated 6 April, at the monastery of Arbroath, where Bernard, chancellor of the kingdom, was the abbot. But, in spite of later traditions and pageants, there was very probably no actual meeting of barons at that place. There are signs that a decision to send a baronial letter – and perhaps also its general outlines – were agreed in a meeting at Newbattle Abbey about the middle or end of March.[5] The document was not issued by a parliament – no clergymen are formally involved in it, and no members of the burgess estate.

The text employs in a prominent manner the papal *cursus* or prose-rhythm structure of wording.[6] It was therefore intended to impress its hearers at the papal court. In addition, its content is heavy with biblical allusions and one classical quotation, from Sallust. It was evidently composed by a highly educated and diplomatically trained author or authors.

As a joint baronial letter to the pope, the Declaration belongs to a European tradition of such communications, running well back into the thirteenth century. Similar letters, either joint or duplicated texts from a group, had emerged from Scotland itself, from France, England and Ireland since as long ago as the year 1205.[7] As I remarked in 1977, 'Scottish barons did not become subject in 1320 to a dramatic nationalist brainstorm. They and the governmental advisers of the time were doing something much more interesting than merely expressing a protest . . . They did not create in the Declaration a unique vehicle for expressing their feelings [on a national basis]. They did intelligently recollect and efficiently put to use a method which had been employed by other European politicians for more than a century past.'[8] The Scots were in line with European diplomatic practice when operating at this high and tricky level of contact with the Holy Father.

These are some of the main features now generally accepted among scholars as being firmly established. But I must add here one question which has not been resolved – and never will be, fascinating though it may seem. Who wrote the Declaration of Arbroath? The traditional answer has been that it was composed by Abbot Bernard, the chancellor. I have suggested that that was unlikely, although clearly he must have had some hand in its preparation. First, there is no evidence that Bernard was a university student or a graduate. Further, high officials in the Middle Ages did not automatically sit down to draft public documents any more than Tony Blair or George W. Bush actually write all the words which we hear coming from their mouths. Since I poured cold water on the name of Bernard as author, two other candidates for authorship have been hustled on to the stage.[9] One, Alexander Kininmonth, later bishop of Aberdeen, was involved in contemporary diplomacy, acting as an envoy of Robert I to the pope in Avignon shortly before 27 September 1320. The other is Walter Twynholm, next chancellor of the kingdom after Bernard. Either could have drafted it. However, trying to identify an author seems somewhat pointless. I wish to underline again the evidence that the English royal chancery, from at least the mid-fourteenth century, had on its staff writers of 'special letters', that is, those sent to the pope or other high foreign dignitaries. The Scottish royal secretariat had similar experts, at least by the later fifteenth century and therefore perhaps also earlier.[10] What matters is that Scotland had the expertise on hand to produce a highly competent, indeed strikingly able, epistle when international negotiations demanded one. This was not a remote, heathery, northern outpost, administered by rough barons and half-educated clerics. The authorship issue matters rather less than many historians seem to think. The quality of the production is what we should observe and admire.

The crux of the present survey lies in the question: what was the contemporary significance of the Declaration? I shall not pursue here in minute detail all the circumstances from which it emerged; but shall simply sketch some elements of the background.[11] The great Scottish victory at Bannockburn did not result in English acknowledgement of Robert Bruce's kingship and the independence of his kingdom. The situation was three-cornered. Robert I and Edward II were in a stalemate, since Robert did not have the power to force England to concede all that he wanted. Meantime Pope John XXII was desperately anxious to produce Anglo-Scottish peace so that the monarchies of Europe could be drawn actively into his scheme for another crusade – forlorn hope though it proved to be. He had declared a solemn papal truce between Scots and English, which Bruce broke by recapturing Berwick in April 1318. The pope therefore despatched at him a hailstorm of threatening papal bulls. Robert Bruce had seriously angered the spiritual head of Christendom and had to get himself out of a very tight diplomatic corner – the Declaration of Arbroath was the result. It emphasised the ancient and independent history of the Scots and their kingdom, along with Bruce's right to the crown, both *de facto* and *de jure*. It declared the unswerving support of the barons and community for their monarchy and their freedom. Their determination was so profound that even if Bruce gave up the fight against the English attempts at domination, they would throw him out, make another man their king, and continue the struggle.

The scholarly disputes of recent years around all this seem to me to be more about emphasis than about fundamentals. To borrow the words of Ditchburn and Brotherstone: 'Duncan and Simpson acknowledged the nationalist sentiment in the Declaration, but neither dwelt on it . . . For [them] the Declaration was, primarily, a pragmatic response to a pressing diplomatic difficulty.'[12] The same point was made to me, in slightly different terms, by a friend who read a draft of my 1977 article: 'Your general approach towards the Declaration is comparatively cool, though not hostile.' I confess that in 1977 I perhaps failed to emphasise with enough clarity and vigour that I accepted the existence of a set of Scottish political sentiments which are enunciated in the Declaration. I personally hesitate, unlike some writers, to use the term 'nationalism' in the context of the central Middle Ages.[13] 'Patriotism' could be a more acceptable word. But since the early thirteenth century there had been growing in the kingdom what I would describe as a 'sense of Scottishness'. This phrase is deliberately a rather generalised one. What exactly it amounted to is very hard to explain with precision. Certainly before the death of Alexander III in 1286 the Scots did not have to shout about what it meant to them. Documents and chroniclers are seldom very specific on the issue. After that date, and especially after 1296, they had to decide what it consisted of and to what extent they were prepared to support or abandon it in the political arena.

The historical task of analysing and expounding this 'Scottishness' has been tackled by distinguished pens, but has not yet, in my view, been accomplished with overall success. For Geoffrey Barrow, the term 'community of the realm' is a central element; but I see that as more of a mere slogan than he would allow. Archibald Duncan takes a somewhat different line of approach towards the same issue when he remarks that 'during the thirteenth century the kings of Scotland had created a political atmosphere whose essential quality was harmony'.[14] Younger scholars have recently been emphasising the complexity and sophistication of the subject. Dauvit Broun has remarked that 'the study of contemporary perceptions of Scotland and the Scots serves to emphasise that the emergence of Scotland [before the Wars of Independence] is not simply about the creation and expansion of a kingdom, but is also the history of an idea which people have engaged with, recreated and adapted'.[15]

In my own efforts to disentangle the diplomatic background and to clarify the documentary minutiae I may have rather left aside some aspects of the pre-existing and underlying attitudes which help to mould and inform the text. Yet these, and the ideas of so-called 'nationalism' in the Declaration, had already been much emphasised by others, Barrow and Nicholson in particular. Following Duncan's acute social analysis,[16] I did say (to be fair to myself) that 'the Declaration genuinely mirrors a political feeling which had become more intense and explicit at the lower levels of society as a result of more than thirty years of internal upset and external interference'.[17]

In trying to relate the words of the Declaration to its *Zeitgeist*, it may be worthwhile to risk a modern parallel. When a party manifesto is drawn up for a general election, how many of the candidates of that party have taken part in drafting every phrase, or even in thinking deeply about every nuance of policy? Yet like the barons of the Declaration, their thinking and that of the central experts writing the manifesto derive from some set of current and shared political ideas. And these ideas have validity for some group of contemporaries. Yet as historians we must attempt to seek critical balance in our comments. As I have remarked, the splendid rhetoric of the Declaration, 'though it may be effective at the time, humanly interesting, and historically full of meaning, cannot be the whole truth'.[18] That critical balance involves both a corpus of ideas and a political and diplomatic situation visible in and around 1320 which was decidedly complex and awkward. The contemporary significance of the Declaration cannot be approached in any simplistic fashion.

It is time now to pass to the issue of what significance the Declaration has had in later times. We can accept at the outset that some ideas and approaches which occur in the Declaration may emerge in later political contexts without specific reference back to that text. But for over 300 years after it was penned, interest in it seems to have been patchy. Those who hail it as a fundamental statement about the constitutional relationships between the Scottish monarchs and their people should note the cautious approach to such matters by Dr Roger Mason. He feels that the political identity of later medieval Scotland tends to emphasise elements such as a basic loyalty to the crown on the part of most barons, a frequent concern for the 'commonweal' and an interest in chivalric behaviour.[19] He comments: 'As regards radical political speculation, late medieval Scotland is something of a barren desert'.[20] This approach suggests that the Declaration should be seen as an interesting but *ad hoc* production rather than as the foundation of a tradition of political thought.

Turning to the works of later medieval chroniclers, we find that the Declaration occurs in *Chronica Gentis Scotorum* (ascribed to John of Fordoun), written in the 1370s, but it is not in Andrew of Wyntoun's *Original Chronicle* of the early fifteenth century, which is a work in verse. It is given prominence in Walter Bower's *Scotichronicon* of the 1440s and his text gives rise to discussion about details of drafting and composition.[21] Bower unfortunately muddles the context of the Declaration somewhat. He is wrong in maintaining that it was written to forestall a visit to Scotland by papal legates. It was in fact produced some time after such a visit had been attempted but failed to occur. The Declaration appears also in a slightly later chronicle, of the 1460s, based on the *Scotichronicon*. It is known as the *Liber Pluscardensis* and its author inserted in error one and a half texts of the document.[22] Bower's *Scotichronicon* was well known and popular and was reproduced in many MS. copies. From the mid-fifteenth century, therefore, the Declaration could easily have been found and read by any typical educated Scot. But from here onwards copying and comment fail: the Declaration disappears into a cloud until the early seventeenth century. Bower's interest in it can be readily accounted for on the basis of his Anglophobia. But why did his historical successors ignore it?

The most puzzling silence is that of the famous, erudite and prolific academic John Mair. As author of a *History of Greater Britain* (1521), none was better qualified to comment on it and to explain its background.[23] The intelligence and clarity of his remarks on Anglo-Scottish history made him well fitted to provide a discussion. And the passage in the Declaration which claims that the barons and community had the right to choose a king chimes well with his view of Scottish sovereignty that 'the holder had it by consent of those he governed'. But perhaps his elements of radicalism in supporting the authority of church councils, and his disapproval of over-blown papal power, led him to remain silent on a document which fundamentally acknowledges the authority of the papacy, even while criticising one of its actual policies in 1320. I suggest tentatively that there may be a hint that he had seen a text of the Declaration although he does not quote it precisely. Mair puts into the mouth of Robert I a speech to his troops before Bannockburn which contains this passage: 'It is not with us . . . to bring distress within the borders of another country that we take up arms, but to defend our own - that end which all men hold it worthwhile to win with life itself. Our strife today is for our worldly goods . . . for life, for the independence of our native land . . . for all that men hold dear.'[24] It could be argued that here are some remembered echoes of a famous passage in the Declaration. Quotation from it and lengthier comment could have suited some of Mair's approaches. We shall probably never know if he was actually acquainted with it and, if so, why he chose to leave it out.

The absence of the Declaration from well-known and extensive sixteenth-/early-seventeenth-century histories, such as those of John Knox, George Buchanan and David Calderwood, can be more readily accounted for on the basis of their dislike of the pre-Reformation church, and especially of the pope.[25] A document in which a set of Scottish barons offered to His Holiness 'all manner of filial reverence, with devout kisses of his blessed feet' was too much for their Protestant stomachs. Even so, this censoring of the text by Knox and Calderwood remains particularly striking, since both were in the habit of filling the pages of their histories with numerous formal documents. And, as with Mair, the Declaration's apparent emphasis on 'the power of the people' as against their king would have suited Buchanan's most basic set of political theories.

As we move into the seventeenth century we do find references to the Declaration and we must begin to notice the motivations of those who talk of it or quote it. Archbishop John Spottiswood in his *History of the Church of Scotland* (published posthumously 1654; he died 1639) gives an abbreviated text.[26] Like Bower, he muddles the matter of the papal legates and specific papal involvement, but as a Protestant archbishop he had no difficulty in handling a set of historical events in which a pope was centrally involved. His contemporary Sir James Balfour of Denmilne (d. 1658) wrote a set of *Annals of Scotland* (not published until the nineteenth century), in which he lists the barons involved, but does not quote the text.[27] As he was a herald and an antiquary, his interests lay with the ancient family names which occur and he makes no comment on politics or church. But the next author to take an interest prints the Declaration in full and comments at length. This was a famous lawyer, Sir George Mackenzie of Rosehaugh (d. 1691), Lord Advocate of Scotland, known from the harshness of some of his anti-Presbyterian attitudes as 'Bluidy Mackenzie'.[28] He was a man of principle, a powerful patriot and notably learned and cultured. He published the Declaration in his *Observations on the Laws as to Precedency* (1680).[29] One of his principal works was *A Defence of the Antiquity of the Royal Line* (1685). He was concerned to support the independent status of Scottish kingship and was firing an opening salvo in the 'battle of the books' which occurred between Scottish and English polemical historians in the times of tension which led up to the Treaty of Union of 1707.[30] The Declaration was becoming a piece of ammunition in modern political controversy and it is striking that it often comes to the fore when some crisis occurs in Anglo-Scottish constitutional relations. It was reprinted as a pamphlet in 1689, around the time of the 'Glorious Revolution'. It appeared again as a pamphlet in 1746, when a dispute over the kingship of Britain came to a head: a Hanoverian monarch occupied the throne and a Royal Stuart pretender with an army attempted to seize it.

Historians who have sometimes stood back from politics may still represent in their expressed opinions some sense of the spirit of their own times. That notable figure of Enlightenment Scotland, Sir David Dalrymple, Lord Hailes, a first-class judge and an erudite documentary scholar, was horrified by the fabulous nature of the early Scottish history expounded in the text: he criticises 'the prejudices of an ignorant and superstitious age'.[31] Sir Walter Scott's comment introduces a tinge of emotion and romanticism when he calls the Declaration 'a spirited manifesto, [of] strong sense and a manly spirit of freedom'.[32] Andrew Lang in 1900 says in similar vein that '[it] sounds the classic note of national freedom'.[33]

It is unnecessary here to follow the story of the Declaration in detail through the twentieth century and on to today, except to underline that the document has become politicised and has been turned into a favourite text of modern Scottish nationalism. But I must draw attention to another instance of ideas and politics operating in tandem. In the year 1967 two things happened. The first Scottish Nationalist MP to gain a Westminster parliamentary seat for a full term was elected at Hamilton. There was also founded a nationalist body called the 1320 Club, which proved to be somewhat extremist in its views and was eventually banned by the Scottish National Party.[34] A fully nationalist interpretation of the Declaration has come to the fore and is already accepted by many. It would be entirely arrogant if professional historians were to insist that the general population ought to accept their academic interpretations of the document. This is especially so since it is not yet clear whether a consensus on the topic can be reached among the professionals.[35] I personally would simply ask interested folk to study the Declaration with care and to set it against the background of the early fourteenth century. I hold to the view that it is entirely faulty to import twentieth-/twenty-first century concepts such as 'democracy' into that distant era. I support the opinion of Ditchburn and Brotherstone: 'The 1320 letter . . . has been forgotten about too often for too long and is remembered now too inconsistently to be the 'Euclidean' proposition with which Scotland's political future is bound up.'[36] Yet even so we may have reached a stage at which many Scots will continue to knit their own Declaration of Arbroath.

NOTES

1 G. G. Simpson, 'The Declaration of Arbroath revitalised', *Scottish Historical Review*, lvi (1977), 11–33, at 11.
2 See Bibliography below.
3 T. Brotherstone and D. Ditchburn, '1320 and a' That: The Declaration of Arbroath and the Remaking of Scottish History', *Freedom and Authority: Scotland c.1050 – c.1650* (East Linton 2000), 10–31.
4 *Acts of Robert I, King of Scots, 1306–29*, A. A. M. Duncan (ed.) (Regesta Regum Scottorum, vol. V; Edinburgh 1988), 174.
5 J. Fergusson, *The Declaration of Arbroath* (Edinburgh 1970), 17; A. A. M. Duncan, *The Nation of Scots and the Declaration of Arbroath* (London 1970), 28.
6 T. M. Cooper, *Supra Crepidam* (Edinburgh 1951), 49–52.
7 Simpson, 'Declaration revitalised', 22–5.
8 Ibid., 24–5.
9 Kininmonth: G. W. S. Barrow, *Robert the Bruce and the Scottish Identity* (Saltire Society; Edinburgh 1984), 22–3; Twynholm: on this suggestion by Archibald Duncan, see Brotherstone and Ditchburn, '1320 and A' That', 23 and n., where they also report Dr Alexander Grant's continuing belief in Abbot Bernard as principal author.

10 Simpson, 'Declaration revitalised', 25.
11 For a fuller survey, see ibid., 16–22.
12 Brotherstone and Ditchburn, '1320 and a' That', 21.
13 For a variety of views on this term, see *Nations, Nationalism and Patriotism in the European Past*, C. Bjorn, A. Grant and K. J. Stringer (eds) (Copenhagen 1994), especially the comments by Alexander Grant on medieval Scotland, at 68–95.
14 A. A. M. Duncan, *Scotland: the making of the kingdom* (Edinburgh 1975), 614. For relevant and percipient remarks by the same author, see also his *Kingship of the Scots, 842–1292* (Edinburgh 2002), 335–6. Many useful insights can be gleaned even now by careful reading of M. Powicke, *The Thirteenth Century, 1216–1307* (2nd edn; Oxford 1962), 571–85.
15 In 'Defining Scotland and the Scots before the Wars of Independence', *Image and Identity: the making and re-making of Scotland through the ages*, D. Broun, R. J. Finlay and M. Lynch (eds) (Edinburgh 1998), 4–17 at 12.
16 Duncan, *The Nation of Scots and the Declaration of Arbroath*, 15–16, 32.
17 Simpson, 'Declaration revitalised', 32–3.
18 Ibid., 28.
19 *Kingship and the Commonweal: Political Thought in Renaissance and Reformation Scotland* (East Linton 1998), chs 1–3.
20 Ibid., 26.
21 *Scotichronicon by Walter Bower*, D. E. R. Watt (ed.) (9 vols; Aberdeen/Edinburgh 1987–98). There is disagreement between Professor Watt and myself about the relationship of texts of the Declaration: cf. ibid., vol. 7, 166, and Simpson, 'Declaration revitalised', 12–16.
22 F. J. H. Skene (ed.) (2 vols; Edinburgh 1877–80): see i, 201–5, 252–5.
23 See the perceptive discussion of it by Mason, *Kingship and the Commonweal*, 36–77.
24 *History of Greater Britain by John Major*, trans. A. Constable (Scottish History Society 1892), 236.
25 *John Knox's History of the Reformation in Scotland*, W. C. Dickinson (ed.) (2 vols; Edinburgh 1949); George Buchanan, *Rerum Scoticarum Historia* (Edinburgh 1582); David Calderwood, *History of the Kirk of Scotland* (8 vols; Wodrow Society 1842–9).
26 At 53.
27 *Historical Works of Sir James Balfour* (4 vols; Edinburgh 1824–5), i, 98–100.
28 For useful discussion of his career and ideas, see W. Ferguson, *The Identity of Scotland: An Historic Quest* (Edinburgh 1998), 151–8, 165–9.
29 At 20–1.
30 For a valuable study of this previously ignored story, see W. Ferguson, 'Imperial crowns: a neglected facet of the background to the Treaty of Union of 1707', *Scottish Historical Review*, liii (1974), 22–44.
31 Sir David Dalrymple of Hailes, *Annals of Scotland* (3rd edn; 3 vols; Edinburgh 1819), ii, 116.
32 Sir Walter Scott, *History of Scotland* (2 vols; London 1830), i, 140.
33 Andrew Lang, *History of Scotland* (4 vols., Edinburgh 1900–7), i, 230.
34 H. J. Hanham, *Scottish Nationalism* (London 1969), 185–6, 209–10.
35 This point is vigorously made in Brotherstone and Ditchburn, '1320 and a' That', 20–6.
36 Ibid., 30.

ARBROATH ABBEY IN CONTEXT, 1178–1320

Keith Stringer

The history of Arbroath Abbey in the period leading up to the Declaration presents a rich array of issues about the experiences of a major royal monastery and the loyalties, interests and aspirations it represented and served. Fifteen abbots ruled Arbroath between 1178 and 1320. None gained renown for his piety or scholarship and only one, Abbot Bernard (1310–28), was outstandingly prominent in Scottish life. Nevertheless, all the men concerned had multiple and weighty responsibilities, be they religious, social, economic or political. First and foremost, the abbot was charged with upholding monastic discipline and observance to benefit the Christian community at large, including, of course, lay benefactors, who were inspired to 'good works' by the monks' spiritual zeal and merit. More specifically, he was a leader of the reformed Benedictine congregation of Tiron which, from the early twelfth century, was conspicuously involved in reshaping the Scottish Church according to novel western European norms and practices. Like the Augustinians and Cistercians, the order enjoyed the enthusiastic support of the kings of Scots, whose concern for their souls' welfare was fused with a determination to adapt new forces in order to enhance their regal power and prestige. By 1300 the Scottish Tironensian establishment numbered seven houses, though only four of these were abbeys. Kelso, founded by David I, was the oldest, and supplied the original founding community for Arbroath, which – according to a late but authoritative source – David's grandson William I (the Lion) 'solemnly and devoutly' founded on 9 August 1178.[1] Kilwinning in Ayrshire was not a royal abbey, but its founder Richard de Morville was King William's constable; Lindores Abbey in Fife was begun by the king's brother Earl David in c. 1190.

Yet Arbroath was more than simply another product of a European-wide movement for religious renewal and reform. What made it truly unique was its status as medieval Scotland's only monastery to be under the special patronage and protection of that hero of the reformed Church, St Thomas of Canterbury.[2] Arbroath's thirteenth-century liturgical calendar, though incomplete as it survives, naturally gives the abbey's mighty patron pride of place; and it was with the greatest dignity that the abbot presided over the celebration of St Thomas's three feast-days, including the *Regressio de exilio* (2 December) – a rare festival known to have been observed only at Arbroath and Canterbury.[3] He also encouraged devotion to Thomas by soliciting gifts in the name of 'the church of St Thomas the martyr of Arbroath and the monks serving and to serve

God and St Thomas there'; and so intense was his identification with Becket that he might, at least in early records, use (or be accorded) the style 'abbot of St Thomas'.[4] He likewise advertised Arbroath's veneration of the martyr by selecting for the front of the abbey's beautiful common seal – the badge and sanction of its corporate authority – a powerful (and largely accurate) pictorial narrative of the momentous event that affirmed Becket's sanctity: his murder by King Henry II's knights in Canterbury Cathedral on 29 December 1170 (Fig. 1). St Thomas was thus proclaimed, through his suffering and sacrifice, as the supreme exemplar of contemporary reforming zeal; and no better indicator exists of the importance of Thomas's cult as a focus for the abbey's devotions, and for its self-image and identity.[5]

It is a commonplace that Becket's cult spread with astonishing rapidity to the furthest corners of Latin Christendom.[6] By the date of Arbroath's foundation, or shortly after, he was venerated by lay rulers, churchmen and ordinary folk as far afield as Iceland, Sweden, Poland, Hungary, Sicily and Spain. In 1174 Henry II himself underwent penance at St Thomas's tomb in the crypt of Canterbury Cathedral, and won his divine support to such apparent effect that, on the very next morning, William I's invasion of Northumberland was brought to an abrupt halt by his defeat and capture at Alnwick. In 1179 Louis VII of France was another royal pilgrim to Canterbury; and already it had become a great pilgrimage shrine to rival Compostela and Rome. Among Europe's churchmen, it was often the Cistercians who took a lead in propagating Becket's cult, and Scotland was no exception. In Abbot Jocelin of Melrose (1170–4), later bishop of Glasgow (1174–99) and as such a good friend of the Tironensians at Kelso, Becket had a fervent admirer. That part of the Melrose Chronicle written at Jocelin's bidding contains a graphic account of the martyrdom, in which Thomas's sanctity was accentuated by drawing explicit parallels with Christ's life and death; so, too, did the Chronicle highlight Becket's holiness by stressing that 'great and unprecedented miracles were performed in England by the blessed martyr'.[7] According to the miracle-evidence compiled at Canterbury soon after 1170, Thomas's clientele already embraced a significant Scottish contingent, including a noble lady called Eda who was cured of lameness at his tomb. Others were helped at a distance: John of Roxburgh, a former Canterbury pilgrim, was plucked from the River Tweed; Hugh Ridel was saved from choking on a bone; a retainer of the Steward left his bed for the first time in two years; a servant of Earl David was delivered from death's door; the wife of a nobleman called Osbern was raised from the dead. Often, use was made of water from Canterbury tinged with Becket's blood, as when Mary of Elgin was restored to health, and an unnamed woman regained her sight, thanks to a phial of the 'water of St Thomas' supplied by Bishop Simon of Moray (1171–84), himself a former Melrose monk.[8] And, throughout western Europe, myriad churches, chapels and altars were dedicated to St Thomas. For medieval Scotland itself, James Murray Mackinlay listed some eighteen dedications, the earliest examples including chapels at Harlaw (lost, near Kelso), Crawford (Lanarkshire) and – probably – Dumfries.[9] Compared to Arbroath, these of course were minor Becket commemorations; but they serve to underscore the pervasive impact of the martyr's cult. In England, by 1216, no fewer than nine new monasteries had been founded in his honour.[10] At least four of

FIGURE 1

The Common Seal of Arbroath Abbey, thirteenth century (an engraving, c. 1850, of the obverse; the actual size of the seal is 81mm across). The 'Arbroath' version of Becket's martyrdom is a fairly comprehensive interpretation. No particular exemplar can be identified, but there is a close correspondence with the details given in eye-witness accounts. The key components are: four knights covered in armour and brandishing drawn swords; an altar; the blow to Edward Grim's arm as he held Becket's archiepiscopal cross; Becket prostrated with his hands outstretched as if in prayer; the coup de grâce *to his head; the knight's shattered sword.*
(Reproduced with permission of the Trustees of the National Library of Scotland)

these – Baswich Priory, Beauchief Abbey, Hagnaby Abbey and Lesnes Abbey – predated Arbroath; and by 1178 there were also in existence St Thomas's Priory at Rouen and St Thomas's Priory (afterwards Abbey) at Dublin. In brief, the founding of Arbroath as St Thomas's monastery in Scotland – within eight years of his death and six years of his canonisation – provides a specially potent indication of how far the contemporary Scottish Church had become integrated into the western European religious scene.

But if Arbroath's foundation needs to be set in the context of almost universal veneration for St Thomas, it is also important to address from the viewpoint of the abbot and convent the benefits – and indeed the real or potential drawbacks – of involvement in so popular a cult. The most obvious advantage was that King William sought to honour the saint by investing heavily in his new abbey – so much so that Arbroath not only became one of Scotland's richest monasteries, but arguably represents the most outstanding single act of devotion to Becket in the history of late twelfth-century Europe as a whole. Previously William had met his religious obligations by spreading his favours widely among his predecessors' foundations, most notably the Benedictine house of Dunfermline, the Augustinian convents of Cambuskenneth, St Andrews and Scone, and the Cistercian abbeys of Coupar Angus, Kinloss and Melrose.[11] He thus linked his spiritual welfare with no particular monastery; and none of his donations was specially generous. But between 1178 and his death in 1214 approximately 28 per cent of his surviving acts for the religious (55 out of *c.* 200) were written for Arbroath. Other houses continued to receive individual grants of churches, rents or property in land.[12] But while Arbroath did not entirely monopolise the king's pious affections, it was far and away his most substantial religious project, probably intended from the first to be his mausoleum, and certainly a very clear message that his kingship was inseparably linked with St Thomas and his cult.

Why was William I so devoted to the bishop-martyr? Fourteenth-century Arbroath tradition stressed William's friendship and admiration for Thomas in life and the king's anguish on news of his death, and a similar emphasis is found in an earlier form in the so-called Lanercost Chronicle.[13] But such claims smack of the formulaic, and take no account of the fact that William had no sympathy for Thomas's radical views on clerical exclusiveness.[14] Less prosaic explanations depend on recognising that Becket's cult had several layers of meaning that could be adapted and exploited to promote the well-being of the Scots monarchy – no doubt with the guidance and encouragement of that Becket enthusiast Bishop Jocelin of Glasgow. In the first place, Arbroath's foundation can be seen as a penitential response to a miracle of divine judgement that had punished William for – in the words of Gerald of Wales – 'mercilessly invading northern England with a horde of barbarians'.[15] As Matthew Strickland has expressed it, 'The seemingly miraculous correlation . . . between Henry [II]'s public act of atonement at Becket's tomb on 12–13 July 1174, and William the Lion's capture by English forces at Alnwick, convinced many . . . that Becket had become reconciled with the king and was supporting him against his enemies.'[16] On this perspective, therefore, William was a contrite sinner anxious to avoid any further humiliations by placating a mighty and vengeful saint. Moreover, his veneration of the martyr automatically won him prestige as a pious monarch, and thereby underpinned his sacral majesty as a king who (from *c*. 1174) officially claimed to rule by God's grace. Indeed, his association with St Thomas helps to explain the remarkable gesture made by Pope Lucius III in 1182 when he awarded William the Golden Rose, and no doubt contributed significantly to his later fame for regal holiness.[17]

But, to take the argument a step further, it is no less likely that King William was also consciously competing with Henry II in a bid to recruit St Thomas's divine help to advance his own political agenda at the expense of the English 'super-state'. After all, despite Henry's skilful manipulation of the cult, Becket was readily perceived by contemporaries as a potent symbol of legitimate and successful resistance to English royal oppression. As Stephen Langton was to preach in 1220, 'St Thomas . . . did not flinch from challenging the tyrant's anger . . . in order to safeguard the Church, to protect his people, and to defend liberty.'[18] It is thus crucial to remember that in 1178 the kingdom of Scotland remained under English overlordship by the terms of the treaty of Falaise imposed on the captive William in 1174; and William surely aimed not merely to appease Becket but to enlist the saint's aid to validate his own kingly rights and dignity against a too-intrusive English crown. If so, it was only appropriate that in 1189 Scotland was formally restored to full independence at Canterbury itself, where no doubt William gave heartfelt thanks to St Thomas for his deliverance.[19] And, significantly, this defining event in Scottish history appears to have prompted a spate of fresh royal grants to Arbroath.[20] Relatedly, it was hardly a coincidence that Arbroath's foundation came when William needed the support of the papacy to defend the Scottish Church from Henry II's intention to bring it under the metropolitan authority of York. So, in this sense, the memory of Becket's fearless defence of ecclesiastical freedom was harnessed specifically to protect the rights of the *ecclesia Scoticana* from English domination; nor, given the martyr's bitter rivalry with Roger of Pont l'Évêque, was there a 'better' saint to deploy against St Peter of York.[21] Martyr cults, as has been well said, 'lend legitimation to whoever may claim them. So martyrdom . . . is always open to appropriation, to competition, to contestation.'[22]

At the outset Arbroath was thus in the highly privileged position of being seen by William I as having a focal role in the fortunes of the Scots monarchy; and that helps to account for the royal favour lavished on it. Furthermore, St Thomas's perceived potency as a heavenly intercessor evidently had a wide currency within Scottish society from which the abbot and monks could – and did – reap further benefits. Yet, conversely, it is possible to exaggerate the long-term value of Becket's cult to Arbroath. A major drawback was the unchallenged (and unchallengeable) fact that the cult had its physical and emotional focus at Canterbury. Accordingly, even in Scotland, Arbroath could not control access to the saint's supernatural power in the way that, say, Glasgow Cathedral commandeered the cult of St Kentigern, or St Andrews Priory capitalised on veneration for St Andrew. A late description of the abbey (1517) reveals that 'relics of St Thomas the martyr and other saints' were preserved in silver reliquaries kept behind the high altar; but we are not told what these Becket remains comprised, or when and how they had been collected.[23] Perhaps Arbroath had quickly acquired secondary relics like Becket's comb and the fragment of his shift (hair shirt?) mentioned in Glasgow's relic list of 1432.[24] Even this is debatable, however; and, certainly, one does not have to look far to find Arbroath freely admitting that it was ill-equipped to provide its patron's cult with a Scottish base. Thus, in 1358 Abbot William wrote to the prior of Christ Church, Canterbury, asking him to spare, 'from the morsels of your ample table', a relic of St Thomas.[25] It was a stark admission that Arbroath had no special right to be regarded by Thomas's devotees as a major cult centre; and long after 1178 individual Scots still wanted the kind of direct physical contact with Becket that only pilgrimage to Canterbury and offerings at his tomb could bring. That applied right across the social spectrum. In 1201 the luckless William, a baker from Perth, was murdered near Rochester while travelling to Becket's tomb.[26] In c. 1240 the Fife freeholder Michael Scot, either at Canterbury itself or on his return home, granted an annual of 20s. from Rumgally near Cupar for lighting the martyr's shrine.[27] Among the elite, Alan of Galloway, Robert de Brus and Walter the Steward did not endow Arbroath; instead, they expressed their devotion to the martyr by attending the translation extravaganza of 7 July 1220 when Becket's remains were moved to a resplendent new shrine chapel – a nice illustration of how far, even for leading Scottish nobles, Becket's cult was rooted elsewhere.[28] Scottish royal pilgrims to Canterbury included Alexander II (1223), Queen Joan (1237) and Queen Marie de Coucy (1276); nor can it escape notice that in 1279 Alexander III honoured St Thomas by arranging for Arbroath to pay to Christ Church 100s. annually, so that thirteen paupers could be fed in the priory's hall every Tuesday, which was the martyr's special day.[29] Even in the late medieval period it was not unusual for Scots of all classes to follow the pilgrims' road to Canterbury; and as late as 1445 Alexander son of Stephen of Aberdeen, a cripple from birth, was cured at Becket's shrine so completely that he threw away his crutches and danced for joy for three days.[30]

Again, it must be underlined that Becket was and remained a quintessentially English saint – as a Swedish hagiologist was to put it in 1414, 'France accords a cult to Denis, England to Thomas, Sweden to Siegfried.'[31] Yet more crucially, while Becket's thaumaturgic powers remained within reach of all, his cult was increasingly promoted and controlled – or rather was effectively usurped and hijacked – in order to bolster the authority of the Plantagenet monarchy. In consequence he gradually lost his credibility as a protector-saint against the might of the English crown; and few Scots kings after William I troubled to cultivate a genuine special relationship with him. It was thus one thing for England's Thomas to become patron saint of the duchy of Brunswick, or co-patron of the kingdom of Hungary; quite another for him to be co-opted in the popular imagination as one of Scotland's national saints. So far indeed were the Scots from monopolising Becket's heavenly aid that he was conscripted by Edward I for the religious campaign mobilised in support of his assaults on Scotland (1296–1307). Thus it was that while Edward presented most of the Scottish regalia to Edward the Confessor's shrine in Westminster Abbey, one of John Balliol's crowns was sent as a thanksgiving to Canterbury.[32] On 7 July 1300 Edward marked Becket's translation feast with an offering to St Thomas's altar in the church of Applegarth in Annandale; on 12 July, in the king's private chapel at Caerlaverock, another offering was made to the martyr, to celebrate or hasten the fall of Caerlaverock castle. In 1303 St Thomas was again invoked to assist the English army's safe passage across the Forth, and his translation was afterwards observed in the chapel of the prince of Wales at Perth.[33] Furthermore, in 1317–19 Edward II is found requesting (albeit unsuccessfully) papal approval to be anointed with the sacred oil of St Thomas, specifically with a view to enhancing the power of the English crown to confound its enemies.[34] If to this we add the fact that the contemporary Scots propaganda machine made limited use of Becket in order to regain a spiritual advantage, then we may speculate that, politically, Arbroath's connection with St Thomas had become something of a liability. It was certainly less potent and resonant than other, more transparently patriotic, monastic affiliations were; and, above all, Becket's association with the kingdom followed a very different trajectory from that of the blessed Andrew, who by 1296 'was fully established . . . not simply as patron and protector of the Scots, but as a Scot himself'.[35]

All this is not to suggest that Becket's cult had merely a transitory importance in Scottish religious life, still less that he ceased to be an essential part of the narrative of Arbroath's history. His aura cast a long shadow over its corporate memory and identity; and the monks continued to proclaim allegiance to St Thomas as 'noster patronus' until the very eve of the Reformation.[36] Nonetheless, Arbroath was careful to increase its authority and appeal by associating itself with a broader heavenly constituency. The abbey came to have altars dedicated to the Virgin Mary, St Catherine, St James, St Lawrence, St Nicholas and St Peter. In 1287, for example, Walter the clerk, a burgess of Arbroath, provided for a lamp to burn in perpetuity at St Peter's altar; while in the same year Alexander Comyn, earl of Buchan, arranged for St Mary's altar to be lit by two candles for the celebration of divine services.[37] Indeed, at Arbroath, the Virgin gained particular importance as a spiritual reference point, even a semi-patronal significance. The reverse of its common seal displayed an image of Mary and the Child, while in the formulas of King Robert I's charters for the abbey, Thomas's name was normally joined with hers.[38] Thomas was generally held to have a close relationship with Mary in the hierarchy of saints; and of the nine English monasteries dedicated to Becket by 1216, three were also under her patronage.[39] But it remains the case that special reverence for the Virgin emerged later at Arbroath; and that the monks were in part responding to pressures from within local society is indicated by the fact that when in *c.* 1285 Reginald Cheyne founded Fyvie Priory as a dependent cell of Arbroath, it was dedicated 'in honour of Jesus Christ, the Blessed Virgin Mary, and All Saints'.[40] Even more strikingly, from the start, the abbot and convent were at pains to enhance their status by linking their fortunes with the glories of the 'Celtic' Church. Enough of Arbroath's thirteenth-century calendar survives to show that liturgical prominence was given to St Vigean (Fechin), whose ancient church, about one mile from the abbey, had passed to the monks in 1178 and subsequently served as the burgh church of Arbroath.[41] A further dimension to the abbey's harnessing of traditional religious culture is suggested by the fact that at least three of its parish churches claimed to preserve the primary relics of local saints: Aberchirder (St Marnan), Banchory (St Ternan) and Glamis (St Fergus).

Indeed, it is known that later the convent carefully promoted these cults, and perhaps that was already the case before 1320.[42]

But, most famously, Arbroath – for all its status as a new Tironensian house dedicated to western Christendom's most recent saint – secured from King William on (or soon after) its foundation custody of the *Breccbennach*, a relic of St Columba, and undertook to have it borne for service with the Scottish army. The customary identification of the *Breccbennach* with the Monymusk Reliquary has recently been challenged; but there seems no reason to query that it was regularly carried forth as a battle standard when the Scots king went to war, or that at Bannockburn itself it was seen to perform its intended role as both a rallying point and a source of spiritual inspiration and protection.[43] We also find that in Robert Bruce's battlefield address – if the Bannockburn verses ascribed to Abbot Bernard can be trusted – the king invoked the aid of St Thomas as well as of St Andrew and the other saints of Scotland.[44] For all that the kingdom was under the care of the latter, and St Andrew especially, there is in fact good independent evidence that Becket did not lack adherents at Robert I's court. In 1328, for example, none other than Thomas Randolph arranged to found in his honour a chapel with five chaplainries at Elgin Cathedral.[45] Yet it may be surmised that if contemporaries attributed to Arbroath a role in Bannockburn's outcome, most thought first of St Columba rather than of St Thomas. No unambiguous friend of Scotland he.[46]

★ ★ ★

We must turn now from the sources of Arbroath's spiritual authority to its economic and socio-political power. The huge bulk of its surviving documentation amply testifies to the fact that the abbot was a great territorial lord. It is also a tribute to the conscientious administration of successive superiors – despite occasional exceptions like Abbot Henry, appointed in 1285, whose behaviour was investigated by Pope Nicholas IV following allegations that, among other transgressions, he had misappropriated the abbey's resources to provide his sisters and nieces with dowries.[47] Surviving today in three different Scottish archives are no fewer than six Arbroath Abbey cartularies and registers, the contents of which were published by Patrick Chalmers and Cosmo Innes in a magnificent two-volume edition printed for the Bannatyne Club in 1848 and 1856.[48] Overlooked by these editors was yet another Arbroath cartulary, now British Library, MS Additional 33245 – an early sixteenth-century compilation which contains copies of many documents which would otherwise be lost.[49] It is a rich source for the history not only of the abbey, but of medieval north-eastern Scotland as a whole; and while historians have long been aware of its existence, and have published extracts from it, there is still a pressing need for a comprehensive scholarly edition. The earliest cartulary, unfortunately surviving only in a fragmentary state, is the 'Ethie Manuscript', a composite work originating in the mid-thirteenth century. Next comes the 'Registrum Vetus' or 'Old Register'. Although by no means a full record of all the muniments stored at Arbroath, it is a most impressive achievement, and was almost certainly begun by the abbey's archivists on the instructions of Abbot Bernard in the early fourteenth century. So, by Scottish

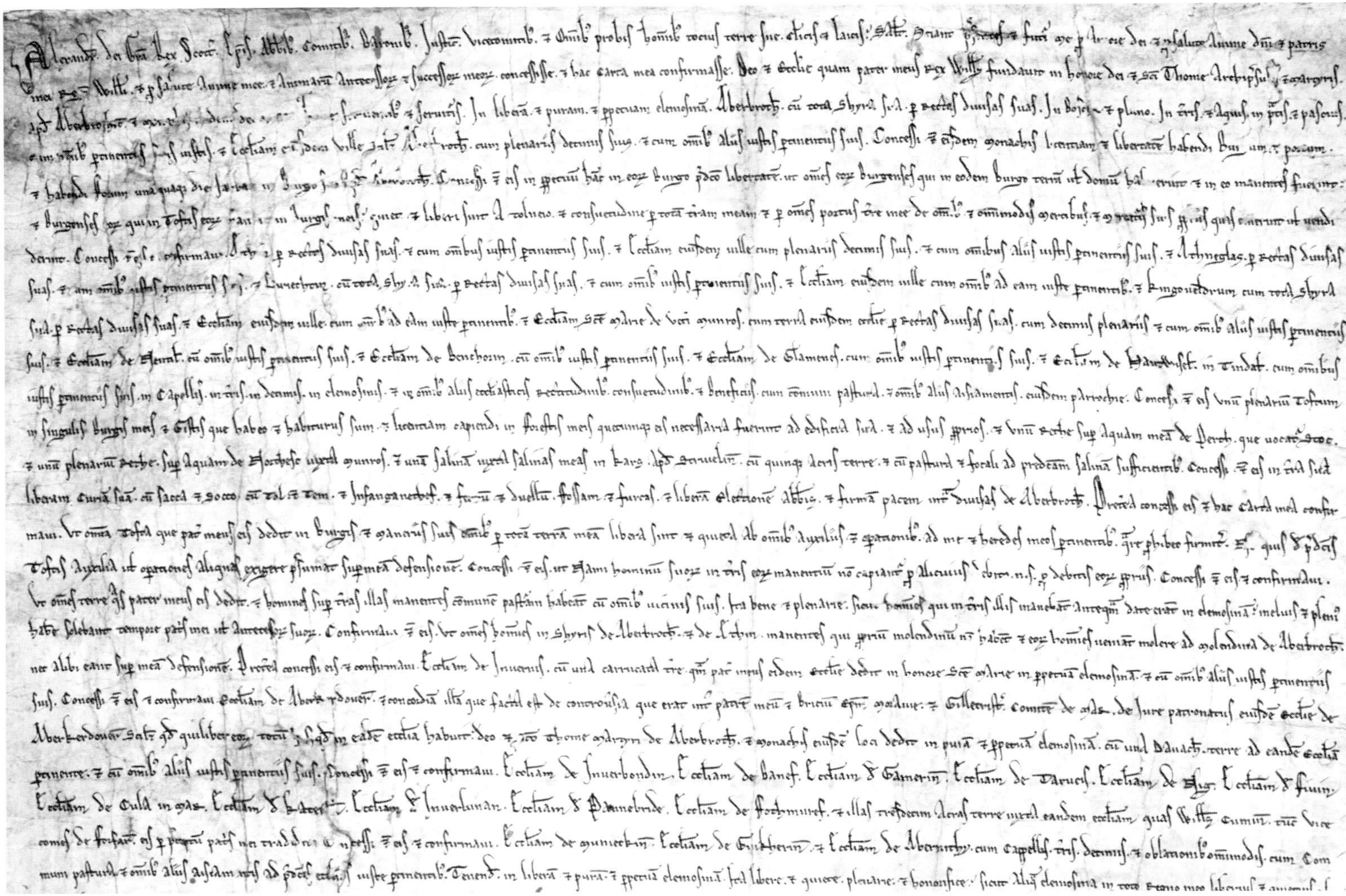

FIGURE 2

General Charter of Confirmation by King Alexander II to Arbroath Abbey, 17 February 1215 (National Archives of Scotland, Register House Charters, RH 6/25 [top part only; size reduced]). This, by a significant margin, is the earliest of Arbroath's title-deeds to survive as an original. It was written in a formal but fluent court hand by a professional royal scribe; another example of his work is Alexander II's general confirmation for Melrose Abbey, 3 April 1215: NAS, Melrose Abbey Charters, GD 55/174 = Liber Sancte Marie de Melros (Bannatyne Club 1837), i, no. 174. Some text has been lost due to rubbing. (Reproduced with permission of the Keeper of the Records of Scotland) standards, the process of sorting, classifying and transcribing the abbey's title-deeds began comparatively early.[50] That reflects an important shift to more regular and orderly business methods, with the clear aim of upholding the abbey's rights of lordship, and generally reinforcing its economic and political authority. It is also the case that but for such bureaucratic initiatives the abbey's history would today be very poorly recorded, for the vast majority of its original deeds are now gone. For instance, only thirteen original royal charters for Arbroath survive for the entire period 1178–1329, and all but one are acts of Robert I.[51] The exception is a confirmation by Alexander II issued on 17 February 1215, ten weeks after the burial of William I in front of the abbey's high altar. It remains a fine production, despite the loss of the royal seal and a large gash in the sheet of parchment at the bottom left. It confirms only King William's grants to the abbey, and the sheer length of the text (c. 1,700 words), not to mention the size of the document (410mm wide and 550mm deep), gives an immediate index of the scale of William's generosity.[52] A second substantial confirmation by King Alexander, known only from the British Library manuscript, was issued on 1 March 1215 to ratify gifts made to the abbey by the king's subjects.[53]

Taken together these two charters show that by 1214 Arbroath had an interest in no fewer than thirty-five parish churches, of which twenty-five had been donated by King William. Its core real estate included the Angus 'shires' of Dunnichen, Ethie, Kingoldrum and Arbroath itself, all formerly part of the royal demesne. William had also given a toft in every royal burgh, and a clutch of highly valuable privileges – including permission to take in the king's forests whatever the monks needed for building or other uses, and the right to have a dependent burgh at Arbroath. Donations had also poured in from numerous magnates and lairds. By 1214 or thereabouts, however, the high watermark of gift-giving had essentially been reached. Some valuable grants came later, as when Alexander II gave the land of Nigg (Mearns) on the completion and final consecration of the abbey church in 1233.[54] But it was Arbroath's earliest endowments that formed the basis of its great wealth, and the accompanying map largely represents the position as it already existed at the close of King William's reign. Another key point to note is the marked regional basis of Arbroath's holdings. Its possessions peppered the countryside of Angus and Mearns; there were important clusters along the rivers Dee and Ythan in Aberdeenshire, and along the Deveron in Banffshire. Outlying concerns included the church of Inverness; small interests at Auchterhead Muir in Clydesdale and at Kingledoors in Tweeddale; and, more remarkably, the valuable church of Haltwhistle (Northumberland), granted to Arbroath by King William in his capacity as lord of the Liberty of Tynedale. Overall, then, Arbroath's concerns were widely scattered, but the concentration of its property between the Tay and north Banffshire is still manifest; and one important reason for this is supplied by its foundation date, for in south-east Scotland by 1178 the crown and other parties had already given generously to reform monasteries begun earlier in the twelfth century, and in this part of the kingdom few resources could be spared for newcomers like Arbroath.[55]

Other considerations help to explain the distribution of Arbroath's holdings. Those who followed William I's example as benefactors of the abbey included prominent

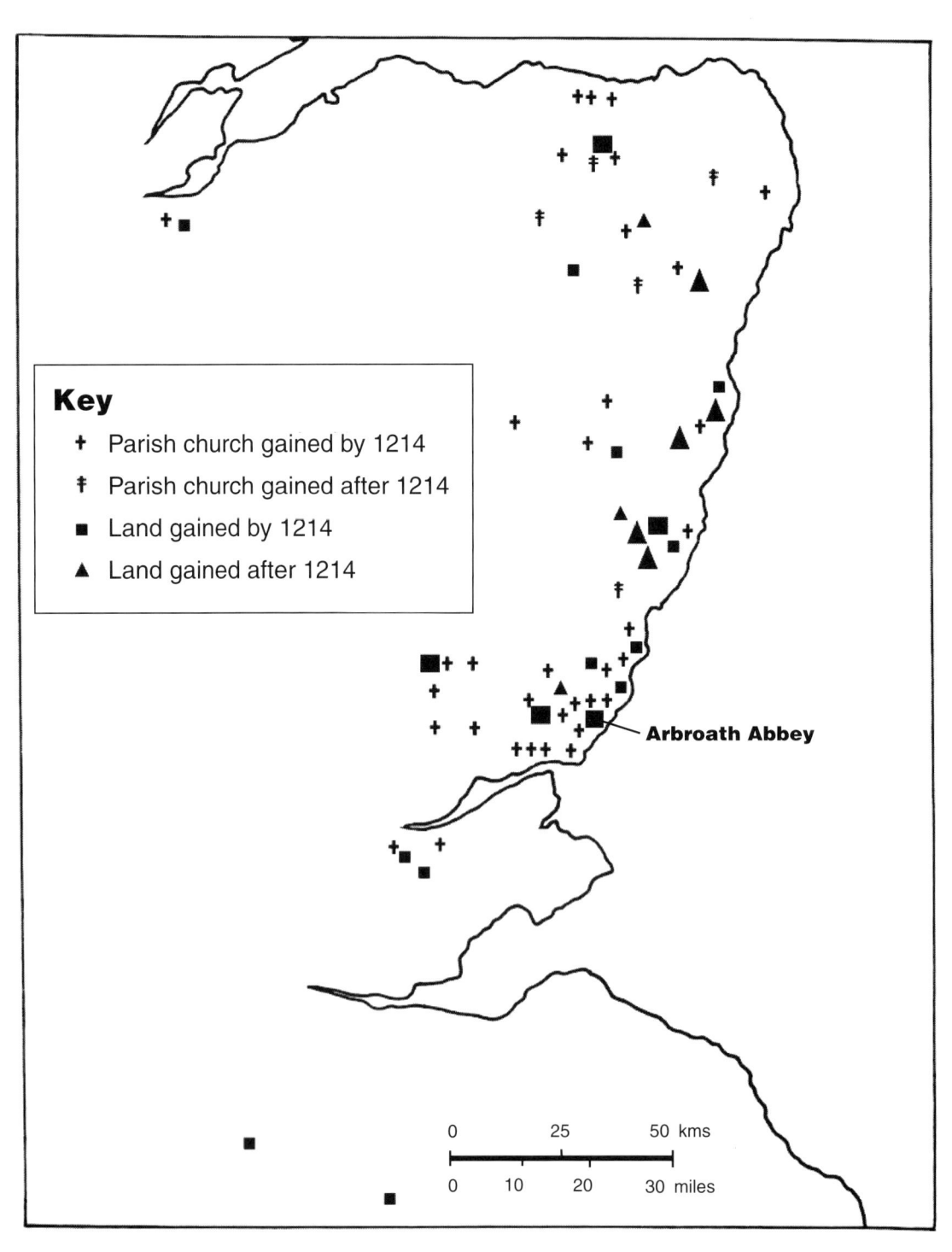

FIGURE 3
The Main Possessions of Arbroath Abbey, 1178–1320.

members of the Scottish royal family like his brother Earl David and his illegitimate son Robert of London, and an impressive array of royal officials such as Hugh of Roxburgh (chancellor) and Walter de Berkeley (chamberlain). Gift-giving by the king's lieges was thus closely linked to the strength of an individual's royal connections and service, and thereby tended to confirm Arbroath's status as the main religious focus for William's kingship. But it was also, and no doubt even more so, determined by landholding patterns and the ties of locality. In southern Scotland the convent's supporters included Thomas son of Thancard of Thankerton, William de Vaux of Dirleton, and (in the 1260s) Henry of Stirling, a burgess of Berwick. But most benefactors belonged to a court-oriented nobility whose background and affiliations reflect the evolving nature of lordship and society in eastern Scotland north of the Tay. The native comital families of Angus, Buchan and Strathearn are all represented; so, too, is that of Lennox, for, by 1230, Earl Maoldomhnaich had assigned to the monks – 'my beloved brethren' – an annual of four oxen and promised an additional twenty oxen on his death. But he was the only earl to favour Arbroath who was not closely connected with the North East. More prolific still were the gifts made by Anglo-Norman lords who had recently settled as crown tenants in the region and often took a leading role in its governance. This cohort of donors included William Comyn, earl of Buchan and justiciar of Scotia, John de Hastings and Humphrey de Berkeley, sheriffs of Mearns, Philip de Melville, sheriff of Mearns and (later) Aberdeen, and Thomas Durward, sheriff of Inverness – as well as members of the Frivill, Malherbe, Melville, Montfort, St Michael and other families.[56]

Yet the nature and scale of the abbey's resources also reflected, and were in part moulded by, William I's concern to project his authority more effectively into the northern reaches of the realm. During the course of his reign Angus, Mearns and parts of Aberdeenshire experienced in full measure those state-making processes that had already paid dividends for the Scottish monarchy in its southern heartlands. Ecclesiastical change was, it is true, merely one aspect of a broad-based programme of power-building.[57] But the fact remains that it was not just Arbroath's relationship with St Thomas that made it important for William's kingship; and his decision to locate the abbey on the Angus coast underwrote a major shift in the geography of royal influence and control. That Arbroath's regional interests and involvements made its abbot a colossus in the affairs of the North East can hardly be gainsaid. Thus it was that on a busy day in 1212 Bishop Malvoisin of St Andrews issued no fewer than twelve charters confirming to Arbroath its churches in his diocese; while in Aberdeen diocese no other religious house controlled as many churches.[58] Moreover, the abbot claimed – and exercised – regality powers, and thereby ruled the abbey's lands and their inhabitants with quasi-royal jurisdiction, including the right to hear pleas of the crown.[59] As exceptional as it was comprehensive, such a franchise was yet another hallmark of Arbroath's prestige and authority, and contributed very significantly to its role as a governmental force. The abbots also proclaimed their power – and indeed Arbroath's wealth and spiritual virtue – through one of the most impressive monastic building campaigns (c. 1190–1233) Scotland had yet seen. The abbey church incorporated the most fashionable Scottish and northern English architectural motifs, with its design partly modelled on recent work at St Andrews Cathedral, Jedburgh Abbey and Hexham Priory. Its magnificent twin-tower west façade rivalled that of Dunfermline Abbey (completed by c. 1170), and even today retains much of its awe-inspiring grandeur.[60] In sum, Arbroath's foundation heralded a radical reordering of the regional power structure: the abbey mastered space and people, and acted as a major focus for the reinforcement and expansion of royal authority in line with the desired norms prevailing elsewhere in the king's territories. Thus, as successive abbots asserted their leadership from 1178, so were the north-east Lowlands integrated more firmly into the kingdom's core.

Even a brief look at the abbot's activity as an estate manager amply confirms the importance of Arbroath's impact and influence. There was no division of goods between the abbot and convent. On his shoulders therefore rested the heavy burden of defending and exploiting all the monastery's property, and he needed to be vigorous, active and watchful. In particular, numerous boundary disputes required his attention in the thirteenth century, and he usually secured the best outcome that circumstances allowed.[61] As for Arbroath's churches, most were fully appropriated to its own uses with the minimum of delay, and on terms distinctly favourable to the abbey. In 1248 Abbot Walter defeated the attempt by Bishop Albin of Brechin to recover six churches which he claimed for his mensa; and when in 1250 Bishop Ramsay of Aberdeen tried to prevent monastic appropriators in his diocese from engrossing the bulk of parish revenues, he likewise met his match in Abbot Walter, who orchestrated a swift and effective counter-attack in concert with the abbots of Kelso and Lindores.[62] Arbroath's abbots also took good care to protect their fiscal and judicial liberties; negotiated convenient additions to the abbey's demesne properties; consolidated important granges in Angus at Conon, Ethie and Letham; retained premises or hospice rights at Inverness, Forres, Cullen, Aberdeen, Perth, Dundee and other centres; and expanded the range of economic activities and opportunities by securing from the English crown licences to trade free from toll throughout England, save only in London.[63] In later sources we get a further glimpse of what the abbot's life might involve when we read of frequent abbatial progresses beyond the Mounth (eastern Grampians) because so many of the abbey's properties were situated there; that during his arduous travels the abbot was often cut off by floods; and that in the dark winter months his working day was sometimes reduced to a mere six hours.[64]

More important still, the record evidence for Arbroath provides invaluable insights into the anatomy of a medieval regional community: how it functioned in terms of its hierarchies, allegiances and solidarities; how its political culture and identity were developed and reinforced; and how major tensions were contained or resolved. The abbot's orbit brought him as a matter of course into the company of other senior Scottish clergy, notably the bishop of St Andrews who was Arbroath's immediate ecclesiastical superior and official visitor. Abbot Henry (1179–1207) set a pattern by taking a close interest in the affairs of Arbroath's sister-house at Lindores; his successors (from 1239) were canons of Dunblane Cathedral.[65] The abbots and monks likewise played a pivotal role in the affairs of lay society. They provided a source of intercessory prayer, or more specific favours such as rights of confraternity, corrodies associated with spiritual benefits, the enrolment of grantors' names in the abbey's obit-book, and burial within its precincts.[66] True, the relationship between a medieval monastery and its wider 'family' of benefactors can only be described as the opposite of exclusive, for 'almost no one put all their eggs in one basket and trusted their souls and those of their family to one set of monastic professional prayers'.[67] But Arbroath's ability to respond to the needs of lay piety was just one aspect of its dealings with a broad cross-section of the region's nobility. For all that their donations to the abbey declined in volume after *c.* 1220, it continued to furnish them with a means of demonstrating through benefactions to a royal monastery the strength of their loyalty and devotion to the crown;[68] it likewise enabled its supporters to express and underwrite through gift-giving their status in regional society, and even to articulate a sense of communal attachment and cohesion. Hospitality was also provided at the abbey's guest-house for large numbers of people, many of them no doubt well-to-do.[69] Again, the abbot interacted with local notables in settling disputes over land or rights on land, either by clarifying the vague terms in which grants to the monastery had first been recorded, or by buying out residual family claims;[70] and he affirmed his authority by bringing local freeholders under his lordship through grants in feu of isolated or otherwise dispensable property. Inevitably the abbot also needed to secure alliances with powerful laymen whose ambitions threatened to cut across his own. When in the mid-thirteenth century a large portion of the abbey's demesne in Mearns and Aberdeenshire was feued to John Wishart, sheriff of Mearns, and to three successive justiciars of Scotia – Alan Durward, Philip of Meldrum and Alexander Comyn – it can only be concluded that this occurred largely on the magnates' own terms. Nonetheless, the abbot attempted to bind them firmly into his service as influential well-wishers – in Comyn's case, by insisting on his solemn oath to give good counsel and advance the abbey's interests against all men save the king. In fact, it has to be supposed that by *c.* 1260 the abbot – like the superiors of English Benedictine houses – had a formal private council, and that Comyn had been appointed to it, especially in order to further the abbey's business in the courts.[71] In such ways, and others, did the abbots of Arbroath play a full and important part in regional society, and thereby help to shape and redefine its structures of social control and political power.

Something has thus been seen of the dominance the abbot sought and achieved within his region – a dominance that was all the more complete because only two other major monasteries, Coupar Angus and Scone, were situated north of the Tay. Nor does this exhaust the range of the abbot's activities and involvements. He attended the councils of papal legates and the provincial council of the Scottish Church; he met with other Benedictine abbots in general chapter, to take advice and to issue legislation for upholding the regular life.[72] As a member of Scotland's political elite, he also participated in the wider business of the realm, be it in parliament or by periodically acting as the king's envoy in diplomatic exchanges with other royal courts.[73] He was required to send his tenants to the royal army 'for the defence of the king and realm'.[74] He might move on to benefit the kingdom through service on the episcopal bench, as did three of the thirteenth-century abbots: one, Ralph de Lamley, as bishop of Aberdeen (1239–47), and two, William and Nicholas, as bishops of Dunblane (1284–96; 1301–7).

But where does all this leave the abbey in terms of its national importance? To start with, its prominence within the realm as a whole can meaningfully be registered only by assessing its standing relative to that of the dozen or so other great monasteries in thirteenth-century Scotland. As for its wealth, such statistics as exist indicate that it was easily the richest Tironensian house – not even Kelso, with perhaps only half Arbroath's income, approached it. Nor did any of the Cistercian abbeys enjoy similar economic influence – even the grandest, Coupar Angus and Melrose, were in Kelso's league rather than Arbroath's. Only St Andrews Cathedral and Dunfermline Abbey had equivalent revenues, as is partly confirmed by the observation of a fourteenth-century English commentator to the effect that Arbroath and Dunfermline were the wealthiest and most magnificent abbeys in Scotland.[75] Materially speaking, therefore, Arbroath was exceptionally strongly placed, though its ascendancy was not unchallenged. But when measured by other criteria, the abbey's prestige and power in thirteenth-century Scotland were arguably less secure. The Vatican Archives name five Scottish monasteries which before *c.* 1300 had a special relationship with Rome as tributary houses. One of these *census*-payers was Arbroath, but it enjoyed only the temporal protection of St Peter and remained subject to episcopal jurisdiction; Kelso – and, so it claimed, Lindores – alone had the greater status of 'Roman liberty', which conferred exemption from all spiritual authority save the Pope's.[76] Nor did the abbot of Arbroath receive from the papacy the privilege of wearing the bishop's mitre until 1396; by contrast, the abbots of Kelso and Dunfermline were so privileged in 1165 and 1245, respectively.[77]

What also needs to be underscored, of course, is that Arbroath's association with St Thomas could never bring it the kind of spiritual reputation and influence enjoyed by the great monastic shrine churches at St Andrews and Dunfermline, whose fame as national focal points of pilgrimage and devotion was undisputed. So, too, would it be unwise to overstate the continuing strength of Arbroath's royal connections. About 17 per cent of Alexander II's extant acts for the religious were directed to the abbey – but the vast majority deal with routine matters; while Alexander III (1249–86) appears to have taken hardly any interest in Arbroath at all.[78] To be sure, the abbey enjoyed considerable kudos as King William's burial church. But no further royal burials took place at Arbroath. Alexander II is said to have loved the abbey with special affection because his father rested there;[79] yet in 1249 he was interred by his request at Melrose. Unquestionably, the great royal mausoleum was Dunfermline, the resting-place by 1286 of no fewer than six kings of Scots from Malcolm III onwards; and its superiority as the official spiritual home of Scotland's ruling dynasty – the Scottish equivalent to Westminster Abbey, so to speak – was firmly underwritten by the holy Queen Margaret's canonisation and enshrinement (1249–50). In brief, for all its crucial regional significance, after 1214 Arbroath ceased to be such an important focus for the aspirations of Scots kingship: William I's immediate successors might occasionally extend its endowments and privileges, but they did not give it preferential treatment; royal interest and attention were diverted elsewhere; and in consequence the abbey's standing in Scottish society declined. Nor is it irrelevant to note the erratic attendance patterns of Arbroath's thirteenth-century abbots at the royal court, which suggest that they were more isolated from mainstream Scottish political life than the heads of royal abbeys in south-east Scotland.[80] Relatedly, whenever the king and his court visited Angus in the period 1178–1286 they normally resided at Forfar, and Arbroath was much less of a focus for central government than were those monasteries, notably Jedburgh, Kelso and Scone, whose proximity to royal castles and burghs put them more firmly on the king's itinerary.[81]

But this qualified assessment has to be radically revised when we turn to Robert I's reign (1306–29) which, for a potent combination of reasons, saw a decisive reinforcement of Arbroath's status and influence. First of all, the initial phase of the Wars of Independence had a catastrophic impact on the Scottish monastic establishment; but not all monasteries suffered equally. The brunt fell on those in Lothian where, quite apart from the severe disruption and extensive losses inflicted on individual houses, the important abbeys of Dryburgh, Holyrood, Jedburgh, Kelso and Melrose were effectively swallowed up into an English 'pale' from 1296 to 1314. North of the Forth, any roll-call of monasteries seriously damaged by English soldiery would have to include Scone (1298), Dunfermline (1303), Coupar Angus (1305) and perhaps St Andrews (1304) – but probably not Arbroath.[82] Its possessions certainly did not survive the 'guerra Scotie' unscathed, and its pro-English abbot John of Angus, appointed in 1303, was not expelled by the Scots until 1309.[83] Yet, relatively speaking, it does not seem to have fared too badly, and the fortunes of war arguably left it with an unrivalled pre-eminence as Scotland's greatest (or least impoverished) monastery.

Furthermore, there was a major shift in the abbey's fortunes due to the remarkable personality, ability and connections of the abbot who succeeded the ousted John of Angus in 1310. And so we turn now to Robert Bruce's chancellor Bernard, who was to hold the offices of chancellor and abbot concurrently for the next eighteen years. At first sight it may seem as if the crown was cynically exploiting church resources to reward a 'civil service' careerist; yet that was far from the case. Admittedly Bernard was no Becket, who – famously – had resigned the chancellorship of England on his elevation to Canterbury, and had thereby bluntly rejected involvement in worldly affairs as incompatible with service to the Church. But, unlike Becket, Bernard found a way of serving both kingdom and Church to their mutual advantage. As chancellor he was in charge of all aspects of the written governance of the realm, and he had onerous fiscal duties besides. Highly regarded by Bruce, he was also one of the king's leading advisers, if not his chief counsellor; and it can confidently be concluded that he played a vital part in reviving the authority of the Scottish crown in the face of English aggression. But Bernard was also the former abbot of Arbroath's sister-house at Kilwinning and thus, by vocation and training, as much a dedicated churchman as he was a highly talented chancellor.[84] Such was the respect in which he was held by ecclesiastical contemporaries that he had a central role 'in the process by which . . . the clergy came to present a united front of patriotism to the papacy, to England, and to the other nations of western Christendom'.[85] Nor was he remembered at Arbroath only for his reputation as a great royal servant and statesman. He devoted much energy to restoring the abbey's position after the difficult days of Abbot John, whom he contemptuously dismissed as a 'mere monk of war'.[86] He took stern action against tenants who owed large arrears of rent or had otherwise defaulted; he retained professional canon lawyers for expert legal advice; and he overhauled Arbroath's policy on demesne leasing to protect against dilapidations and safeguard its rights of re-entry. He also issued a code of injunctions to restore monastic discipline at Fyvie Priory; and generally spared no effort to put the abbey's affairs on a sounder basis.[87] So it was that Bernard won high praise for living a laudable and honest life; for ruling the abbey in both spiritual and temporal matters vigilantly and wisely; and for committing his own resources, including his stipend as chancellor, to advancing its interests.[88]

On one reading, of course, Bernard's career can be seen as part of that continuum represented by Arbroath's multi-faceted contributions to the well-being of the Scots kingdom ever since 1178. Yet the main point is surely that the abbey's original association with the safety of the realm was now decisively reasserted and enhanced. It is indeed striking how closely Arbroath's history, and the strength of its links with the monarchy, were tied to the kingdom's fluctuating fortunes *vis-à-vis* the English crown. William I had firmly associated Arbroath with the defence of his regal rights and independence; now, when new and graver dangers threatened, the abbey assumed a yet more critical role as the effective monastic focus for upholding the Scottish monarchy. The first to acknowledge as much was Bruce himself. Little about the phraseology of the thirty-three surviving acts he issued for Arbroath suggests the same kind of wholehearted devotion to Becket's cult as that displayed by King William; and he had no intention of making the abbey his mausoleum. But there is no mistaking that Robert I, of all William's successors, showed the greatest enthusiasm for Arbroath – mainly no doubt because Bernard was his right-hand man, and partly because, as a 'usurper' king, he wanted to stress the legitimacy of his kingship by linking himself and his line with an illustrious royal predecessor. Thus was the special bond between Arbroath and the realm purposefully highlighted and reaffirmed. No other monastery, not even Robert's chosen burial churches of Dunfermline (for his body) and Melrose (for his heart), received greater attention; nor was it mere coincidence that, probably at the king's instigation, the convent had William's tomb lavishly embellished with an effigy made of Frosterley marble.[89] Moreover, not only was Bernard 'the clerical hero of Robert I's reign',[90] but the abbey became a hub of governmental operations – for a major office of state, the royal chancery itself, was housed there on a semi-permanent basis from 1312 until 1328, when Bernard demitted the chancellorship (and the abbacy) on his elevation to the bishopric of the Isles.

Thus, on virtually all fronts, Arbroath was transformed – however transiently – into what can only be described as a national, rather than a regional, 'capital'. Alas, matters cannot be brought to a resounding conclusion by baldly proclaiming, as did an older generation of historians, that the substance of the Declaration of Arbroath was agreed by a royal council held at the abbey on 6 April 1320, and that Abbot Bernard himself was the author of its celebrated rhetoric – all that can safely be inferred is that the final text was no doubt drafted by a chancery scribe working at Arbroath.[91] Nonetheless, the fact remains that by 1320 Arbroath Abbey had gained an unprecedented importance in

Scottish regnal affairs and, by the same token, it was then contributing in the fullest possible measure to Scotland's unity, identity and independence as an embattled yet essentially well-founded medieval nation-state. The Declaration of Arbroath, for all its difficulties of interpretation, can in that sense be construed as a fitting memorial to 'the church of St Thomas of Arbroath and the monks serving God there'.

NOTES

1. This unique reference to Arbroath's foundation date – presumably the day on which the founding colony arrived from Kelso – has hitherto escaped the notice of the abbey's historians. It occurs in a letter (1358) of Abbot William of Arbroath printed in *Literae Cantuarienses*, J. B. Sheppard (ed.) (Rolls Series 1887–9), ii, no. 851. Arbroath's first abbot, Reginald (1178–9), is known to have received the benediction after *c*. May 1178: *The Heads of Religious Houses in Scotland from Twelfth to Sixteenth Centuries*, D. E. R. Watt and N. F. Shead (eds) (Scottish Record Society 2001), 3.

2. Kilwinning's foundation may also have been prompted by Becket's martyrdom, for Richard de Morville's brother Hugh was one of the assassins: G. W. S. Barrow, *The Anglo-Norman Era in Scottish History* (Oxford 1980), 77. But the abbey was dedicated to St Mary and St Winnin.

3. The calendar, for January–April and November–December, remains unpublished and is in British Library, London, MS Additional 8930, fos. 1r–3v; see further *English Benedictine Kalendars after A.D. 1100*, F. Wormald (ed.) (Henry Bradshaw Society 1939–46), i, 65 and n. 2. Arbroath specified St Thomas's feast of 29 December – observed at the abbey with an octave – for the payment of a rent of three stones of wax; an annual of one pound of incense was due on his translation (7 July): *Regesta Regum Scottorum*, ii: *The Acts of William I, King of Scots, 1165–1214*, G. W. S. Barrow (ed.) (Edinburgh 1971), no. 203; BL, unpublished Arbroath Abbey cartulary, MS Addit. 33245, fo. 147v.

4. See, e.g., K. J. Stringer, *Earl David of Huntingdon, 1152–1219: A Study in Anglo-Scottish History* (Edinburgh 1985), 241–3; *Reg. Regum Scott.*, ii, no. 254. A variety of forms was used in Arbroath charters for the abbey's designation. The formula quoted in the text was often shortened to 'the church of St Thomas of Arbroath and the monks serving God there'.

5. The earliest records of this seal seem to be of mid-thirteenth-century date: *Liber S. Thome de Aberbrothoc* (Bannatyne Club 1848–56), i, nos. 307, 365. Descriptions are given in H. Laing, *Descriptive Catalogue of . . . Ancient Scottish Seals* (Bannatyne and Maitland Clubs 1850), 173; W. de G. Birch, *Catalogue of Seals in the . . . British Museum* (London 1887–1900), iv, 129–30; and J. H. Stevenson and M. Wood, *Scottish Heraldic Seals* (Glasgow 1940), i, 169. The depiction of the death scene mirrors some well-established Becket iconography; note especially the parallels with two frequently illustrated artworks: the miniature in an English psalter of perhaps *c*. 1200 (BL, MS Harleian 5102, fo. 32r), and the early thirteenth-century 'Becket' window of Chartres Cathedral. As for representations of the martyrdom on monastic seals, the closest similarities in design known to me are to be found on the seal of Langdon Abbey (Kent): R. H. Ellis, *Catalogue of Seals in the Public Record Office: Monastic Seals*, i (London 1986), 48, with photograph at plate 21. Birch, *Catalogue of Seals*, iv, 130, notes that otherwise Arbroath's seal has a connection with that of Milton Abbey (Dorset). A recent exploration of the visual images used to promote Becket's cult is R. Gameson, 'The early imagery of Thomas Becket', in *Pilgrimage: The English Experience from Becket to Bunyan*, C. Morris and P. Roberts (eds) (Cambridge 2002), 46–89.

6 There is a vast literature on the swift diffusion of Becket's cult. Particularly helpful for present purposes are R. Foreville, *Thomas Becket dans la tradition historique et hagiographique* (London 1981), and A. Duggan, 'The cult of St Thomas Becket in the thirteenth century', in *St Thomas Cantilupe, Bishop of Hereford: Essays in his Honour*, M. Jancey (ed.) (Hereford 1982), 21–44.

7 *The Chronicle of Melrose*, A. O. Anderson et al. (eds) (London 1936), 39–40. Cf. A. A. M. Duncan, 'Sources and uses of the Chronicle of Melrose, 1165–1297', in *Kings, Clerics and Chronicles in Scotland, 500–1297*, S. Taylor (ed.) (Dublin 2000), 149–50, 157; and, for further insights into Jocelin's association with Becket's cult, see A. A. M. Duncan, 'St Kentigern at Glasgow Cathedral in the twelfth century', in *Medieval Art and Architecture in the Diocese of Glasgow*, R. Fawcett (ed.) (British Archaeological Association 1998), 9–12. B. D. Hill, 'Archbishop Thomas Becket and the Cistercian Order', *Analecta Cisterciensia*, xxvii (1971), 64–80, sets the broader context.

8 *Materials for the History of Thomas Becket*, J. C. Robertson and J. B. Sheppard (eds) (Rolls Series 1875–85), i, 296–8, 326–8, 384–5, 478, 497; ii, 225, 266–7. Bishop Jocelin was sent by King William to verify John of Roxburgh's story. Bishop Simon, who is said to have recounted the last two miracles to the custodian of Becket's tomb, was certainly in England in c. 1173 and 1176: Stringer, *Earl David*, 279, n. 103; *Annals of the Reigns of Malcolm and William, Kings of Scotland*, A. C. Lawrie (ed.) (Glasgow 1910), 206–7. Hugh Ridel, described as 'filius cujusdam castaldi regis Scotorum', was probably an otherwise unrecorded son of another Hugh Ridel, the steward of the honour of Huntingdon and an Anglo-Scottish landholder (Stringer, *Earl David*, 25, 128). A boy from Berwick who sought a cure at Canterbury in the early 1170s is mentioned in Reginald of Durham, *Libellus de Admirandis Beati Cuthberti Virtutibus*, J. Raine (ed.) (Surtees Society 1835), 270–1.

9 J. M. Mackinlay, *Ancient Church Dedications in Scotland: Non-Scriptural Dedications* (Edinburgh 1914), 282–8. Note also the reference to the chapel of St Thomas in the barony of Naughton (Fife) in 1440: *Illustrations of the Topography and Antiquities of the Shires of Aberdeen and Banff* (Spalding Club 1847–69), iii, 267.

10 A. Binns, *Dedications of Monastic Houses in England and Wales, 1066–1216* (Woodbridge 1989), 119, 140, 143, 149, 158, 161, 164–5, 170.

11 *Reg. Regum Scott.*, ii, nos. 10, 22, 97–8, 111, 134, 148, 154, 159, 161, 166.

12 Chiefly the abbeys of Cambuskenneth, Coupar Angus, Dunfermline, Kelso and Kinloss, and the priories of Manuel and Paisley: ibid., nos. 208, 221–2, 237, 242, 254, 278, 304–5, 323–4, 349, 371–2, 391, 397, 407, 409, 420, 433.

13 *Literae Cantuarienses*, ii, no. 851; *Chronicon de Lanercost* (Bannatyne and Maitland Clubs 1839), 11.

14 Cf. G. W. S. Barrow, *Scotland and its Neighbours in the Middle Ages* (London 1992), 87: 'In comparison with royal treatment of the Scottish church in [William I's] time, the Constitutions of Clarendon read like a Gregorian tract.' The two men had certainly met at Henry II's court – their acquaintance probably went back to the Toulouse campaign of 1159 – and it was reported that when in 1171 William expelled Becket's murderers from Scotland, they were lucky to escape with their lives (Lawrie, *Annals*, 73, 159; *Becket Materials*, iv, 162). But that is as far as the evidence goes; though a strong (or at least stronger) case could be made from contemporary sources for an affinity between Malcolm IV and Becket: see Lawrie, *Annals*, 110, supplemented by Reginald of Durham, *Libellus de Vita et Miraculis S. Godrici*, J. Stevenson (ed.) (Surtees Society 1847), 237.

15 Gerald of Wales, *Opera*, J. S. Brewer et al. (eds) (Rolls Series 1861–91), viii, 164. For a review of contemporary reports of Scottish atrocities in northern England during the war of 1173–4,

see M. Strickland, *War and Chivalry: The Conduct and Perception of War in England and Normandy, 1066–1217* (Cambridge 1996), 302, 324–7.

16 Ibid., 65; see also M. Strickland, 'Arms and the men: war, loyalty and lordship in Jordan Fantosme's *Chronicle*', in *Medieval Knighthood IV: Papers from the Fifth Strawberry Hill Conference, 1990*, C. Harper-Bill and R. Harvey (eds) (Woodbridge 1992), 205–6. The connection between Henry II's Canterbury pilgrimage and William I's capture was stressed by most contemporary writers, including the Melrose chronicler: *Chron. Melrose*, 41.

17 Cf. A. A. M. Duncan, *The Kingship of the Scots, 842–1292: Succession and Independence* (Edinburgh 2002), 114.

18 Quoted in Duggan, 'Cult of St Thomas', 40–1.

19 The Quitclaim of Canterbury was issued on 5 December 1189. There is no firm evidence that William I performed devotions at Becket's tomb, though he arrived in time for the *Regressio* feast (2 December); and Richard I apparently solicited the saint's protection before he departed on 5/6 December to join the Third Crusade: H. E. J. Cowdrey, 'An early record at Dijon of the export of Becket's relics', *Bulletin of the Institute of Historical Research*, liv (1981), 253.

20 *Reg. Regum Scott.*, ii, nos. 318, 327–8, 332, 339, 355–7.

21 William I's relations with Becket's former protector Pope Alexander III were, of course, far from uniformly cordial, not least in 1180–1. But the argument for linking the king's promotion of the cult to Scottish-papal diplomacy seems to be strengthened by the case deployed in A. D. M. Barrell, 'The background to *Cum universi*: Scoto-papal relations, 1159–1192', *Innes Review*, xlvi (1995), 119ff., which indicates that the bull *Super anxietatibus* (July 1176) was less conclusive for the independence of the Scottish Church than has been thought. See also D. Broun, 'The Church and the origins of Scottish independence in the twelfth century', *Records of the Scottish Church History Society*, xxxi (2001), 28–9. Duncan, 'St Kentigern at Glasgow', 10, makes the interesting suggestion that Bishop Jocelin's commitment to Becket's cult helped to secure for the Scottish bishops Canterbury's support against York at the council of Northampton (January 1176). More importantly, his devotion to the martyr had been amply rewarded when in 1175 Pope Alexander granted to the church of Glasgow protection and exemption as a special daughter of Rome. Jocelin also led the Scottish mission to Lucius III in 1182, and brought back – with the Golden Rose – Arbroath's first papal privilege, dated at Velletri on 27 March: *Scotia Pontificia: Papal Letters to Scotland before the Pontificate of Innocent III*, R. Somerville (ed.) (Oxford 1982), no. 115; *Arbroath Liber*, i, no. 220.

Dr Dauvit Broun has also kindly reminded me that the founding of Arbroath coincided more or less closely with the onset of the dispute over the succession to St Andrews following Bishop Richard's death in May 1178; and suggests that King William and his advisers calculated that their opposition to John Scot would cause less affront to the papacy because Arbroath provided reassurance that William intended to act with greater restraint in imposing his will on the premier see of his kingdom than Henry II had done.

22 M. Rubin, 'Choosing death? Experiences of martyrdom in late medieval Europe', in *Martyrs and Martyrologies*, D. Wood (ed.) (Studies in Church History 1993), 153.

23 *Vetera Monumenta Hibernorum et Scotorum Historiam Illustrantia*, A. Theiner (ed.) (Rome 1864), no. 926.

24 The presence of these Becket relics at Glasgow has been attributed to Bishop Jocelin: Duncan, 'St Kentigern at Glasgow', 11–12.

25 *Literae Cantuarienses*, ii, no. 851.

26 Although never formally canonised, William of Perth inspired an English cult of some importance: C. R. Cheney, *Pope Innocent III and England* (Stuttgart 1976), 59. Two Becket

ampullae – pilgrim souvenirs which would have contained curative water from Canterbury – were found during recent excavations at High Street, Perth; see P. Yeoman, *Pilgrimage in Medieval Scotland* (London 1999), 113, 118.

27 G. W. S. Barrow, 'Some east Fife documents of the twelfth and thirteenth centuries', in *The Scottish Tradition*, G. W. S. Barrow (ed.) (Edinburgh 1974), 30–1.

28 K. J. Stringer, 'Periphery and core in thirteenth-century Scotland: Alan son of Roland, lord of Galloway and constable of Scotland', in *Medieval Scotland: Crown, Lordship and Community*, A. Grant and K. J. Stringer (eds) (Edinburgh 1993), 93. The attendance of these magnates at the translation – a great state occasion – was closely linked to the regularisation of Anglo-Scottish relations following the war of 1215–17; cf. R. Eales, 'The political setting of the Becket translation of 1220', in *Martyrs and Martyrologies*, Wood (ed.), 127–39. But Brus and the Steward, whose father Alan son of Walter (d. 1204) had been a Canterbury pilgrim, both made offerings to St Thomas's shrine before they returned home: G. W. S. Barrow, 'Early Stewarts at Canterbury', *The Stewarts*, ix (1953), 230–3.

29 Walter Bower, *Scotichronicon*, D. E. R. Watt *et al.* (eds) (Aberdeen and Edinburgh 1987–98), v, 117, 161; *Calendar of Documents relating to Scotland*, J. Bain *et al.* (eds) (Edinburgh 1881–1986), ii, nos. 67, 80; G. W. S. Barrow, 'A Scottish collection at Canterbury', *Scottish Historical Review*, xxxi (1952), 16–17. For the importance of Tuesdays in Becket's cult and commemoration, see Duggan, 'Cult of St Thomas', 23, n. 8, 40, n. 105.

30 S. C. Wilson, 'Scottish Canterbury pilgrims', *Scot. Hist. Rev.*, xxiv (1926–7), 258–64; D. Webb, *Pilgrims and Pilgrimage in the Medieval West* (London 1999), 220–2, 224; B. Ward, *Miracles and the Medieval Mind: Theory, Record and Event, 1000–1215*, revised edn (Philadelphia 1987), 217–18. There was a noteworthy Scottish presence at Canterbury for the celebration of the 1420 Jubilee of St Thomas; see R. Foreville, *Le jubilé de saint Thomas Becket du XIIIe au XVe siècle (1220–1470)* (Paris 1958), 180.

31 Quoted in A. Vauchez, *Sainthood in the Later Middle Ages*, trans. by J. Birrell (Cambridge 1997), 139.

32 As reported by William Rishanger; see A. J. Taylor, 'Edward I and the shrine of St Thomas of Canterbury', *Journal of the British Archaeological Association*, cxxxii (1979), 26 and n. 22. At Carlisle in 1297 the future King Robert I was required to confirm his loyalty to Edward I by swearing a special oath on the sword used to kill Becket, one of the most precious relics of Carlisle Cathedral: *The Chronicle of Walter of Guisborough*, H. Rothwell (ed.) (Camden Third Series 1957), 295.

33 *Liber Quotidianus Contrarotulatoris Garderobae, 1299–1300*, J. Topham *et al.* (eds) (London 1787), 41–3; *Cal. Docs. Scot.*, ii, nos. 1413, 1441. See further on Edward I's special veneration of St Thomas, Foreville, *Le jubilé*, 15, n. 4; M. Prestwich, 'The piety of Edward I', in *England in the Thirteenth Century*, W. M. Ormrod (ed.) (Harlaxton 1985), 124; and N. Vincent, *The Holy Blood: King Henry III and the Westminster Blood Relic* (Cambridge 2001), 167, n. 38. Arbroath appealed to Edward I's reverence for Becket in the hope of safeguarding its property and rights: *Rotuli Scotiae in Turri Londinensi . . . asservati*, D. Macpherson *et al.* (eds) (Record Commission 1814–19), i, 39a–b; The National Archives: Public Record Office, London, Chancery Miscellanea, C 47/22/13/2 (a much-damaged document). A similar example concerning Edward III and the church of Haltwhistle (Northumberland) is in *Reg. Regum Scott.*, v: *The Acts of Robert I, King of Scots, 1306–1329*, A. A. M. Duncan (ed.) (Edinburgh 1988), no. 376.

34 Edward II was advised that while in exile Becket had received from the Virgin Mary an ampoule of miraculous holy oil for the consecration of English kings; see J. R. S. Phillips, 'Edward II and the prophets', in *England in the Fourteenth Century*, W. M. Ormrod (ed.)

(Woodbridge 1986), 196–201. It was used to anoint most of England's late medieval monarchs from Henry IV onwards.

35   M. Ash and D. Broun, 'The adoption of St Andrew as patron saint of Scotland', in *Medieval Art and Architecture in the Diocese of St Andrews*, J. Higgitt (ed.) (British Archaeological Association 1994), 22. The ambivalence towards St Thomas's cult from the Welsh perspective is demonstrated in K. Williams-Jones, 'Thomas Becket and Wales', *Welsh History Review*, v (1970–1), 350–65.

36   *Arbroath Liber*, ii, nos. 428, 443, 605. According to the description of Arbroath Abbey in 1517 (Theiner, *Monumenta*, no. 926), its Becket relics were then much venerated; while the high altar was adorned with a gilded altar-piece or retable containing images of Christ, the Virgin and Child, St Thomas, and King William. The additions made at Arbroath in the early sixteenth century to a printed Cassinese breviary, now at Downside Abbey (Somerset), include Becket's translation and the *Regressio*. The former was one of only four feasts to which the annotator gave the highest grading ('prime dignitatis'), the others being the consecration of the abbey church (8 May), the translation of St Benedict, and the presentation of the BVM: J. B. L. Tolhurst, 'Notes on a printed monastic breviary used at Arbroath Abbey', *Innes Review*, v (1954), 108–9, 113.

37   BL, MS Addit. 33245, fo. 80v; *Arbroath Liber*, i, no. 319, with earlier references (and grants) to St Mary's altar, *c.* 1220–84, at BL, MS Addit. 33245, fos. 138r, 152v, 160r; *Arbroath Liber*, i, no. 256. For the other altars, see BL, MS Addit. 33245, fo. 62r; *Arbroath Liber*, ii, nos. 267, 753. The 1517 description gives a total of twelve altars, but does not record their dedications.

38   Cf. *Reg. Regum Scott.*, v, 15. The Arbroath charters of Alexander II supply two instances of the Virgin and St Thomas as joint beneficiaries: *Arbroath Liber*, i, nos. 101 (1233), 266 (1246). The earliest example in surviving non-royal acts is provided by BL, MS Addit. 33245, fo. 160r (a charter of Alexander Comyn dated 1255). An addition to Arbroath's thirteenth-century calendar, in an early fourteenth-century hand, is 'Oblacio beate Marie virginis' (21 November): BL, MS Addit. 8930, fo. 3r. This feast, added to the abbey's printed breviary as the *Presentatio* and there given great prominence (n. 36 above), does not often occur in early Benedictine calendars. It was kept at Christ Church, Canterbury, from the twelfth century (*English Benedictine Kalendars*, i, 78), whence it may have reached Arbroath.

39   Binns, *Dedications of Monastic Houses*, 143, 161, 165.

40   *Arbroath Liber*, i, no. 235; I. B. Cowan and D. E. Easson, *Medieval Religious Houses: Scotland* (2nd edn; London 1976), 67.

41   BL, MS Addit. 8930, fo. 2r. Less significant is the appearance (at fo. 2v) of the principal feast of St Bridget (Bride), patron of the abbey's churches at Abernethy and Panbride. The observance of this festival (1 February) was almost universal; and for later evidence of its low grading at Arbroath ('xii lectiones') relative to St Vigean's feast ('in cappis'), see Tolhurst, 'Monastic breviary', 106. Also entered in the thirteenth-century calendar (fo. 3r) is the main feast of St Machutus (Malo), whose inclusion can probably be attributed to Kelso's influence, for he was patron of its cell at Lesmahagow.

42   Mackinlay, *Ancient Church Dedications*, 76, 107, 212. Almost half the feast-days added to Arbroath's printed breviary were for the commemoration of 'Celtic' saints. These include the three saints mentioned in the text – and Adomnán, Anglesius (Englat), Brendan, Constantine, Machonus (Conan), Murdoch and Nathalan, who were patrons of the abbey's churches at Forglen, Tarves, Inverboyndie, Dunnichen, Inverkeilor, Ethie and Meldrum, respectively: Tolhurst, 'Monastic breviary', 105, 107–9, 111–13. It may be added that Anglesius of Tarves was an entirely bogus construct, as is explained in W. J. Watson, *The History of the Celtic Place-Names of Scotland* (Edinburgh 1926), 318–19.

43 D. H. Caldwell, 'The Monymusk Reliquary: the *Breccbennach* of St Columba?', *Proc. Soc. Antiq. Scot.*, cxxxi (2001), 267–82. Dr Caldwell's reappraisal is thoughtful and important, but I gather that a rejoinder will soon be published. The relevant month for Columba's feast (9 June) is missing from Arbroath's thirteenth-century calendar; later the abbey gave it the relatively high grading 'xii lectiones in cappis': Tolhurst, 'Monastic breviary', 109.
44 Bower, *Scotichronicon* (Watt), vi, 365.
45 *Registrum Episcopatus Moraviensis* (Bannatyne Club 1837), no. 224.
46 It should be added, however, that David II was said to be devoted to St Thomas 'ex magna causa': *Reg. Regum Scott.*, vi: *The Acts of David II, King of Scots, 1329–1371*, B. Webster (ed.) (Edinburgh 1982), nos. 116, 123, and cf. *Rotuli Scotie*, i, 887b, 892a, 900b, 917a, for his safe-conducts to visit Canterbury. In the fifteenth and early sixteenth centuries, popular veneration of Becket expressed itself in the foundation of a chantry at Aberdeen and altars at Brechin, Glasgow and Perth, as well as hospitals at Aberdeen, Edinburgh and Hamilton: Mackinlay, *Ancient Church Dedications*, 286–8; Cowan and Easson, *Medieval Religious Houses*, 169, 178, 181.
47 Theiner, *Monumenta*, no. 338. In *c.* 1267 Abbot Robert lost the confidence of his monks for unspecified shortcomings, and they expelled him: Bower, *Scotichronicon* (Watt), v, 359.
48 G. R. C. Davis, *Medieval Cartularies of Great Britain* (London 1958), nos. 1117–18, 1120–3, describes the cartularies and registers edited in *Arbroath Liber*, for which Cosmo Innes was in fact primarily responsible. The 'Ethie MS' (no. 1117) is now deposited in Dundee City Archives; the 'Registrum Vetus' (no. 1118) and the 'Registrum Nigrum' (no. 1120) remain in the National Library of Scotland; and three later registers (nos. 1121–3) are now in Angus Local Studies Centre (formerly Angus Archives), Montrose.
49 Davis, *Cartularies*, no. 1119. There is a modern transcript (1815) in NLS, General Hutton's Collections, MS Advocates 9A.1.18, made when the cartulary was at Panmure House. How it escaped the attention of Cosmo Innes remains a puzzle. For mention of a now lost 'paper register' of Walter Paniter, abbot of Arbroath (1410–49), see *Arbroath Liber*, ii, nos. 121–3.
50 Only eight, possibly ten, surviving Scottish cartularies are earlier than *c.* 1320, and only the 'Registrum Vetus' of Glasgow Cathedral certainly predates the 'Ethie MS': Davis, *Cartularies*, 129ff.
51 *Reg. Regum Scott.*, v, nos. 19, 28*A*, 28*B*, 29, 31, 112, 153, 164, 213–14, 221, 390.
52 National Archives of Scotland, Register House Charters, RH 6/25. The text of this original charter remains unpublished. It is copied in the 'Registrum Vetus' and (incompletely) in the 'Ethie MS', whence *Arbroath Liber*, i, no. 100.
53 BL, MS Addit. 33245, fos. 43r–44r. The exemplar for Alexander II's confirmations was apparently William I's great confirmation of 25 February 1213 (*Reg. Regum Scott.*, ii, no. 513), which largely quotes the 'foundation charter' of 1178? (ibid., no. 197), but adds properties subsequently granted to Arbroath by the king and other parties.
54 *Arbroath Liber*, i, no. 101.
55 Still useful is the account of Arbroath's possessions and rights given in A. J. Warden, *Angus or Forfarshire: The Land and People, Descriptive and Historical* (Dundee 1880–5), ii, 57–62.
56 This paragraph is based on *Arbroath Liber*, i, passim. See also BL, MS Addit. 33245, fos. 61r, 141v.
57 Cf. Stringer, *Earl David*, 30–5, and 56–103, passim.
58 *Arbroath Liber*, i, nos. 153–64; I. B. Cowan, *The Medieval Church in Scotland*, J. Kirk (ed.) (Edinburgh 1995), 113–15. In *c.* 1212 Bishop Ralph of Brechin issued on the same occasion a set of eight charters concerning Arbroath's churches in his diocese: *Arbroath Liber*, i, nos. 174, 179–85.

59 *Reg. Regum Scott.*, v, 39–41.
60 R. Fawcett, 'Arbroath Abbey', and J. P. McAleer, 'The west front of Arbroath Abbey: its place in the evolution of the twin-tower façade', both in *Medieval Art and Architecture in the Diocese of St Andrews*, Higgitt (ed.), at 61–9, and 70–83, respectively; J. H. Lewis *et al.*, *Jedburgh Abbey: The Archaeology and Architecture of a Border Abbey* (Society of Antiquaries of Scotland, Monograph Series 1995), 170.
61 For example, *Arbroath Liber*, i, nos. 227–30, 232, 294, 307, 366.
62 I. B. Cowan, *The Parishes of Medieval Scotland* (Scottish Record Society 1967), 30; P. C. Ferguson, *Medieval Papal Representatives in Scotland: Legates, Nuncios, and Judges-Delegate, 1125–1286* (Stair Society 1997), 151; Stringer, *Earl David*, 100.
63 Liberties: *Arbroath Liber*, i, nos. 108–11, 231, 246–7, 270, 274, 320–1, 335, 339–40, etc.; additions to demesne (notably at Banchory-Devenick, Fordoun, Laurencekirk and Tarves): ibid., nos. 102, 252, 261–4; BL, MS Addit. 33245, fos. 110v, 112r, 145r–152v, 153v–154r; granges: *Arbroath Liber*, i, no. 318; BL, MS Addit. 33245, fo. 86v; premises/hospice rights: *Arbroath Liber*, i, nos. 347–8, 357, 367; ii, nos. 5, 7, 14; licences: *Cal. Docs. Scot.*, i, nos. 398, 2231; BL, MS Addit. 33245, fo. 47r–v. It might be added that when the deposed King Henry VI was in exile in Scotland in 1461 he renewed the trading permits originally issued to Arbroath by King John and Henry III, and for love of St Thomas granted to Abbot Malcolm Brydy and his monks the status of denizens of England, and that in peacetime their servants and tenants were to be received there as 'veri Anglici et indigene Anglicane' (ibid., fos. 47v–48v).
64 *Calendar of Scottish Supplications to Rome, 1447–1471*, J. Kirk *et al.* (eds) (Edinburgh 1997), no. 871.
65 *Arbroath Liber*, i, nos. 241, 358; *Chartulary of the Abbey of Lindores*, J. Dowden (ed.) (Scottish History Society 1903), nos. 107, 127; Stringer, *Earl David*, 241–4, 252.
66 Confraternity: *Arbroath Liber*, i, nos. 63, 133, 138, 339, 342; BL, MS Addit. 33245, fos. 63v–64r, 132r–v, 160r; corrodies: *Arbroath Liber*, i, no. 261; BL, MS Addit. 33245, fos. 148r, 149r; obit-book: *Arbroath Liber*, i, no. 133; burial: ibid., nos. 138, 339.
67 C. Holdsworth, *The Piper and the Tune: Medieval Patrons and Monks* (Reading 1991), 25.
68 It was not unusual for Arbroath's lay benefactors to associate their grants with the spiritual welfare of the Scottish royal family: e.g., *Arbroath Liber*, i, nos. 72, 81, 89–91, 93, 112, 116, 119, 122, 130, 242, 309, 319.
69 Ibid., nos. 248, 280–1; Theiner, *Monumenta*, no. 213. According to the 1517 description of the abbey, more than 300 visitors could easily be accommodated (ibid., no. 926).
70 Unpublished examples include BL, MS Addit. 33245, fos. 147r–v, 152r, 153v–154r.
71 *Arbroath Liber*, i, nos. 247, 251, 257, 271–2, 311; BL, MS Addit. 33245, fos. 151v–152r, 160v. The words of Comyn's oath of allegiance – 'consilium, patrocinium ac defensio' – compare very closely with those of the oath sworn by the counsellors of the prior of Christ Church, Canterbury, in the late thirteenth century; note also the reference to the 'parliamentum conventus' held at Arbroath in 1327: R. A. L. Smith, *Canterbury Cathedral Priory: A Study in Monastic Administration* (Cambridge 1943), 72; *Arbroath Liber*, i, no. 320. But, to complete the story, in 1315 the Comyn feu reverted to Arbroath because of the failure of Earl Alexander and his heirs to fulfil their obligations; while in 1346 it was remembered that Alan Durward had violated the terms of his infeftment by alienating his feu without the abbey's consent: *Reg. Regum Scott.*, v, no. 49; *Arbroath Liber*, ii, no. 21.
72 *Charters of the Abbey of Coupar Angus*, D. E. Easson (ed.) (Scottish History Society 1947), i, no. 11; *Liber S. Marie de Calchou* (Bannatyne Club 1846), ii, no. 427; 'Miscellaneous monastic charters', D. E. Easson (ed.), in *Miscellany of the Scottish History Society*, viii (1951), 5–6; *Arbroath*

Liber, i, no. 356. See also D. E. R. Watt, 'The provincial council of the Scottish Church, 1215–1472', in *Medieval Scotland*, Grant and Stringer (eds), 143.

73 *Documents Illustrative of the History of Scotland, 1286–1306*, J. Stevenson (ed.) (Edinburgh 1870), i, no. 92; *Cal. Docs. Scot.*, i, no. 292; ii, no. 839; *Reg. Regum Scott.*, v, 200.

74 *Arbroath Liber*, ii, no. 208; cf. ibid., i, nos. 250, 340.

75 *Flores Historiarum*, H. R. Luard (ed.) (Rolls Series 1890), iii, 311. Given the chronology of the build-up of monastic endowments, the values extrapolated in Cowan and Easson, *Medieval Religious Houses*, from the accounts of the Thirds of Benefices (1561) supply a useful indication of the relative economic status of Scotland's monasteries three centuries earlier. St Andrews (£12,500), Arbroath (£10,924) and Dunfermline (£9,630) head the list, a long way above the next group: Paisley (£6,100), Holyrood (£5,600), Coupar Angus (£5,590), Scone (£5,350), Melrose (£5,180), Kelso (£4,830?) and Lindores (£4,790). Otherwise, this part of the text is based on the patchy evidence of thirteenth-century taxation returns, notably 'Bagimond's Roll', A. I. Dunlop (ed.), in *SHS Misc.*, vi (1939), 25–77, and *Arbroath Liber*, i, no. 300.

76 Stringer, *Earl David*, 96. The other *census*-paying houses were Jedburgh and Monymusk.

77 Cowan and Easson, *Medieval Religious Houses*, 58, 67–8.

78 Those of Alexander II's acts which indicate a particular bond between the monarchy and the abbey are *Arbroath Liber*, i, nos. 100–1, 110, 266.

79 Ibid., no. 258.

80 Significantly, an exception must be made of Abbot Henry (1179–1207) who, to judge from charter witness-lists, was often in attendance at William I's court, normally (though not exclusively) at royal centres in Fife and Angus: *Reg. Regum Scott.*, ii, nos. 254, 272, 286, 317, 344, 352, 358, 398, 404, 421; *Registrum de Dunfermelyn* (Bannatyne Club 1842), no. 147; *Lindores Chartulary*, no. 107; Stringer, *Earl David*, 252.

81 See the maps of place-dates of royal charters in *Atlas of Scottish History to 1707*, P. G. B. McNeill and H. L. MacQueen (eds) (Edinburgh 1996), 161–3. Exceptionally, three of Alexander II's charters were issued at Arbroath, though all during the same visit in March 1246: *Arbroath Liber*, i, no. 264; BL, MS Addit. 33245, fos. 46v, 150r. It may be significant, however, that occasionally King Alexander is found at Forfar on or shortly before one of Becket's feasts: *Arbroath Liber*, i, nos. 101, 103–4; W. Fraser, *History of the Carnegies, Earls of Southesk, and of their Kindred* (Edinburgh 1867), ii, no. 26.

82 Scone: *Liber Ecclesie de Scon* (Bannatyne and Maitland Clubs 1843), no. 124; Dunfermline: *Flores Historiarum*, iii, 311–12; cf. *Cal. Docs. Scot.*, ii, no. 1687; *Reg. Regum Scott.*, v, no. 44; Stevenson, *Documents*, ii, no. 627; Coupar Angus: *Memoranda de Parliamento, 1305*, F. W. Maitland (ed.) (Rolls Series 1893), no. 355; cf. *Coupar Angus Chrs.*, i, nos. 101, 103; St Andrews: *Cal. Docs. Scot.*, ii, nos. 1654, 1687, 1704.

83 Watt and Shead, *Heads of Religious Houses*, 5. For specific references to war disruption, real or feared, concerning Arbroath, see *Memoranda de Parliamento*, no. 388; *Reg. Regum Scott.*, v, no. 13; *Arbroath Liber*, i, nos. 280, 329, 331, 339, 351, 355.

84 *Reg. Regum Scott.*, v, 202–3. As Archie Duncan has put it, 'Abbot Bernard was no career chancellor battening on monastic resources, but a professed and committed Benedictine monk' (ibid., 203).

85 G. W. S. Barrow, *Robert Bruce and the Community of the Realm of Scotland* (3rd edn; Edinburgh 1988), 269.

86 *Arbroath Liber*, i, no. 333.

87 Ibid., nos. 324–59, passim.

88 Ibid., no. 358.

89 Here the text follows the arguments in G. S. Gimson, 'Lion hunt: a royal tomb-effigy at Arbroath Abbey', *Proc. Soc. Antiq. Scot.*, cxxv (1995), 901–16. A date of *c.* 1340 is suggested in G. Henderson, 'A royal effigy at Arbroath', in *England in the Fourteenth Century*, Ormrod (ed.), 88–98. For acts of Robert I which suggest preferential treatment for Arbroath, stress its role in safeguarding the spiritual welfare of the royal dynasty, or otherwise indicate its importance as a source of support for his kingship, see especially *Reg. Regum Scott.*, v, nos. 4, 13, 14, 19, 20, 28, 49, 74–5, 112, 153, 164, 175, 203, 221, 260, 376. The king's special affection for Arbroath was commended by Pope John XXII in 1329: *Arbroath Liber*, i, no. 282.
90 Barrow, *Robert Bruce*, 268.
91 For a recent review of the relevant historiography, see T. Brotherstone and D. Ditchburn, '1320 and a' that: the Declaration of Arbroath and the remaking of Scottish history', in *Freedom and Authority: Scotland c. 1050 – c. 1650*, T. Brotherstone and D. Ditchburn (eds) (East Linton 2000), 19ff.

INDEX

Page numbers in italics refer to notes.
Declaration in index subheadings refers to Declaration of Arbroath

A

Aberchirder parish church 122
Abercromby, Patrick 15
Abernethy, Laurence of 8
Absalon, archbishop of Lund 3
Act of Annexation (1587) 79
Act of Proscription (1747) 19
Adrian, pope 3
Ailp´n, king of Scots 5
Airlie, earl of 91
Alan of Galloway 121
Albin, bishop of Brechin 128
Alexander II, king of Scots 121, 125, 130
Alexander III, king of Scots 121, 130
Alexander III, pope *135*
Alexander, son of Stephen of Aberdeen 121
American Declaration of Independence 13, 14, 20, 22, 24, *31*
Anderson, James 14–15, 42
Anderson, Joseph 86
Andrew of Wyntoun 4
Applegarth, Annandale 121
Arbroath
    churches 128
    official guide book (1950) 93, 96
    shire of 125
Arbroath Abbey
    abbots and their role 116, 123, 127–9, 130, 131–3
    abbot's house 50, 71–3, 80, 82–3, 84
    architecture 50–79
    cartularies and registers 123
    cloister and claustral ranges 69–70
    common seal 117, 118, 122
    confirmation by Alexander II (1215) 124, 125

Arbroath Abbey (*continued*)
    conservation 79–84
    conventual buildings 50, 69–70, 80
    dating evidence 50–2
    destruction 80
    economic and socio-political power 123–33
    endowments/benefactors 125–7, 129
    gatehouse range 73–7, 80, 82
    guest houses 77–8, 129
    history (1178–1320) 116–41
    ownership 79–80, 81, 82–3
    possessions 125–7
    sacristy 51, 53, 67, 68–9, 80
    and St Thomas of Canterbury 116–22
    600th anniversary of Declaration 89–90
    650th anniversary of Declaration 104, 105
    source of spiritual authority 116–23
Arbroath Abbey Church 50, 51, 52–69, 79, 80, 127–8
Arbroath Pageant 91–101
    600th anniversary of Declaration 87–91
    costumes 87–8
Arbroath Pageant Society 91
Ascherson, Neal 21, 22
Australia, Tartan Day 19

B

bagpipes 23
Balfour, Sir James 35, 40, *47*, 113
Balliol, Edward 1
Balliol, John, king of Scots *see* John, king of Scots
Banchory parish church 122
Bannockburn, battle of 110, 123

Barbour, John, *Bruce* 7–8
Basire, Isaac 15
Becket, Thomas, saint 116–22, 123
Benedictines 116
Berkeley, Humphrey de 127
Berkeley, Walter de 127
Bernard, abbot of Arbroath 30, 71, 109, 116, 123, 131–2
Bernard de Linton 16
Bisset, Baldred 4, 5, 6
  processus (1301) 33, 36, 37
Boniface VIII, pope 33, 35
Bower, Walter 6, 112
Braveheart (film) 21, 22
Brecbennach 123
Bridget (Bride), saint *137*
Brinkburn Priory, Northumberland 60, 65
Brodie, J., *About Arbroath* 16–17
Bruce, Duncan, *The Mark of the Scots* 20, 22
Bruce, Edward 1
Bruce, Robert, grandfather of Robert I 37, 44
Bruce, Robert, king of Scots *see* Robert I
Brus, Robert de 121
Brydy, Malcolm, abbot of Arbroath *139*
Buchanan, George 113
Burnet, Gilbert, bishop of Salisbury 14, *29*
Burns Federation 17
Burns, William 15–16
Burton, John Hill 15
Byland Abbey, Yorkshire 65

C

Caerlaverock Castle 122
Calderwood, David 113
Caledonian Foundation, USA 20
Canada
  Scots in 18
  Tartan Day 17–19
Canterbury
  cathedral 116–17
  Christ Church 121
  pilgrims to 117, 121
  Quitclaim *135*
Celestine V, pope 33
Cheyne, Reginald 122
Chronicle of Melrose 8
Cinaed mac Ailp´n, king of Scots 5

Clans of Scotland Inc. 20
Clans and Scottish Societies of Canada (CASSOC) 17
Clement V, pope 33–5, 38, 39, 40
Clergy, Declaration of *see* Declarations of the Clergy
Coalition of US Scottish Organizations 19, 20
Columba, saint 123
commemorations of Declaration
  600th anniversary 86–91
  650th anniversary 101–6
community, use of word 36, 37
community of the realm 111
Comyn, Alexander, earl of Buchan 122, 129
Comyn, William, earl of Buchan 127
Coupar Angus Abbey 130, 131
crusades 32, 34

D

Dalrymple, Sir David, Lord Hailes 15, 113–14
Daniel, Samuel 14
David, earl, brother of William I 127
David II, king of Scots *138*
Declaration of Arbroath
  authorship 109–10, 132
  facsimile (1970) 102, 106
  mythologisation 13, 14, 16–23
  origins of Scots 3–5, 6–7
  printed versions 26–8
  significance 2–3, 108–15
  600th anniversary celebrations 86–91
  650th anniversary celebrations 101–6
  translation into English xiii, 13–14, 15, 25
declarations 14
Declarations of the Clergy
  1309 14, 16, 32, 35–40
  1310 40–4
  translation 44–5
Denmark 3
Dryburgh Abbey 131
Dunblane Cathedral 128
Duncan, Alison 22
Duncan, Archie 102
Dundee, council of Scottish church 40
Dunfermline Abbey 65, 128, 130, 131
Dunnichen, shire of 125

Durward, Alan 129
Durward, Thomas 127

E
Eda (noble lady) 117
Edward I, king of England 1, 2, 14, 32–3, 35, 37, 121–2
Edward II, king of England 1, 8, 34, 38, 40, 110, 122
Eirik, king of Denmark 3
Ethie, shire of 125
Ethie Manuscript 123

F
Fechin, saint 122
Fergus, saint 122
Fergusson, Sir James 103, 104, 106
Forbes, Murray *31*
Fordun (Fordoun), John of 6, *16*, 112
Fountains Abbey, Yorkshire 65
Fraser, Neil 19
freedom
   national 2, 3, 24
   use in Declaration 15, 38, 44
   use in letters to Philip IV 38
Frivill family 127
Fyvie Priory 122, 132

G
Galloway, Alan of 121
Galt, John 15
Gardner, Provost D. A. 95
Geoffrey of Monmouth 3
George III, king of Britain 14
Gibson, Colin 93–6
Glamis parish church 122

H
Hague, Euan 20–1
Hailes, Sir David Dalrymple, lord 15, 113–14
Haltwhistle church, Northumberland 125
Hamilton family 79–80
Hastings, John de 127
Henry II, king of England 3, 117, 119, 120
Henry VI, king of England *139*
Henry, abbot of Arbroath 123, 128, *140*
Henry of Huntingdon, *History of the English* 4
Henry of Stirling 127

Herder, Johann Gottfried 7
Hexham Priory, Northumberland 60, 61, 66, 128
Hill Burton, John 15
Historia Brittonum 4
Holyrood Abbey 131
Hugh of Roxburgh 127

I
Iceland, Tartan Day 23
independence, ancient 2–3, 6, 7
Inglis, Alan 87–8, 90
'Instructions' (1301) 33, 35, 36
Ireland, Scots and 4, 6
Irish Remonstrance (1317) 2–3, 16
Isidore, bishop of Seville 3

J
James VII, king of Scots 14
Jedburgh Abbey 60, 65, 128, 131
Jefferson, Thomas 14
Joan, wife of Alexander II 121
Jocelin, abbot of Melrose, later bishop of Glasgow 117, 119, *135*
John (Balliol), king of Scots 5, 33, 35, 37, 44
John XXII, pope 17, 38, 109
John of Angus, abbot of Arbroath 131
John of Roxburgh 117
Johnston, Thomas, Secretary of State for Scotland 93

K
Kelso Abbey 116, 130, 131
Kilwinning Abbey 116, 131, *133*
king-list 5–6
Kingoldrum, shire of 125
kings
   Pictish 5
   Scottish 5–6
Kininmonth, Alexander 109
Knights Templar 34, 40
Knox, John 113

L
Lamberton, William, bishop of St Andrews 33, 34, 37, 40, 42
Lamley, Ralph de 129
Lanercost Priory, Cumberland 65

Lang, Andrew 114
Laon Cathedral, France 68
Lennox, Maoldomhnaich, earl of 127
A Letter from the Nobility, Barons & Commons of Scotland 13–14
Liber Pluscardensis 112
liberty, in translations 15
Lindores Abbey 116, 128, 130
Linton, Bernard de, abbot 16
Lochbren, Easter Ross 42
Lott, Trent, US senator 20, 21
Louis VII, king of France 117
Lucius III, pope 120, *135*

M
McAlpine, Gerry 19
MacDonald, Miss Duncan 19
Machutus (Malo), saint *137*
Mackenzie, Agnes Mure, and Arbroath Pageant 91, 99–101
Mackenzie, Sir George, of Rosehaugh 113
Mackenzie, Major-General Lewis 19
Mair, John 112–13
Malherbe family 127
Malvoisin, bishop of St Andrews 127
Maoldomhnaich, earl of Lennox 127
Margaret, wife of Malcolm III (St Margaret) 130
Marie de Coucy, wife of Alexander II 121
Marnan, saint 122
Mathews, A. T. 16
Maule, William 81
M'bain, J. M. 16
Meldrum, Philip of 129
Melrose Abbey 131
Melrose Chronicle 8, 117
Melville family 127
Melville, Philip de 127
Mirvisch, 'Honest' Ed 18
monarchy, concept of 24
Montfort family 127
Monymusk Reliquary 86, 123
Moray, Thomas Randolph earl of *9–10*
Morville, Richard de 116

N
nationality, concept of 7–8, 24, 110–11
Navarri 4

New Zealand, Tartan Day 19
Newbattle Abbey 109
Nicholas IV, pope 123
Nicholas, bishop of Dunblane 129
Nigg, Mearns 125
Nixon, William 82
Nova Scotia 17, 18

O
Ochterlony of Guynd family 80
origins of Scots 3–5, 6–7

P
pageants 86–7
    Arbroath 87–101
Paniter, Walter, abbot of Arbroath 51, 68
Panmure, earls of 80, 81
papal Curia (1301) 2, 4
papal jurisdiction 32–3
the people, authority of 36, 37
Perth, William of 121, *135–6*
Philip IV, king of France 32, 33, 34–5, 38–40
Phipps, Joanne 20
Picts 4–5, 6

Q
Quasimodo (Low) Sunday *29*
Quitclaim of Canterbury *135*

R
Ralph, bishop of Brechin *138*
Ralph de Lamley, bishop of Aberdeen 129
Ramsay, bishop of Aberdeen 128
Randolph, Thomas, earl of Moray *9–10*
Red Sea, crossing of 3–4
Reformation 17
Reid, Robert 82, 83
remonstrances 16
Ridel, Hugh 117, *134*
Robert I, king of Scots 1–2, 34, 35, 37, 38, 109, 131, 132
right to kingship 7, 15, 32, 35, 38, 44–5, 110
Robert, abbot of Arbroath *138*
Robert of London 127
Robertson, A. Linton 91
Ross, William, Secretary of State for Scotland 101, 102

INDEX

Roxburgh
   Hugh of 127
   John of 117

S

St Andrews 35, *47*
   abbey 131
   cathedral 60, 64, *84*, 128, 130
St Bridget (Bride) *137*
St Columba 123
St Fergus 122
St Machutus (Malo) *137*
St Margaret 130
St Marnan 122
St Michael family 127
St Ternan 122
St Vigean (Fechin) 122
Sallust 24, 38, 109
Saltire Society 100–1, 102, 103
Saxo Grammaticus 3
Scimus fili (papal bull) 33
Scone Abbey 129, 131
Scot, Michael 121
Scota, daughter of Pharaoh 4
Scots, origins 3–5, 6–7
Scott, Sir Walter 15, 90, 91, 106, 114
Scottish Claim of Right 14
Scottish Education Department 101, 102
Scottish Home and Health Department 101, 102
Scottish National Party (SNP) 101–2, 103, 106, 114
Scottish Office 101, 103, 104, 106
Scottish Record Office 102–3, 106
Scottish Studies Foundation, Canada 18
Scottishness 7–8, 110–11
Scythia 2, 3
Shepherd, George 91
Simon, bishop of Moray 117
Sinclair, William, bishop (elect) of Dunkeld 42
Soules, William de 1
Soules conspriracy 1–2
sovereignty 1, 2–3, 7, 8, 24
Spain, Scots and 3, 4
Spottiswood, John 113
stamps, commemorative 102, 103–4
Stevenson, Robert 81
Stewart, Andy 96, 98

Stewart, James 34
Stewart, Robert, grandson of Robert I 1
Stirling, Henry of 127
succession, royal *9–10*, 37

T

Tartan Day 13, 17–24
   United States 13, 19–23, 24
   websites 22–3
Templars *see* Knights Templar
Ternan, saint 122
Thomas, son of Thancard of Thankerton 127
Thomas of Canterbury, saint (Thomas Becket) 116–22, 123
Thornton, Frank 91, 96
Tironesians 116
Tranter, Nigel 17
Twynholm, Walter 109
Tyninghame House 15

U

Umfraville, Sir Ingram de 8
United States
   Declaration of Independence 13, 14, 20, 22, 24
   (National) Tartan Day 13, 19–23, 24
   Scots in 20
University of Guelph, Ontario 18

V

Vaux, William de 127
Vienne, Council of 34, 39, 40, 42
Vigean, saint 122

W

Wallace Award *31*
Walter, abbot of Arbroath 128
Walter the clerk, burgess of Arbroath 122
Walter the Steward 121
Watson, Jean 17
Wegner, Fritz 103
Whigs, invocation of Declaration 14, 15
Whithorn, bishop of 34
William I (the Lion), king of Scots 117
   and Arbroath Abbey 65, 50, 51, 116, 119, 120, 125, 127
   devotion to Thomas of Canterbury 119–20
   tomb/Frosterley effigy *82*, 132

William, abbot of Arbroath 121
William, bishop of Dunblane 129
William of Perth 121, *135–6*
Wilson, Brian, MP 21
Wilson, James 24

Wishart, John, sheriff of Mearns 129
Wishart, Robert, bishop of Glasgow 34, 42
Witherspoon, John 24
Wyntoun, Andrew of 4, 112